THE EVERYTHING

PARENT'S GUIDE TO

CHILDREN WITH AUTISM

Know what to expect, find the help
you need, and get through the day

Adelle Jameson Tilton

Adams Media
Avon, Massachusetts

Publishing Director: Gary M. Krebs
Managing Editor: Kate McBride
Copy Chief: Laura MacLaughlin
Acquisitions Editor: Bethany Brown
Development Editor: Karen Johnson Jacot
Production Editors: Khrysti Nazzaro
                    Jamie Wielgus

Production Director: Susan Beale
Production Manager: Michelle Roy Kelly
Series Designer: Daria Perreault
Cover Design: Paul Beatrice, Frank Rivera
Layout and Graphics: Colleen Cunningham
Rachael Eiben, Michelle Roy Kelly,
John Paulhus, Daria Perreault, Erin Ring

An Everything® Series Book.
Everything® and everything.com® are registered trademarks of F+W Publications, Inc.

Published by Adams Media, an F+W Publications Company
57 Littlefield Street, Avon, MA 02322 U.S.A.
www.adamsmedia.com

ISBN: 1-59337-041-5
Printed in the United States of America.

J I H G F E D C B A

Library of Congress Cataloging-in-Publication Data
Tilton, Adelle Jameson.
The everything parents guide to children with autism / Adelle Jameson Tilton.
      p.   cm.
(Everything series book)
ISBN 1-59337-041-5
1. Autism in children. 2. Autistic children–Care. 3. Parents of
autistic children. 4. Child rearing. I. Title. II. Series: Everything series.
            RJ506.A9T54   2004
     618.92'85882–dc22   2003020364

This publication is designed to provide accurate and authoritative information with regard to the subject matter covered. It is sold with the understanding that the publisher is not engaged in rendering legal, accounting, or other professional advice. If legal advice or other expert assistance is required, the services of a competent professional person should be sought.
      —From a *Declaration of Principles* jointly adopted by a Committee of the American Bar Association and a Committee of Publishers and Associations

Many of the designations used by manufacturers and sellers to distinguish their products are claimed as trademarks. Where those designations appear in this book and Adams Media was aware of a trademark claim, the designations have been printed with initial capital letters.

Cover photo ©Lisette Le Bon / Superstock

This book is available at quantity discounts for bulk purchases.
For information, call 1-800-872-5627.

All the examples and dialogues used in this book are fictional, and have been created by the author to illustrate situations.

Welcome to

THE

EVERYTHING

PARENT'S GUIDES ®

A S A PARENT, you're swamped with conflicting advice and parenting techniques that tell you what is best for your child. THE EVERYTHING® PARENT'S GUIDES get right to the point about specific issues. They give you the most recent, up-to-date information on parenting trends, behavior issues, and health concerns— providing you with a detailed resource to help you ease your parenting anxieties.

THE EVERYTHING® PARENT'S GUIDES are an extension of the bestselling *Everything*® series in the parenting category. These family-friendly books are designed to be a one-stop guide for parents. If you want authoritative information on specific topics not fully covered in other books, THE EVERYTHING® PARENT'S GUIDES are the perfect resource to ensure that you raise a healthy, confident child.

Visit the entire Everything® series at everything.com

THE EVERYTHING® PARENT'S GUIDE TO

Children with Autism

Dear Reader,

My personal journey into autism started with my son. I, like many other parents, was not very familiar with the condition and my exposure was limited to what I had seen on television or in films. I soon discovered that those portrayals of ASD (autism spectrum disorders) were not quite the same as living with autism on a daily basis.

If you have a child who has just been diagnosed, you are not alone. If you have a grandchild, nephew, niece, or other family member who is autistic, and you do not quite understand all the issues, you are also not alone. The most important thing anyone can do for a child with autism is to learn. You are entitled to grieve, of course. No one would choose this for his or her child. After that, it is time to move on, become educated, and educate others.

Life can be normal again. It may not seem like it in the beginning, but it will get easier. It has been said by some that autism is the most devastating of all disabilities, but viewed differently it becomes a challenge with an unlimited world of opportunities just waiting to be seized.

Adelle Jameson Tilton

au•tism (ô′tĭz′əm) ▶ *n.* Autism is a condition affecting the processing, integrating, and organizing of information that significantly impacts communication, social interaction, functional skills, and educational performance. There are many manifestations and degrees of severity within the autism spectrum.

Dedication

My husband, my North Star
Floyd
Forever and a Day

• • •

Acknowledgments

Jonathan. As we worried about your future, you went on to create it.

Laura, Carl, and Hannah—explaining autism to strangers, repeatedly watching "Thomas the Tank," and accepting your brother "as is."

Carl—a wonderful father and friend.

My parents—for your support and love.

Erin, Crystal, fish faces, New Moons, and loyalty.

Dr. Michael Goldberg, Dennis Debbaudt, Marc, Lenny, Monica, ASA . . . an endless list.

Fr. Isagelos Yaza—because.

Avram and Joe—you understood irretrievable loss.

Bill Stetson—for tomorrow.

Bill Harper—for laughter.

Jack—I haven't forgotten.

My husband, Floyd Tilton. As an autism expert, you brought so much to so many. You helped, you listened, you reported, you advised, you taught, and somehow you were never too busy to be a husband and parent. The difference you made is phenomenal. You are always there, Floyd, and you always will be.

• • •

Contents

Foreword xiii

CHAPTER 1: **The World of Autism** 1
What Are Autism Spectrum Disorders? 1
Classical Autism 2
PDD-NOS 5
Asperger's Syndrome 6
High-Functioning Autism 9
Rett Syndrome 10
Other Spectrum Disorders 12

CHAPTER 2: **Diagnosis: ASD** 13
Age of Onset 13
Typical Symptoms 14
Your Emotional Reaction 18
Increase in Incidence 21
A National Epidemic 23
Possible Causes 23

CHAPTER 3: **Other Coexisting Medical
Conditions** 29
Tourette's Syndrome 29
Obsessive-Compulsive Disorder 31
Seizures 34
Hearing and Auditory Response 34
Vision Problems 38

Other Physical Challenges 40
Other Mental Challenges 41

CHAPTER 4: **Behaviors** 43
Obsessive-Compulsive Behaviors 43
Flapping 46
Anger and Aggression 48
Elopement—The Escaping Child 51

CHAPTER 5: **Communication** 55
The Nonverbal Person 55
Lacking Conceptual Images 57
Receptive Speech 59
Expressive Speech 61
Sign Language 62
Communication Boards 64
Other Communication Methods 66

CHAPTER 6: **Meltdowns** 69
Autistic Meltdowns Vs. Temper Tantrums 69
Handling a Meltdown in Public 73
Defusing a Meltdown 75
Behavior Modification 78
Discipline 80
Medications 80

CHAPTER 7: **ASD and Effects on the**
Parents' Marriage 83
How Mom Is Affected 83
How Dad Is Affected 85
Keeping ASD from Affecting the Marriage 87
Maintaining and Creating Intimacy 88
The Importance of Faith 89
Making Your Spouse a Priority 91
Children as a Priority 91
Valuing Extended Family 92

Handling Your Work 93
Friends, Hobbies, and Everything Else 95

CHAPTER 8: *The Single Parent and*
             the ASD Child **97**
Unique Challenges 97
Working and Caring for an ASD Child 100
Finding Reliable Day Care 104
Future Relationships 105
The Possibility of a Stepparent 106
Concerns of Women 108
Concerns of Men 108

CHAPTER 9: *ASD and the Effects on Siblings* . . **111**
Older Siblings 111
Younger Siblings 114
Growing Up Too Fast 116
The Isolated Sibling 117
The Social Impact of Having an ASD Sibling 118
Considering Future Children 119

CHAPTER 10: *ASD and the Extended Family* . . **123**
Grandparents 123
The Unique In-Law Problem 126
Other Family Members 128
Celebrating Family Holidays 129
Special Occasions 132

CHAPTER 11: *Dealing with Society* **135**
Shopping 135
Religious Services 138
School Functions 139
Restaurants 141
Vacations 143

CHAPTER 12: *Starting School* 147
What You Need to Know about the Law 147
Integration and Special Education 149
Individual Educational Program 151
Further Education 154
Parents' Expectations 157

CHAPTER 13: *Child to Teenager* 159
Physical Changes of Puberty 159
Emotional Changes of Puberty 161
Sexuality 162
Menstruation 165
Birth Control 168
Inappropriate Behaviors 169

CHAPTER 14: *Life as an ASD Adult* 173
Living Independently 173
Residential Living 176
Providing After You Are Gone 179
Guardians 181
Financial Protection 184

CHAPTER 15: *Assistive Techniques and*
                 Technologies 187
A Mind Like a Computer 187
Daily Life with the Computer 189
Hardware That Helps 190
Useful Software 192
Service Dogs 193
Homemade Assistive Devices 196
Learning Through Toys 197

CHAPTER 16: *Challenging Obstacles* 199
Communicating Needs 199
Illness 201
Running Away 204

A Missing Child 205
Safety Concerns 206
Toilet Training 207

CHAPTER 17: *Intervention for ASD Children* . . 213
Who's Who Among Physicians 213
Selecting the Right Physician 216
The Importance of Qualified Therapists 217
Possible Treatment Programs 221
The Experts Vs. the Parents 224

CHAPTER 18: *Financial Assistance* 227
Social Security Benefits 227
Supplemental Security Income 228
Medical Coverage 232
Creative Financial Assistance 234
Respite Care 236
Custody Issues 238

CHAPTER 19: *Support for Parents* 241
The Importance of Support 241
What Is Support? 242
Finding the Right Support Group 245
Forming a Support Group 247
Support on the Internet 250

CHAPTER 20: *The Future of Autism* 255
Struggling for Unity 255
The Role of the Individual 256
Looking for Answers 257
The Impact on Society 259
Awareness Issues 261

APPENDIX A: *Glossary* **263**
APPENDIX B: *Additional Resources* **271**
Index **281**

Foreword

U PON GRADUATING UCLA Medical School in 1972 I
was politely told by one of my professors that if I saw
one autistic child in my lifetime of practice it would be
one too many. Today 75 percent of my practice are children labeled
on the autistic spectrum. This percentage of patients in a standard
pediatric practice would have been unheard of twenty years ago.
Why? Were there fewer children then being diagnosed? Did the
criteria for diagnosis change? Is there really an increase in autism?
Does any parent with a child on the spectrum believe their child
could have gone to school un-noticed years ago?

We are presently experiencing a worldwide epiphenomena of
increases in neuro-immune mediated disorders in adults and children. Perhaps, not so coincidently, at the same time a worldwide
increase in the diagnosis of Autism Spectrum Disorders (ASD)—a
situation that, as it reaches epidemic levels, is essentially incom-
patible with any concept of a developmental or genetic disorder.

Adelle Jameson Tilton renders an authoritative effort at
explaining how living with a child on the spectrum can be.
She presents a multitude of situations and challenging obstacles one might run into and how to handle them. From
toilet training to puberty to life as an adult on the ASD
spectrum, Adelle gives rational sound advice on getting
through the situations. Her insight and understanding
of these situations shows through when explaining the

difference between a temper tantrum and a meltdown. As Adelle delineates, a tantrum is a power play looking for a reaction, while a meltdown is the child totally out of control—not looking for a reaction from you. The real risk, if you have a child who practices elopement, or runs away, is that such a child might become a danger to himself or herself. Adelle Tilton cannot overstate the dangers of this risk enough.

With the reality that 50 to 75 percent of families with a disabled child end in divorce, Adelle Tilton gives real advice for problems formed within the family. *The Everything® Parent's Guide to Children with Autism* assists in understanding how the disabled child will affect the rest of the family and the relationship of the parents, with a focus on what to look out for to take care of everyone's feelings. Adelle's advice is very practical knowledge that she gained firsthand from having a child of her own on the spectrum.

As Adelle discusses the issues and problems of society, schooling, intervention and support, I encourage all readers to think what it would mean if society, our school system, educators, therapists, etc., understood that many of these children are ill and could be treated, and maybe perhaps even be intelligent, high functioning, potentially normal individuals. While there is no "cure" for autism, in clinical practice, I have seen many children improve from this diagnosis who are currently functioning fine in normal classrooms! While I would encourage parents to utilize this book for many helpful tips and insights, I would also encourage them to focus on the "medical" aspects of their child's problem.

As a pediatrician, I constantly see the stressful effects of a chronically ill child on both the child and the family—the loss of hope as parents are told they must accept their child's diagnosis and learn to live with it. In reality, these children deserve real medical work-ups, not just a label based on symptoms, a "waste basket" diagnosis and then to be "followed" for further observation. I cannot count the endless number of children I have seen who are iron deficient, have thyroid problems or have slow viruses altering their brains that can be addressed and treated. Allergies and immune sensitivities contribute to the central nervous system dysfunction of most of these children. Many of them do not feel well, and, as Adelle Tilton states, do not know how to tell you. These children are not oblivious to pain (as some mistakenly think); rather many are daily in a level of constant pain! What other world do they know? Have they ever had a chance to feel well? Do they have a model of normality to strive for? No.

With further advances in brain imaging tools such as NeuroSpect scans (a brain scan that shows precise blood flow to various areas of the brain) and immune profiling, researchers and physicians will begin to understand why the brain is receiving the wrong messages and figure out how to correct it in many cases (hint: Most of these children are *not* miswired to start with). Many disorders causing ASD symptoms turn out to be treatable medical disorders. It is important to remember to look at the whole child, and get thorough medical evaluations: Deal with and treat medical issues that deserve therapy, while reading and utilizing the wealth of information in *The Everything® Parent's Guide to Children with Autism*.

I congratulate Adelle on her exceptional effort, and wish to close with advice I was given in my first pediatric lecture, "Listen to the Mother." As parents, follow *your* instincts. Believe in yourselves and your children; the medical system will have to listen.

Michael J. Goldberg, M.D., F.A.A.P.
Director, NIDS (Neuro-Immune Dysfunction Syndromes)
    Research Institute

CHAPTER 1

The World of Autism

L EARNING ABOUT autism spectrum disorders is a bit like learning an unfamiliar language. It is a new world, and the customs and behaviors may seem foreign. From the moment a physician gives the diagnosis, everything changes.

In all likelihood, as a mom or dad, this will not be the parenting experience you had hoped for. There are pitfalls and disappointments along the way. However, the good news is that this world can be navigated successfully, and it can be the beginning of something different, full of adventure and accomplishment.

What Are Autism Spectrum Disorders?

Often referred to as ASD, autism spectrum disorder is a broad classification of conditions sharing similar objective symptoms. Objective symptoms are those that can be observed by someone other than the patient, whereas subjective symptoms are those that only the patient experiences. For example, in the case of influenza, an objective symptom might be a fever or a rash; a subjective symptom might be fatigue or pain.

Many times ASD is referred to as PDD (pervasive developmental disorder). Historically, ASD has been the more commonly used term in Europe and has recently been accepted as the proper term in the United States as well. This differs from PDD-NOS, which will be discussed in more detail later in this chapter. All of the various conditions within the spectrum are labeled, and there are differences in how the various conditions manifest themselves.

ASD in its widest definition refers to the class of disorders in which there are several similar impairments. Experts believe that all autism spectrum disorders are as individual as fingerprints. No two children with autism display the disorder in exactly the same way. The variety of symptoms and behaviors displayed by children with ASD do certainly bear this out.

Classical Autism

Autism is the most commonly known of the spectrum disorders. First written about in the 1940s by Dr. Leo Kanner, a psychiatrist at Johns Hopkins University, autism was rarely seen by physicians. Characterized primarily by communication and socialization difficulties, classical autism is a very isolating and frustrating condition.

 ESSENTIAL

The word *autism* originates from the Greek word *autos*, meaning "self." This disorder was named autism because it was believed to be an excessive preoccupation with oneself originating from a mother who would not love her child. This theory has been proved false, and autism is now recognized as a medical disorder.

Classical autism is part of the ASD, or PDD, category. It is the best known of the pervasive development disorders, and it is one of the largest classifications within ASD as well, rivaled only by PDD-NOS (pervasive development disorder "not otherwise specified"). ASD is a syndrome. A syndrome is a group of symptoms that indicate a condition. Syndromes, by their very nature, have many characteristics, and each patient will display or not display those symptoms in very different ways. As such, each case of autism will be different.

The Signs and Symptoms of Autism

Autism has a set of signs and symptoms that appear differently in each child, and parents must remember that what is considered autistic in one child may not appear in another child who is also considered autistic. This is part of the time-consuming nature of the diagnosis of autism. Without a definitive lab test such as blood work, diagnosis is a process of defining and understanding the symptoms as displayed. As a rule, children with autism exhibit the following signs and symptoms that characterize all autism spectrum disorders to a great degree:

- Expressive and receptive communication and social deficits.
- Insistence on routine and resistance to change.
- Appearing to be "off in their own little world."
- Resistance to physical closeness such as hugging.
- Attachment to "odd" toys such as kitchen utensils.
- Parallel play (playing beside other children rather than inter-actively with them) and lack of imaginative play.
- Sudden and apparently unexplainable anger and tantrums.
- Repetitive behaviors and obsessive-compulsive disorder.
- Splinter skills (excelling in a particular skill that is above the apparent IQ level).
- Appearing to have sensory overload in normal environments.

The Struggle with Communication

There is a marked reduction in verbal communication, or a child may have no speech at all. Echolalia is a speech pattern seen in autism spectrum disorders in which a child echoes back the words spoken to him or her. It is an attempt to understand language. For example, instead of responding to a question with an answer, the question is repeated back.

Children with autism also have difficulties with nonverbal communication skills. It is problematic for a child with autism to understand, use, and interpret subtle nonverbal language cues, such as facial expression or tone of voice, and translate those into meaningful language.

The difficulty with communication often accentuates the other deficits in autism. Frustration is a common problem with a child unable to communicate his most basic needs, and the result of frustration is often anger. A child will either struggle to communicate or withdraw even further if he is unable to convey thoughts and feelings to others.

The Problem with Conceptual Thinking

Children with autism also struggle in a profound way with conceptual ideas and thought patterns. For example, a child with autism may associate leaving the house with putting on a coat. Now imagine that same child was outside without a coat on and the temperature dropped dramatically, and it began to snow. Although the child might have a coat with her, even in her hands, she will not put on the coat. Why not? She associates the coat with leaving the house, not with a solution to cold weather, and the concept of using the coat for protection is nonexistent.

Because of the difficulty the child has in understanding concepts, he or she becomes limited in many ways. The child does not recognize that other people have their own thoughts, feelings, attitudes, and beliefs, and the child becomes even more isolated. Much of the maturing process for children is based on conceptual thinking, and the inability to think conceptually adds to the communication difficulties of a child with autism.

The Theory of Mind (TOM)

At some point in a child's development, he becomes aware that he is an individual. More importantly, he realizes that other people are individuals as well. Unfortunately, this moment never comes for children with autism. People with autism are unable to understand that every individual has her own thoughts and perspectives on the world. It is part of the self-involvement typical of ASD. It causes social problems, communication difficulties, and can come across as cold and unfeeling.

TOM is the ability to recognize that other people have their own thoughts and feelings. If the theory of mind is disrupted, it is not a sign of poor intellect or mental retardation. It seems to be related to language and social function; feelings are generally communicated through language and subtle social clues (such as facial expression and body language), and these are the primary areas that are deficient in autism and its related disorders.

ALERT!

People with autism experience all of the same emotions that others do. The difficulty comes from their inability to recognize those emotions in others and to express empathy for those emotions. Do not think if your child does not display feelings that she doesn't have them. She does.

Anger and Aggression

Although not all children with autism display aggression, it is a very common symptom, and temper outbursts and outright tantrums are common. These can range from a brief explosion to a full-fledged meltdown. Children with autism may also strike out through hitting and/or biting as well as by destroying objects and possessions.

A child with autism throwing a temper tantrum is not a child acting "spoiled" or "bratty." Unfortunately, parents of children with ASD hear these terms quite often. These behaviors are a symptom of a disorder, not a result of poor parenting skills.

PDD-NOS

PDD, as mentioned previously, stands for pervasive developmental disorder. NOS means "not otherwise specified." In real-life terms, this means that the physicians know that the child's disorder is within the pervasive development category or on the autism spectrum, but it does not neatly fit into any particular category. As such, it is classified as a PDD that has no further specification—it isn't quite autism, isn't quite Asperger's, and isn't quite CDD (childhood disintegrative disorder), or any other PDD.

 ESSENTIAL

If your child has been diagnosed PDD, ask the physician why this diagnosis was given rather than autism or Asperger's syndrome. A PDD diagnosis may stand between your child and benefits she is entitled to.

PDD-NOS has essentially the same set of signs and symptoms that autism does, but the severity of the symptoms is not as extreme as that found in autism. A child who has PDD-NOS may initiate speech, using language that is appropriate to the context of the social situation. There will be deficits compared to the milestones of normal childhood development; however, they will not be as blatant as a child who has autism. Echolalia is heard less often and auditory processing skills are more advanced.

Social skills in a PDD-NOS child are also less of a challenge. These children are able to interact at varying degree with parents, siblings, other adults, and children. Imaginative play may still be limited but interactive play is somewhat more common than it is with a child who is autistic.

Asperger's Syndrome

Dr. Hans Asperger first documented Asperger's syndrome at the same time Dr. Kanner was writing about autism. Both physicians were unaware of the other's work, as open communication between German and American scientists was not possible during World War II. The two physicians, however, arrived at the same conclusion at a time when ASD had not yet been officially identified. European physicians diagnosed Asperger's syndrome, and American physicians diagnosed Kanner's syndrome, which was the name initially given to autism.

It was not until the early 1980s that Asperger's was brought into American diagnostic procedures, and it was a full decade later that Dr. Asperger's original paper on the topic was translated into English. It was during the early 1990s that Asperger's syndrome was placed on the autism spectrum and became a disorder independent of other spectrum disorders. Several signs distinguish Asperger's syndrome from other disorders on the spectrum:

- Essentially normal speech development with phrases used by age three.
- Essentially normal cognitive development.
- Essentially normal development in self-help and curiosity about the world.
- Gross motor skills are often delayed and clumsiness is common.
- Eye contact, facial expression, body language inappropriate to the social situation.
- Difficulty establishing and maintaining peer relationships.
- Difficulty expressing emotions and relating to others with those emotions.
- Intense and persistent association with particular subjects, objects, or topics.
- Repetitive mannerisms such as flapping.
- Insistence on routine.

Although the symptoms of Asperger's syndrome seem very similar to that of autism, the normal development of speech and motor skill difficulties distinguish this disorder. Keeping in mind there are varying degrees of severity in Asperger's, it becomes easier to understand why diagnosis of this particular form of a high-functioning ASD may be delayed for many years. There are adults who are just now receiving the diagnosis of Asperger's, having been thought of as odd or eccentric for decades.

The Subtle Cues of Communication

The most obvious symptom in Asperger's syndrome is the socialization impairment. So much of our society's communication is based on unspoken cues, such as hand gestures, body language, eye movement, and even the pauses taken in conversation. All of those convey emotions and messages that may be subtle, but they are crucial to understanding the meaning of what a person is saying. For a person with Asperger's, those nonverbal cues are totally missed, as they live in a literal world where words have only literal meanings.

It is possible for people with Asperger's to learn social mannerisms by rote, but they do not generally understand the meaning behind them, and consequently, socialization suffers. Often people will misunderstand what a person with Asperger's is trying to say because of the literalness of the conversation. These misunderstandings can lead to hurt feelings and anger.

 **ALERT!**

It is common to hear people with Asperger's syndrome refer to themselves as "Aspies." This is not a derogatory term; however, it should be used only with someone who is close, such as a family member.

Asperger's Vs. Autism

One challenge for parents is distinguishing Asperger's syndrome from autism in a very young child. If the parents have no other children, they may not have a frame of reference for comparison, or they might not realize how disordered the structure of the Asperger's social world is. In addition, if a child is very talkative and seems somewhat advanced in her interests, the parents may think the child is unusually gifted rather than narrowly and persistently focused on a subject, object, or topic.

It is important for the child to have an early diagnosis that is accurate so appropriate intervention can begin. Testing by qualified medical professionals can determine where a child falls on the autism spectrum and what treatments and therapies should be initiated. As with all disorders on the spectrum, early intervention offers the best hope for a promising future.

High-Functioning Autism

High-functioning autism (HFA) is a disorder on the autism spectrum that is often confused with Asperger's syndrome. It is, however, a distinct disorder. There is controversy about HFA because of the standard used to separate it from classical autism.

Statistically, many experts feel that approximately 75 percent of children with autism are mentally retarded. The technical standard for determining high-functioning autism and classical autism is the presence of mental retardation. In the past, a child with autism who was retarded was considered to have classical autism, and if retardation was not present, the disorder on the spectrum was high-functioning autism. If your child has a diagnosis of autism, do not assume he or she is retarded, as this may be the furthest thing from the truth. This is a very gray area and extremely difficult to determine for children on the autism spectrum.

 **QUESTION?**

What is IQ?
IQ stands for "intelligence quotient" and is a number derived from standardized tests that are calibrated to a person's age. This creates an accurate rating that will remain consistent throughout a person's life. IQ tests are for those who can communicate and are not always accurate for a person with autism.

The reason that this is a hotly debated issue is because of the difficulty of accurately measuring IQ in nonverbal children, as tests are constructed so that verbalization and the ability to conceptualize are mandatory. If a person is nonverbal and is unable to understand concepts, they will fail miserably at this method of determining intelligence. A score of seventy or below on an IQ test indicates a person is mentally retarded. However, a child with autism may not be measured accurately with the standardized IQ testing. Many physicians feel that children are inaccurately labeled as being retarded, which makes the line between classical autism and high-functioning autism harder to determine.

In everyday life, for parents, teachers, and most medical professionals, high-functioning autism is autism that is less debilitating than classical autism. If spectrum disorders could be viewed on a scale, high-functioning autism would fall between classical autism and PDD-NOS. As stated before, there is a fine line between HFA and Asperger's—the primary difference is in the motor skills. Although there are always exceptions, children with classical or high-functioning autism will not have the deficits in motor skills that a child with Asperger's displays.

Rett Syndrome

This spectrum disorder is unique, as it affects girls almost exclusively. Until recently, it was thought that a male fetus could not survive the disorder, and therefore all victims were female. Research now shows that although Rett syndrome is rare in boys, it should not be excluded as a diagnosis just because of gender. Rett syndrome is a genetically caused disorder.

A gene mutation causes Rett syndrome, and the degree of the mutation determines the severity of the condition. If a boy does have Rett syndrome, he will display the symptoms differently than a classic Rett syndrome girl, and therefore DNA testing is required to determine this disorder in boys. Rett syndrome is a rare condition, affecting only 1 in 100,000 children. The diagnosis of Rett syndrome is made by the observation of symptoms similar to autism. However, the differences between the two conditions become more apparent as the child ages, due to the dramatic regression exhibited in Rett syndrome. Indicators of Rett syndrome include:

- Frequent hand-wringing motion, which is unique to this disorder
- Major milestones as an infant achieved
- Loss of skills and abilities beginning at age two with increase in hand-wringing
- Loss of the ability to walk
- Profound retardation
- Social skills decreasing with age

Girls with Rett syndrome are often misdiagnosed as being autistic when they are very young because of the similarities of symptoms. It is as the child ages, between the ages of five and ten, that the differences become apparent. The distinctive hand-wringing is indicative of the disorder, and it interferes with normal motor functioning. It can interfere with the child's ability to perform simple tasks necessary in the activities of daily living. The child may have difficulties feeding herself, dressing, playing, or engaging in activities typical of any young child.

 **FACT**

There are gender tendencies in autism spectrum disorders. Seventy-five percent of children with autism and PDD-NOS are boys. Asperger's syndrome affects boys at a ratio of 10 to 1 over girls. Fragile X and childhood disintegrative disorder are also more prevalent in boys. The only ASD to affect girls almost exclusively is Rett syndrome.

Girls diagnosed with Rett syndrome, or those with Rett syndrome but improperly diagnosed as being autistic, will benefit from the same therapies used for other spectrum disorders. Because it is common for Rett syndrome to be overlooked as the cause of the child's difficulties until the child is older, parents should proceed with therapies for children with autism. Working with the strengths and abilities of the child will ease the issues of the disability later in life. If the diagnosis of Rett syndrome is confirmed, parents need to prepare for the physical and mental limitations that will occur as the child matures.

Other Spectrum Disorders

There are other less-known disorders on the autism spectrum such as childhood disintegrative disorder, fragile X syndrome, auditory processing disorder, hyperlexia, Williams syndrome, Prader-Willi syndrome, and Landau-Kleffner syndrome. There are also a handful of disorders that seem to fall among the better-known disorders. Most of these disorders are characterized by some of the same symptoms as other disorders on the spectrum, but they are less severe in their number and/or intensity. Other disorders are rare and seldom diagnosed in the face of other, more accepted diagnoses.

It is common for various physicians and therapists not to commit to the diagnosis of autism or one of its cousins, saying instead that a child is "autistic-like." This is usually reluctance on the part of the physician to deliver a diagnosis. It is difficult for a physician to tell parents that their child has a disorder that will not disappear over time. There was a time in our society when labeling a child with such a disorder was a stigma not only for the child, but also for his or her siblings and the entire family. Those days are behind us, or are at least on the way out, and a parent should not hesitate to push for an accurate diagnosis so that the best intervention can begin.

The journey begins, as poets say, with a single step. Of course, that first step is the hardest one to take. But once the journey has begun, your small beginning steps will become more sure and certain, and your progress will show.

CHAPTER 2

Diagnosis: ASD

ACTUALLY RECEIVING THE DIAGNOSIS of a disorder on the autism spectrum is often the most difficult step you, as a parent, will encounter. As previously mentioned, many professionals are reluctant to place the label of autism on a child. Many others are not qualified to recognize the autism spectrum, and if the disorder is not dramatic, they may attribute the presenting symptoms to a behavioral or psychiatric disorder. It is imperative that a parent be assertive in obtaining an accurate diagnosis if he or she believes some form of autism is present.

Age of Onset

Autism is not discriminating. It affects children of both sexes, and it strikes all races and ethnic groups. Virtually all children with autism show the symptoms and can be diagnosed between the ages of two to four. The most common age for children to display the behaviors and traits of autism is between fifteen and twenty months. Although some children are born with certain qualities that cause their parents to take note and observe them for unusual behavior, it is most common for a child to develop normally up to about sixteen months and then begin to regress, losing skills that had been mastered. It is common for children with ASD to have normal speech and behavior patterns for a child of fifteen to twenty months and then lose that behavior and speech, retreating into a world that they alone occupy.

However, the issue is not so much about at what age autism strikes as it is about getting an early diagnosis. A correct diagnosis for a child at a very young age means treatment and intervention at a very young age. Those interventions can make all the difference in a child's future. If a child receives therapy and treatments beginning at approximately age two or three, the long-term outlook is much better. The future is a much brighter one for the entire family.

The problem can often be the failure of parents to recognize that there is a problem. Parents see their children day after day and may not recognize that their son or daughter is not reaching the developmental milestones. This is where the extended family can help and often raise the alarm about issues with the child. Grandmothers are often the ones to see the delays and point them out.

Typical Symptoms

Although each child will display his particular type of ASD in a unique way, there are symptoms that form a consistent basis upon which to diagnose the disorder. The different degrees of these symptoms will determine the particular diagnosis of which disorder it is. Although, for example, all spectrum disorder patients will have communication deficits, a classical autism case will display those speech issues differently than a child who has Asperger's syndrome.

The three main categories that characterize ASD are social interaction, communication, and patterns of behavior, interests, and activity. Within these three categories are four criteria that are then used to determine if the diagnosis of an ASD is appropriate. At least one of the signs within each category along with a minimum of six signs from all of the categories must be met for a diagnosis of ASD.

Children with autism usually display the signs readily whereas pervasive developmental disorder, which is diagnosed with fewer than six signs, may be more elusive. The same symptoms exist but in a milder form. Sometimes parents need to seek out consultations with several experts to determine the exact diagnosis in less extreme cases.

 **FACT**

The diagnosis of all mental diseases and disorders in the United States are standardized through manuals that medical professionals have collaborated on to achieve uniformity. The *DSM-IV*, published by the American Psychiatric Association, is the manual used to diagnose autism spectrum disorders. This stands for the *Diagnostic and Statistical Manual of Mental Disorders*, 4th edition. In other words, whether a patient sees a physician in New York City or Cleveland, Ohio, the same standards are applied to diagnose a particular disorder.

Social Interaction

How a child interacts socially is the first of the three categories examined to ascertain whether an autism spectrum disorder is present. The physician will be involved, and it is likely a psychologist or psychiatrist may examine the child as well. Other experts will be consulted if needed. Doctors will look for:

- Reduction or absence of eye contact, facial expressions, and/or body language
- Inability to form friendships within a peer group
- Unwillingness or inability to share enjoyment or accomplishments with others
- Inability to relate and share emotions on a social level

The impairment of social skills in a child with autism becomes obvious to a parent when a child is young. As a child matures, the interaction skills within the peer group isolate the child further, as he or she is unable to relate to other children and adults.

Communication

Communication is the second area experts analyze to determine if autism or a related condition is present. This exam involves a physician, speech therapist, and possibly other experts such as a psychologist or psychiatrist. The communication difficulties in an ASD child are typical to most of the conditions on the spectrum. These include:

- Reduction, absence, or loss of expressive (spoken) language.
- No attempt to replace language with another method of communication.
- Inability to converse with another person even if speech is present.
- Repetitive use of words, or echolalia (echoing words without meaning).
- Absence of imaginative play typical to a specific age group.

Communication is imperative for a human being to function successfully. This impairment may be the most blatant and painful for parents to understand and cope with on a day-to-day basis. A child may have had language at a young age, perhaps saying "mommy" or "daddy" or identifying various objects within the house, and then lose those words completely.

 FACT

The behaviors of autism may seem strange at first, but upon consideration, you will see that they reflect the child's effort to establish predictability and order in his or her world. A world with limited language, or no language at all, is out of control. A repetitive behavior can help the child gain some control.

A child may be suspected of being deaf because of the total lack of response to spoken language. It is common for the diagnostic trail to begin with a parent or grandparent asking for an auditory test because of the child's apparent lack of hearing.

However, when the tests show that the child's hearing is normal, further testing will lead to the ASD diagnosis.

Patterns of Behavior, Interests, or Activity

Although the last area discussed, behavior patterns are by no means the least important. The behaviors in a child with ASD are very distinctive and will be an indicator of where on the spectrum a child places. This exam involves a physician, possibly a pediatric neurologist, various therapists, and possibly experts in the mental health field. They will look for characteristics such as:

- Intense preoccupation with a particular activity
- Compulsive engagement in routines that serve no practical function
- Repetitive movements such as flapping, spinning, and/or body movements
- Intense preoccupation with parts of a whole—for example, the spinning tires on a bicycle rather than the entire bicycle

The behaviors of ASD are perhaps the best known of the signs and symptoms. Films have illustrated behaviors exhibited by people on the autism spectrum, so the public is familiar with this set of symptoms. Most children with autism appear perfectly normal to the bystander until certain behaviors such as flapping or spinning indicate that autism or a related condition is present. These behaviors are an early indicator as well, and they may be what prompt parents to seek a medical opinion.

 ESSENTIAL

The intensely repetitive use of a VCR to watch the ending credits of a film is a common behavior in children with ASD. They will often spend an hour or more rewinding the tape to view the words as they move by on the screen. Music accompanying these credits is even more appealing.

Your Emotional Reaction

When parents first absorb the information about their child being somewhere on the autism spectrum, they experience various stages of coping. You will, too. Never allow anyone to make you feel guilty for experiencing these emotions. There has been a loss—a loss of dreams, potential, and hopes for a future that will be different than anticipated. You most likely will experience guilt, denial, hopelessness, depression, sadness, anger, desperation, and any number of emotional reactions, and all of these reactions are normal.

Loss of Dreams

When a couple learns of a pregnancy, it is almost impossible not to have expectations for the child growing in the mother's womb. It is also natural to project dreams of this child's future: playing baseball, camping, school band . . . the list of possibilities is as varied as the families to which the children are born.

When a diagnosis of a disability is given, so many of the preconceived notions of what life could have been like for this child are lost. The feeling of loss is tremendous. It is a devastating blow to parents. The imagined arguments over curfews, borrowing the car, going to college, and bringing home a boyfriend or girlfriend for the first time become anticipated events that just slip away from the future like water through open fingers. This loss of dreams is not unlike a death, and all of the hopes of the future have to be calibrated into a new pattern of thought.

Guilt

Parents invariably turn inward when something goes wrong with their child. It is a natural reaction. Mom may question every aspect of her pregnancy and wonder what she did to cause the autism or what she could have done to prevent it. Mom may look in the mirror and analyze every moment to find what she did wrong to cause this to happen to her child. Dads, too, will find ways to blame themselves and turn inward, hating themselves for a perceived or imagined wrong they may have done.

It is important to understand that ASD is not caused by parental neglect. You did not cause this. It is even more important for health care providers to realize parents are going through this grieving process and that guilt makes the ability to cope with ASD that much more difficult.

 **FACT**

Feeling guilt without reason can have the same effect as excessive stress. The person may experience headaches, depression, and other physical and emotional symptoms, and/or participate in harmful activities such as overeating or substance abuse in an attempt to remove the pain. There is no reason you should feel guilty: Autism is no one's fault and there is no blame.

Denial

When a situation arises that exceeds a person's ability to cope, such as the diagnosis of a terminal disease, denial is often the result. It is human nature to handle a devastating situation by simply pretending it does not exist. This is not a failure on the part of the person to "handle it." In many ways, this shows the coping mechanisms are functioning normally in the part of the human brain that only allows a certain amount of stress to be processed at a time. By avoiding a stress overload, the ability to cope is maintained.

Although denial may seem unhealthy to the outsider, and it is unhealthy if you do not slowly begin to accept the situation, it initially serves as a protecting shield. It allows the mind to absorb the facts at a manageable rate. Eventually, acceptance will come about.

If a parent remains in denial, it is important to have intervention through some form of counseling. Counseling can help a person understand that this disability, although it does indeed change life, does not ruin the parent/child relationship. Different is not necessarily the end; it only requires adaptation.

 **ALERT!**

> Everyone has to cope in his or her own way. For some, acceptance comes quickly; for others, it is a lengthy process. There is no right or wrong way to do this. Learning to cope with the diagnosis of autism in your child has to be done at your own pace.

Hopelessness

This aspect of dealing with the diagnosis of autism will wax and wane. At times you will feel you can handle just about anything; at other times you will feel totally helpless to protect and assist your child. Both of these reactions are normal. There will be many times when you can't make life easier for your autistic child, and feelings of hopelessness are natural at such times. Just ride it out and remind yourself that tomorrow will be easier.

Parents tend to look at a child's entire life and, in one day, try to solve all the problems they foresee their child facing. This aggravates the feeling of hopelessness. Time teaches us that problems cannot be solved in one day. It is normal to experience feelings of hopelessness when you cannot easily solve the problems that your child faces. Just remember, these feelings will pass.

Anger

Hearing that a child has a lifelong disorder that has an unknown cause and for which there is no absolute and effective treatment is enough to make anyone angry. Anger is a normal part of loss. Depression is anger turned inward, so it is important to acknowledge anger and displace it properly.

It is only natural to be infuriated with a situation that is out of your control; learn to be gentle with yourself and your family when you feel anger. Talking it over with a therapist or trusted friend can be very helpful. Meeting other parents who are dealing with the same challenges is also helpful. Support groups are set up all over the United States and Canada. Surrounding yourself with people who also have children with autism will help the anger dissipate into actions that are more constructive.

Desperation

This is one of the most common reactions; virtually all parents will experience this emotion. Parents of newly, and not so newly, diagnosed children will do or try just about anything to "cure" ASD. Many spend hours of research on the Internet, in libraries, in public records, or private book collections to find the one thing that may "fix" the autism. It is not unusual to find a parent spending six to eight hours each day on the Internet exploring an unfamiliar treatment.

Because of this, it is important that parents recognize their vulnerability in this area. The tantalizing product that may cure your child is hard to resist. Many less than scrupulous people are out there who are more than willing to sell you the latest autism cure for a "reasonable price," never to be seen again.

Increase in Incidence

Over the past few years, there has been considerable debate regarding statistics that show an increase in the number of children diagnosed as autistic or on the spectrum. Has the number of children with autism increased, or has better diagnostic criteria resulted in the appearance of a higher incidence? This question has the autism community divided.

Autism was documented for the first time in the 1940s and it was theorized that "refrigerator mothers," those mothers who withheld love from their children, were causing autism. Because of that, it was labeled a psychiatric disorder and 50 percent of diagnosed children were institutionalized, forgotten by a society that never knew them in the first place.

Thirty years ago, the incidence of autism was between 1 and 4 per 10,000 children. It was a rare disorder, and few people had ever heard of it. Certainly even fewer had met anyone who had autism.

After 1990

In the recent past, though, the number of children with autism has exploded. It is difficult to find exact statistics on autism, but estimates by some research organizations show that it affects anywhere from 1 or 2 children per 500 to 1 per 100. The CDC reports a range of 2 to 6 per 1,000 children. The CDC reported that during the 2000–2001 school year, there were more than 15,000 children ages three to five years old and more than 78,000 children ages six to twenty-one years old in the United States with autism, as defined in the Individuals with Disabilities Education Act (IDEA). These estimated numbers are lower than the actual count, however, as students in private schools or home schooling environments are not included.

As autism numbers have increased, the general population within the United States has become more interested. During a prime-time newscast, CNN reported that California—the only state that keeps records on the incidence of autism—had documented an increase of nearly 300 percent. However, the CDC states that the exact number of ASD children in California is unknown, despite the existence of Centers of Excellence for Autism and Developmental Disabilities Research and Epidemiology (CADDRE) in that state.

 **FACT**

"Medicine for Autism Today," a neuro-immune dysfunction syndrome (NIDS) project, documented a study that illustrated the dramatic rise in the number of children with autism when they reported a 900 percent increase in cases of autism. Autism, according to this study, is growing faster than any other special-needs disorder in the world.

Better Diagnostics or Legitimate Increase?

The question remains whether the numbers are a true reflection of an increase of actual children with an ASD or if the procedures for diagnosis are simply more accurate now. Could it just be that it is recognized and properly labeled more often because our society has become better educated and therefore more aware of autism and related conditions? Were children who had autism thirty years ago overlooked and therefore not treated? Many parents and researchers find themselves at odds over this point, and the children are in the middle of the debate.

The unanswered question that essentially solves the debate pertains to adults. If autism has not increased in numbers and it is simply being diagnosed more carefully and accurately now, where are all of the adults with autism who were undiagnosed as children? Where are the children with autism who were born forty and fifty years ago?

A National Epidemic

If the increase in the ASD population is in fact an increase in the numbers of actual children affected rather than a reflection of better diagnostics, what does this mean for these children and our society? The documentation showing the percentages of affected children is substantial. Regardless of why the numbers are up, the fact is that there are a lot more children with autism, and it is going to affect our society.

Many people do not feel that the word *epidemic* is appropriate for autism spectrum disorders. Epidemics imply a contagious disease, and although autism and the related conditions are not contagious, they do share other qualities of an epidemic. Strictly defined, an epidemic is an illness or condition that spreads rapidly and affects a large number of people. In common usage, the term implies something that grows unchecked and continues to affect more and more people. Autism certainly fits into that classification.

Possible Causes

Nothing divides the autism community more deeply than a discussion of the potential causes of autism. Perfectly normal and rational adults will come together in meetings and benefits to raise awareness of autism issues and end up in bitter arguments as to what causes autism. Many of the disagreements over the cause of autism have been so hostile that the debates themselves have actually overshadowed the main purpose of the gathering—to raise awareness of the disorder itself.

ALERT!

The most critical problem facing the autism community today is the lack of unity. Without unity, progress cannot be made toward finding any treatment or cure, let alone a cause. The autism community must put their differences aside and work together.

Some organizations have worked hard to achieve unity as the foundation of their structure and have not taken a direct stand on causes. However, many more organizations have sprung up with the express target of catering to what that particular organization and its members have determined to be the trigger of ASD. Although that would seem to be an adequate solution, it has backfired. It does keep people within one organization from attacking one another because of disagreements over theories of cause and treatment, but it has also served to divide the autism community as a whole. This division has been a nearly fatal blow to the cause of autism.

To understand the problems behind the disagreements over cause and treatment, it must be understood that there are some very controversial issues behind autism spectrum disorders. The conflicts over vaccinations, genetics, disease processes, and allergies, to name a few, have driven deeply into the consciousness of parents with affected children. It is human nature to want to blame something or someone for a loss, and it is no less true where autism is concerned.

Many feel there is no one single cause but that a combination of triggers, combined in a unique way during this generation, has caused a cascade effect that has resulted in the condition we call autism and its related disorders.

There is no one proven cause of autism, but there are many suspected triggers. Aggressive research continues to be done in an effort to determine what the cause may be so that the most effective intervention can be put in place.

Neuro-Immune Dysfunction Syndrome (NIDS)/Autoimmune Disease

Interestingly enough, when the number of autism spectrum disorders in the population began to increase, so did the incidences of autoimmune diseases and chronic fatigue syndrome (CFS), as well as attention deficit disorder (ADD/ADHD). It is common to find a family in which one parent suffers from CFS or another autoimmune disorder, an older child has ADD, and a younger child falls somewhere on the autism spectrum. It is as if something came into the environment of the house and attacked, affecting each member of the family differently based on his or her age.

The NIDS theory says that many, if not most, patients who suffer from a variety of autoimmune disorders, as well as autism, actually have a neuro-immune dysfunction. This causes chemical imbalances, which subsequently causes a restriction in the blood flow to the brain. In autism, the area of the brain affected would be the area controlling speech, language, socialization, and obsessive behaviors. The trigger that starts the disease process could be environmental, vaccine related, or an illness.

If this theory holds true, then what is being dealt with is a new disease that has a great potential for treatment. This theory has not yet been proved, but physicians researching NIDS and the treatment of it are seeing relief of the symptoms of autism in their patients. Parents who have chosen these methods of treatment for their children are also seeing improvements they had only hoped for but never expected.

Vaccinations

One of the leading theories behind the cause of autism spectrum disorders is the increase in the number and kind of vaccinations given to very young children. The leading suspect is the MMR (measles, mumps, and rubella) vaccination first given at approximately fifteen months of age. Some leading studies have shown that upon biopsy of the lower gastrointestinal tract of children with autism, measles is found. This, of course, is not normal, and since many children with autism also have bowel diseases, it raises the question of what the connection may be.

The research continues, and in the interim, many parents have decided against immunizations, despite the insistence of health organizations that there is no link between the MMR and autism. There are thousands of anecdotal stories about children who were perfectly normal until shortly after the first MMR immunization. These children spoke in phrases, interacted with people around them, and suddenly became nonverbal and nonresponsive within a few days of receiving the immunization.

 ALERT!

If you choose not to have your child immunized, upon entering school, you will need paperwork that states one of two reasons. You may claim a religious exemption or present a letter from your child's physician stating that he or she believes vaccinations are harmful to your child's health.

Genetics

Many people believe that the cause of autism spectrum disorders will be found to have a genetic basis. The completion of the Human Genome Project will accelerate this line of research. Since many families who have one child with autism later have another one, it has led many to believe that autism "runs" in families. The only autism spectrum disorders that have conclusively been proved to be genetic are fragile X syndrome and Rett syndrome. Both of those disorders can be tested by blood work that looks directly at the chromosomes involved, and the genetic flaw can be identified.

Genetics is a field that is vast and uncharted. The Human Genome Project will enable researchers to delve more deeply into this area than was ever before possible, but it is much like looking for the proverbial needle in the haystack. The one hole in the theory that all autism spectrum disorders are genetic is that human genetics has not mutated very much over the past few thousand years, yet the incidence of autism is much higher now than at any time in history.

Environmental Causes

Another theory that either stands alone or works in conjunction with the other theories is the environmental issues that may have caused autism. The world is now inundated with pollution, food processing, and other toxic elements that were not present in past eras. It is conceivable that humanity has caused this syndrome by environmental abuse.

The most likely link with the environment intertwines with other theories, such as environmental factors combining with a vaccine and affecting DNA in a new way. At this time, like all theories, the truth is unknown. It may be that in the past few decades a new environmental agent has triggered a genetic weakness.

There are no easy answers for parents faced with the diagnosis of an autism spectrum disorder in one or more of their children. It is a challenge that will be faced on a daily basis for the rest of the parent's lives, and the burden will extend beyond the parent's lives. Exploring different options in a unified manner will progress the cause of autism more than any other single effort.

CHAPTER 3

Other Coexisting Medical Conditions

IT WOULD SEEM that autism would be enough to deal with, but other medical conditions often accompany ASD. Some of these conditions are just those that happen to any child. Comorbid conditions are conditions that exist simultaneously within the same person. Other conditions occur with more frequency in an individual with autism and are thus known as associated disorders.

It is common to think that if any other condition arises, it must be part of autism. That assumption isn't always true, and children should be watched closely for symptoms that need medical attention. With the passing years, parents will become more experienced in recognizing less obvious symptoms, such as sore throats and headaches.

Tourette's Syndrome

Often, parents of ASD-diagnosed children question whether or not their child may also have Tourette's syndrome (TS). TS is a neurological condition characterized by repeated and uncontrollable tics and/or vocalizations. This syndrome is diagnosed symptomatically, as there is no laboratory testing available to confirm the diagnosis. Signs include:

- Involuntary tics that are impossible to control for any extended period of time

- Tics that appear in repeated and consistent patterns
- Several motor and vocal tics that may or may not appear simultaneously
- Symptoms occur for more than one year
- Symptoms increase or decrease in severity over time
- Symptoms manifest before the age of eighteen or twenty-one, depending on diagnostic criteria

TS was first documented in the nineteenth century by Georges Gilles de la Tourette, a French physician. It is considered a spectrum disorder in itself, with different degrees of severity. Some people with TS have barely noticeable symptoms and others have problems with normal daily activities, as the rapid movements interfere to a great degree.

There is controversy and confusion as to whether the incidence of Tourette's is higher in children who have ASD. Some of the symptoms of Tourette's appear very much the same as the symptoms of autism. Some confusion may exist in the diagnosis of TS because TS and obsessive-compulsive disorder (OCD) are linked, and OCD and ASD are linked. However, there does not appear to be a dramatically higher occurrence of TS in children with ASD.

 FACT

Tics are the involuntary movements of a portion of a person's body. These can occur anywhere in the body, but the face, neck, and shoulders are the most commonly seen locations for tics. Uncontrollable sounds made by a person are called vocal tics.

Coprolalia and Copropraxia

One of the most recognizable symptoms of Tourette's syndrome is coprolalia—uncontrollable utterances of obscenities. However, this is seen less in autistic children due to the nonverbal issues. It is often combined with a gross motor tic called copropraxia, which is the use of obscene gestures.

Coprolalia only affects 30 percent of patients with TS, although it is the most commonly known symptom of the syndrome. Victims of this syndrome try desperately to mute the socially unacceptable words but, as with other types of tics, doing so only increases the compulsion. Ultimately, this effort increases, rather than decreases, the behavior.

Anxiety disorders are closely related to TS. The affected person can control the tics to some extent; however, this control comes at great expense. Finally allowing the tics to occur after holding back for a period greatly increases their severity and the anxiety in the patient. It becomes a vicious cycle as the patient tries to control the tics for social acceptability. When control is lost, the tics are more dramatic, which increases the anxiety, thus increasing the need to act out the tics.

Autism and Tourette's Syndrome

It is important to determine if a child has autism and Tourette's or if his or her tics may be a part of autism alone. Many children with autism have a series of tics that appear to be out of their control. With the repeated rhythm and compulsion to act out these tics, it is easy to confuse the two syndromes, but the compulsive aspects of autism are enough to cause this behavior.

If a child with an ASD has TS as well, it can be treated with various medications. However, medications should only be used if necessary, and a certain diagnosis is needed before such medications can be prescribed. A qualified physician can determine exactly what the diagnosis is and how to treat the disorder.

Obsessive-Compulsive Disorder

It is surprising to many people that obsessive-compulsive disorder (OCD) is an actual psychiatric disorder in and of itself, separate from autism. All disorders on the autism spectrum do show some degree of obsessive-compulsive behavior. ASD and OCD are closely linked. If a child has ASD, it is very likely she will deal with an element of OCD as well. OCD symptoms can be quite debilitating:

- Thoughts and/or images that are recurring and persistent.
- Anxiety, sometimes severe, that results from the thoughts and images.
- Thoughts and images experienced are not normal worries experienced by all people.
- Patients realize these thoughts are irrational but are unable to stop them.
- Behaviors such as counting, hand washing, or any number of activities done repetitively.
- Behaviors that are compulsive and produce anxiety if not performed.
- Compulsive behaviors not linked in any rational way to the anxiety they are intended to reduce.
- Obsessions and compulsions interfere in a person's daily activities because of the amount of time they involve.

 FACT

Historically, people with OCD have been treated by psychiatrists, as it was and still is considered a mental illness. However, recent research is beginning to cast doubt on the classification of OCD as a mental disorder. It has long been understood that family influences or social pressures do not cause OCD; the theory that a person compulsively counts or checks things because a parent insisted on perfection is not valid.

The Prevalence of OCD

The National Institute of Mental Health estimates that between 2 and 3 percent of the population in the United States is affected by OCD. That means that in the United States, over 3 million people between the ages of eighteen and fifty-four suffer from OCD. OCD affects men and women equally and does not discriminate based on race, economic status, or ethnic background. It usually begins in the adolescent or young adult years, but in many cases it begins in childhood. OCD accounts for 6 percent of the total cost of mental health care expenses.

Current research indicates there is a strong possibility that OCD is caused by a misfiring or "mis-wiring" in the brain. Given the close connection between TS and OCD, it is also possible there is a genetic link. Many people with OCD report having a parent who also had it.

OCD with Other Conditions

In a person with another condition, it is often difficult to separate out what might be OCD and what is part of the original problem. This is particularly true with an ASD. Autism by its very nature includes obsessions and compulsions as part of the matrix of symptoms. Children with an ASD will compulsively put objects in a line, insist that things are ordered in a certain way, and demand that a certain routine be followed, and they will become anxious and belligerent if these behaviors or routines are interrupted.

 **QUESTION?**

Why does my child line up objects on the floor?
There are many theories as to why lining up objects is an almost universal symptom in autism, but it is an obsession and a compulsion. If the lines are disturbed, it is extremely frustrating to a child with autism. It may be an attempt on the part of the child to establish order during times of sensory overload.

If a child is diagnosed as having OCD and is not diagnosed on the autism spectrum, but the parents feel that there is a possibility of autism, it is important to seek a second opinion. If autism is present, even high-functioning autism, and early intervention is not provided, the possibilities of tremendous advancement at a young age may be lost. Do not hesitate to follow your own instincts regarding your child's health. A pediatric neurologist familiar with autism is a resource that should be considered.

Seizures

Of all the conditions that can occur with autism, perhaps none is as frightening to parents as seizures. Parents feel out of control and fearful for their child. It may be more frightening because most seizures in children with autism do not begin until puberty, so the family has not gotten used to handling them. However, it is not as common as many parents fear; it is estimated that 25 to 30 percent of children with autism also have a seizure disorder. Most children on the autism spectrum make great strides during their teenage years, and negative anticipation is not warranted.

Since the seizures most commonly begin at puberty, and hormones become quite active at that time, researchers are looking for the connection between hormones and the chemicals within the brain. This could perhaps lead to testing that would predict which children might have seizures and to treatments that would prevent seizures from occurring.

Hearing and Auditory Response

A child with an ASD is not immune to the normal vision and hearing disorders that any other child may deal with. The problem for parents is recognizing when a problem exists.

Generally, hearing losses are discovered quickly in ASD children because of the suspicion of a child being deaf before an ASD is considered. It is common for parents, and especially grandparents, to question whether a child can hear due to the behavior of the child when a family member speaks to him or her. Normally, children turn their heads to acknowledge their name or to look in the direction of an interesting sound. Children with autism do not always respond to voice, and this may be the first thing you notice.

Hearing tests are very accurate, even on very young children. Audiologists will use special equipment to rule out a hearing loss.

If there is a deficit in hearing, they will then determine what kind of deafness is occurring and how to treat it. If a child has a hearing loss, whether total or partial, it is important to intervene with the appropriate hearing aids, even if a child is totally nonverbal. Speech therapy is an important part of the intervention used for a child with ASD, and a child must hear properly to learn to integrate speech into her life. If she is not hearing sounds properly, it will be even more difficult for her to compensate for and possibly conquer the lack of speech.

There are even more problems if a deaf child is autistic, as the hearing impairment may mask the symptoms of autism, and the autism may not be recognized early in the child's life. This delays intervention and therapy that a child with autism so desperately needs.

 ESSENTIAL

Sign language is the communication tool for the deaf. Although American Sign Language (ASL) is most commonly used, it is not the easiest for an ASD child to learn, as it is very conceptual. Exact Sign Language is more suitable for the way the autistic brain works.

A Deaf Child with Autism

Although it might seem to be splitting hairs, there is a difference in what happens to a child when he or she is first diagnosed as being deaf as opposed to being diagnosed with autism. When a child is deaf, interventions begin for the hearing impairment, but the other impairments particular to autism are not begun. This, of course, is expected if a child is not autistic. But the result can be catastrophic for the family and the child if the child is also autistic.

A child who is deaf and is undiagnosed as being on the autism spectrum will have difficulty with socialization skills, and therapy will be much more difficult. The lack of eye contact will be treated as a behavioral issue rather than as a disorder. The situation can become a very stressful family issue when a child is perceived as uncooperative or belligerent, and meanwhile, the child is forced to wander about alone in the imposed exile of autism.

If you have a child with a hearing impairment, but recognize many of the symptoms on the autism spectrum, it is very important to have an evaluation done to determine if autism is also involved. There are not many profoundly deaf children who are also autistic, but it does happen. The Rose F. Kennedy Center for Research in Mental Retardation and Human Development did a study on forty-six children with deafness and found that nearly half of those children were also autistic but had been undiagnosed as such. The children's progress was suffering severely due to the lack of proper intervention. Therapy must be initiated not only for the hearing loss but also for the autism to ensure the most promising outcome.

An ASD Child with Deafness

A child who has been diagnosed with autism either before or simultaneously with the diagnosis of deafness will have a much better chance at progressing well in therapy. Therapists teaching a child to communicate will use several different approaches to increase communication skills. Perhaps one of the most important therapies a child with autism will have is sensory integration.

 ALERT!

Because of the importance of visual processing for a child with ASD, parents must remember that their child may be watching them at any time. This is good for teaching things to your child, but remember that he will also see you doing things that could be harmful if he did them, such as getting into medications.

Sensory integration is teaching a child how to understand all of the stimuli that enters into the brain from the different senses.

Children with autism can be hypersensitive to sensory input or they can be completely hyposensitive. As stated previously, it depends on the child, where they are on the spectrum, and what particular impairments they are struggling with. The purpose of sensory integration therapy is to train, or "retune," the brain to understand that the different stimuli do indeed fit together into a cohesive whole.

When a child has a hearing loss, one of the senses has been deprived of input. It is a myth that other senses will become stronger to make up for the loss; it only seems that way because people do depend on the other senses more. So, with sensory integration, a therapist will work with a child who is deaf and has autism to learn to lean on the visual, usually with sign language, to place a "visual sound" in her mind. This can then be integrated with the other senses, such as taste, smell, and touch.

As a parent, if your child has a hearing loss as well as autism, understand that the progress will be slow, but there will be progress. The challenges will be great, but the victories will be greater. If you are using sign language and are discouraged because you believe your child never looks at you and there isn't any point to continuing, remember that people with ASD visualize in different ways. She may have been watching you in her peripheral vision and learned more than you realized.

Hypersensitivity to Sound

Another common problem for children with ASD is being hypersensitive to sound. It is not unusual to see a child who is autistic suddenly cover his or her ears in an effort to block out all sound. One theory on this is that people with autism do not discriminate sounds. In other words, they hear all sounds equally. As you sit here reading this book, you are most likely aware of sounds around you: Traffic on the street, the hum of a heater or air conditioner, a radio, a dog barking in the distance, or any variety of the normal sounds of life. If this theory is correct, children with autism hear all of these sounds with equal intensity. It wouldn't take much of that to cause a sensory overload!

 **FACT**

If your child suddenly covers his ears and looks for an escape out of the room, make every effort to lower the sound level or remove him to a quieter room. Sensory overload is painful, and not relieving the situation may result in an anger outburst.

Whether it is not enough sound or too much sound, hearing is an issue for a person with an ASD. This sense is a vital part of functioning in the world, and a child needs to learn how to manage it. Appropriate therapy, especially sensory integration therapy, is vital to success in this area.

Vision Problems

Parents generally look out for vision problems by observing how their child watches television, colors pictures in a coloring book, or gauges distance while playing. A child with autism will do these things in the same manner as other children, so the unique visual problems of a child who has an ASD may be missed.

Identifying the Problem

Most children with autism have some kind of visual problem that results from being on the spectrum. Common indications for visual difficulties include:

- Lack of eye contact
- Staring at objects, especially spinning items such as wheels
- Momentary peripheral glances
- Side viewing
- Scanning objects quickly
- Difficulty maintaining visual contact with an object or person
- Crossed eyes
- Eye movement abnormalities

Vision problems are more typical in their occurrence with sensory disorder patients than in the normal population. Yet, when a child has autism, it is very easy for schools, caregivers, and parents to attribute behaviors to autism when visual problems are the actual culprit. Combined with the problems an autistic child has in integrating visual input with other sensory input, this can lead to difficulties that are very hard to overcome. As an example, when there is difficulty integrating central vision with peripheral vision, processing is less efficient in the brain. This overlaps into other areas and can affect motor, cognitive, and speech skills.

 ESSENTIAL

One easy way for parents to determine if their child is having visual processing problems is to observe how she watches television. Does she press her face sideways to the screen and rotate her eyes around looking for a better angle? If so, an eye exam is in order.

Vision Therapy

Vision therapy is a specialized area of eye care. The specialists who practice in this field are known as developmental optometrists. These doctors are qualified to do vision exams and check for particular vision conditions. They can prescribe special lenses that will help with the integration of a child's vision and can prescribe therapies that will improve vision and sensory integration skills. These therapies are important to maximize the potential of a child's vision, potentially avoid surgery, and alert parents to any eye diseases that require an ophthalmologist.

Visual health is important, but just as important is visual processing. If an individual on the autism spectrum cannot process the information he or she receives through sight, the entire chain of sensory skills will not be in proper working order. The potential effects of poor visual processing can be multiple. Children can have attention span problems, an inability to recognize objects from different angles, and further delays in speech and sensory skills.

The visual abnormalities likely in children with autism can cause a total distortion in how they view the world and how they process that information. It can give a child the feeling that objects bounce or swim, jump unpredictably, are fragmented into tiny pieces, or are overly large. Poor visual processing will contribute to problems with fine motor skills, attention deficits, and a variety of social interaction issues. In order for a person to function as a whole, integrated human being, sensory integration must be functioning, and that begins with vision.

Other Physical Challenges

Some physical issues that accompany ASD are a part of the symptom matrix. Conditions such as encopresis, a bowel disorder characterized by leaky stool, and eczema are common in children with ASD. It is also common for these children to have abnormal reactions to sensations, such as the apparent inability to feel pain or an intolerance to heat or cold. Clumsiness or gross motor skill issues are common in Asperger's syndrome patients. Rett syndrome has its own set of physical issues that result in the loss of the ability to walk.

 FACT

A child with autism is just as likely to break a bone, require stitches, skin a knee, or be subject to any of the childhood injuries all of us go through at young ages. They are susceptible to the same childhood illnesses, perhaps more so if parents have elected to forgo immunizations, and having autism will not make these diseases worse.

Any physical issues that may occur in the family are just as likely, or just as unlikely, to occur in the child with ASD. Migraines, allergies, scoliosis, and any number of issues are not affected in either direction by autism. It may be harder for a parent to determine if a problem is present due to the communication difficulties and the different reaction to pain, but time and experience will teach parents how to cope with these problems.

Other Mental Challenges

ASD is characterized by deficits in mental functioning. The most difficult associated deficit is without a doubt mental retardation. Statistics vary widely on how many ASD children are also mentally retarded—the estimates range from 30 percent to 80 percent. Because of the difficulty in obtaining accurate IQ scores in children with autism, it is also difficult to determine if a child is mentally retarded. The standard for determining retardation is an IQ score of seventy or below.

With such a wide variance on the estimates of retardation occurring in ASD children, it is an area of great concern and great controversy. There is no "standard" retardation seen in ASD children, so the effect may be mild to moderate and even range to profound retardation in some individuals. When the level of retardation is mild, it is difficult to determine if it is truly a retardation issue or a problem with other symptoms of autism.

Retardation is difficult for parents to accept. Often, they emotionally cope with the diagnosis of autism easier than they do the diagnosis of mental retardation in their child. Be aware that many people with autism have extraordinary skills in a few areas. These are known as splinter skills and include such things as the ability to determine the day of the week of any given date in any given year. Splinter skills are remarkable feats of intelligence in very narrow areas. Having them, or not having them, does not indicate retardation one way or the other.

A variety of physicians and therapists should be involved if retardation is suspected. A pediatric neurologist is always the best physician for the primary care in autism, but a psychiatrist, a pediatrician, and a variety of therapists and psychologists should be involved as well. A team approach to a child with multiple deficits will provide for the best outcome.

There are no easy ways through this. Children on the autism spectrum have multiple problems of varying kinds. One child may have virtually no other physical or mental problems and another might have several. Most children fall in between and have a few problems along with the autism.

The most important thing a parent can remember is that not all of this will happen at once, and not all of it has to be solved at once. It is a matter of discovering the issues, determining the best course of action, and then beginning to walk the path. Your goal? Make your child with autism the best person he or she can be!

CHAPTER 4

Behaviors

THE BEHAVIORS OF AUTISM are a hallmark symptom, after lack of speech. Behaviors that are out of the ordinary are the primary symptom in other spectrum disorders such as Asperger's syndrome. The behaviors shown in ASD are particular to the disorder, and although each child is unique in how he or she displays autism, certain behaviors are common. Some of these behaviors will interfere with daily life and others will not. Some can be controlled while others are just a part of the package that is your child.

Obsessive-Compulsive Behaviors

Many behaviors fall into this category, and it is important to remember that although OCD may appear to be the same, it is not. However, autism includes many behaviors that the child with autism is obsessed with and compulsively engages in:

- Lining up objects, such as trains, blocks, cars, or video-tape cassettes.
- Opening or closing doors on cupboards, closets, or doors to the outside.
- Spinning in circles or walking in a circle.
- Hand or arm flapping.
- Rocking the body back and forth.

- Counting objects repeatedly for no apparent reason.
- Hiding or hoarding objects.
- Preoccupation with objects being placed in a chosen location.
- Gestures and facial movements that resemble Tourette's syndrome.
- Narrow selection of food often based on color or shape.

These behaviors have two parts. The first part is the obsession; it is uncontrolled and unwanted thoughts. Because people with autism are either nonverbal or have limited verbal ability, it is difficult to determine if those thoughts are present, particularly in children. The second part manifests as compulsive behaviors; parents, teachers, and medical experts easily see this aspect.

Lines

Some believe that the creation of lines, and the act of lining up objects, is the effort of the person with autism to put a sense of order to what he perceives to be an out-of-control and disordered world. If the sensory overload that children with autism have is common, it is easy to understand in this context. Lines are orderly and creating those lines gives control.

It is believed that people with autism do not have the discriminatory ability to separate environmental input. In other words, when the television is on, the air conditioner is running, the dog is barking, and the phone is ringing at the neighbor's house, autistic people perceive the sounds as all being of equal weight. The same analogy can be applied to the other senses as well. Sensory overload is a common occurrence for children with autism. It could easily be deduced that this "equal opportunity stimuli" would apply to visual input as well.

Lines are the perfect solution if the visual part of the brain is on overload. A line is the shortest distance between two points and that makes it clean and uncluttered. Lines may not be a meaningless compulsive behavior but may be a way of coping with sensory overload through an order that is natural and easily understood.

ESSENTIAL

Some parents discourage the creation of lines and have very frustrated and irritable children. Other parents ignore the lines, as they seem to reduce stress and anger in children who are autistic. The only negative aspect to line creation is the preoccupation and absorption that may result. If that is the case, divert your child's attention into other activities that do not threaten his ability to create his lines. Most of the time, this behavior of creating lines diminishes as a child matures.

Medications

Parents of children with autism are very divided on the use of medications, particularly for issues of behavior, as opposed to seizures or other medical conditions. The medication commonly used for the compulsive behaviors of autism is known as a serotonin reuptake inhibitor (SSRI).

SSRI medications used by patients with autism have been shown not only to reduce compulsive behaviors, but to also aid in other symptoms of autism. Most notably, eye contact improves, social interaction becomes easier, the narrow field of interests grows, and the isolation problems many children with autism have lessen. Tantrums and anger are also reduced with the use of SSRIs. The primary symptom of autistic children being withdrawn and preoccupied within their own world is also lessened, and the medication has a calming effect.

Side effects are generally few and include dry mouth, insomnia, and paradoxically impulsive behavior. These side effects are rare and can be avoided by starting with very small doses and working up to the ideal dose. These medications are not recommended for people who have seizures or heart problems, so a consultation with a physician well acquainted with the use of these medications is prudent. Studies of ten years and longer do not show any long-term problems resulting from the use of SSRIs.

Routine

One way that obsessive-compulsive behavior manifests in a child with autism is through the insistence of routine. A sudden change in the daily routine, or even a small aspect of that routine, can cause a perfectly good day to go downhill fast. Routine is part of autism, and although flexibility can be taught to a certain degree, the need for routine will never disappear completely. Children with autism depend on that routine to know what is going on, what is expected of them, and what they can expect from others.

 **FACT**

In the case of separated or divorced parents, a child may have behavioral problems with the noncustodial parent when that parent has the child for a long weekend. This can lead to questions about the ability of a parent to care for the child. In reality, it is the change in routine that is to blame.

If your child is sensitive to routine changes, minimizing the shock of the change is a wise idea. Sometimes sudden change cannot be avoided, so all a family can do is remember how upsetting those changes are to a child with autism. When an unexpected event causes a routine change, such as a snow day that has canceled school, provide your child with a good movie or a favorite toy that hasn't recently been played with to distract her as much as possible. For the most part you will have to ride it out; it is just one of those things that everyone will learn to adapt to, including your child.

Flapping

Flapping is a behavior that can be considered a form of compulsive activity. It is common in all spectrum disorders, but is particularly strong in autism. It is something that appears around the time of other autism symptoms and is linked to either strong physical actions or emotional activity. Flapping is a rapid and repetitive hand and/or lower arm motion that resembles waving. It is often one of the first symptoms that parents notice, as it is an atypical behavior in children.

 QUESTION?

Is flapping always an indication of autism?
No. While flapping may be one of the earliest symptoms of autism, it is common for all babies to engage in this behavior. The difference with autism can be seen as a child matures. Flapping behavior typically disappears in most children. If a child, at the age of eighteen months to two years, continues flapping, it is something to investigate.

Expressing Excitement

When a child with autism becomes excited, it is common to see this excitement manifested as flapping. Many children will be watching a television program or movie and become so excited that the emotion has to spill out; flapping will be the result. Positive emotions such as excitement, joy, or utter delight are more commonly associated with flapping than negative emotions. Flapping can often herald a loss of control and should be watched and regarded as a signal. Most of the time flapping means nothing more than the emotion it is connected to, but if an emotion is getting too extreme, flapping will usually precede it.

There are times when a child who is irritated or upset will flap. Parents will see a different "character" to this kind of flapping and will learn to recognize that anger or aggression may be building. This is something that only experience can teach. Learning to correctly anticipate behaviors is part of the parenting of a child with autism. As the months and years go by, it becomes much easier to accurately do this, so learn to trust yourself, as no one knows your child as well as you do.

Flapping is also seen in children with autism during physical activity. Most children will pump their arms while running. Children with autism will quite often not reach this developmental milestone and will flap while they run. This is related to the activity and not to any particular emotion.

Other Repetitive Behaviors

Flapping isn't the only repetitive behavior that appears in autism. Autism also causes other behaviors that are unique to the disorder. Such actions as twirling, rocking, head banging, facial contortions, eye movements, and unusual voice patterns are also repetitive stereotypical behavioral patterns. These behaviors are different from tics and other repetitive motion disorders, so a diagnosis of autism cannot be based on the appearance of these behaviors alone.

Behaviors such as head banging and facial contortions disturb parents greatly. It is an out-of-control behavior that displays the undeniable fact that a child is disabled. Lack of speech can be covered up; deficits in learning abilities can be glossed over. It is impossible to ignore a physical action repeated endlessly with no meaning.

Treatment

Physicians have different views on the treatment of flapping and related behaviors. The vast majority feels that if the movement patterns do not respond to the medications a patient with autism is already on, no further treatment will be effective either. SSRIs, Ritalin, and Risperdal are medications often used on patients with autism. SSRIs are often the medication that can halt behaviors specific to autism.

The best way for parents to handle these behaviors is to ignore them. It is unknown why people with autism engage in these behaviors, but it seems to fulfill a need. Interrupting the behaviors will only cause agitation, which can develop into aggression and anger. It is tempting to want to stop these behaviors, but resisting the urge will be less stressful for both parents and child.

Anger and Aggression

Unfortunately, the behavior that is most commonly seen in autism is anger that is expressed through aggression, tantrums, and outbursts.

Meltdowns are an extreme form of an anger display (see Chapter 6 for a more detailed discussion of meltdowns). Of all of the issues in autism, dealing with anger is probably the most difficult.

Anger is caused by frustration, and frustration is an emotion that is prevalent in children with autism. When communication is difficult or not possible, it is only natural to become frustrated. Consider how you feel if you are trying to explain something important to someone who does not speak your language. As you attempt to convey your thoughts and they are not being understood, your frustration grows; you feel frustrated with the situation and with yourself. If you consider that feeling in a child, the only outlet they have is anger, and that is particularly so if the child does not grasp proper social interaction.

Getting Aggressive

Aggression is often the first indication of anger. Children with autism are often aggressive toward other people. They can also become aggressive with pets, toys, and household items.

Anyone and anything can be on the receiving end of the seemingly rude and thoughtless behaviors that occur as a child with autism strives to get his own way. Keeping in mind the frustration a child feels when he is unable to convey his needs and wants, it is easy to understand why he might turn to whatever method will work to have those needs met. Any child, even one who is successfully learning the social graces of our culture, will become pushier than normal when he has to struggle to have his needs satisfied. But a child void of social skills will turn to whatever behavior is successful, and often that behavior is aggression.

 ALERT!

The medication Risperdal is often used to control aggression and anger in children with autism. It is important that parents watch for excessive weight gain and facial tics while their child is on this medication. If these side effects are observed, discuss them with your physician right away.

Tantrums and Outbursts

It is also common for a child on the spectrum who doesn't get her own way to show anger as a form of retaliation, resulting in an outburst or tantrum. When the child is prevented from having what she wants at any given moment, it can result in her hitting or slapping someone without any warning. Parents, siblings, teachers, and caretakers are the usual targets of retaliation. For example if your child wants a particular toy, or to play with something that you have denied her, your child may strike out in anger by hitting or biting.

It isn't unusual for the family dog or cat to bear the brunt of a child's lashing out as well. She may also throw or break things, which only makes the situation worse, as the child then becomes distressed over the broken item. The child has difficulty gaining control over this repeating cycle. Tantrums and outbursts can end as quickly as they began or may take some time to wind down.

Responding to Aggression

When a child has an explosion of anger, parents have to think on their feet. This isn't a problem you can analyze and try to solve—you do need to reflect back on the issue that brought the anger about for the sake of prevention, but the tantrum or outburst you are seeing now has to be dealt with now. It is better to resolve the problem quickly, even if it means giving in to your child's tantrum. It is always unacceptable for a child or adult to strike another person for any reason, at any time. This is the lesson you must convey. The easiest way to teach this is by understanding the cause of the outburst.

If a child loses control over an unmet need that is important, or that an adult did not realize was an issue, the situation will only get more out-of-control if the child is punished. There is enough of a problem with communication without your child feeling that you are punishing him for his attempts to let you know what's on his mind.

QUESTION?

My child is very angry with me. What do I do now?
When someone is out of control, it is hard, but don't get mad.
Try to determine what is frustrating your child. If there is no
discernable cause, there is little you can do other than prevent
damage. Wait it out. It will pass.

Elopement—The Escaping Child

Elopement is something almost all parents of children with autism
have had experience with at one time or another. Elopement in this
case is not a child running off to get married; it is a child with
autism escaping from his home and wandering off alone. It makes
for sleepless nights and jittery nerves. Take the time to view your
house as your child would. How can you prevent elopement?

- Put extra locks on all doors that open to the outside.
- Install a security system that monitors both entering and exiting.
- Install an alarm that hangs on doors for use away from home.
- Get a service animal (a dog is most useful for this problem).
- Establish a routine: The child *never* leaves the house unsupervised.
- Inform trusted neighbors of the possibility of elopement.
- Notify the local police department of the potential problem.

There are other hints that can help your peace of mind at the
same time you are protecting your child's safety. A large family can
work in shifts so that someone always has an eye on a child with
autism. This is particularly important for a child that is bound and
determined to escape. If Mom can't cook dinner or even escape to

the bathroom for a few minutes, stress levels will rise and tempers will get shorter. The entire family must work together to lessen the stress on everyone.

One solution that will work for any person with autism, regardless of age or size, is a double-keyed dead bolt. This type of dead bolt requires a key on either side to lock or unlock it. If you choose this method, the most important thing to develop a habit of doing is to have a key with you *at all times!!* Put a chain around your neck with the key and have a key well hidden near the door. If a fire should break out, having a double-lock dead bolt can turn a safe situation into a deadly trap.

Wearing an identification bracelet is one of the easiest, and most important, steps parents can take to protect their child. MedicAlert has an inexpensive annual program that can protect your child in case of an accident or separation from the family. If you have a bracelet engraved, include the child's name, address, telephone number, allergies, and a physician's telephone number. Above the child's name have printed "Nonverbal Autistic" or "Limited Verbal Autistic" so that people are immediately aware of the child's situation.

 **FACT**

> If you have an identification bracelet made, be sure you purchase one with a secure fastener. It should be made of stainless steel and have enough links on it to grow with your child. Put it on your child's nondominant hand so it won't interfere with things she does.

Special Considerations

If you live near any potentially dangerous situation, such as near water or near a busy road, it is imperative you have a locking safety system even if your child is not prone to elopement. All it would take is one escape and a child with autism could easily drown. Children with autism have been known to walk right in front of a moving car. Children with autism lack the ability to understand danger.

It is also wise to contact the city government for the town in which you live. Special road signs (the bright yellow diamonds) can be placed on both ends of your street that send a warning to drivers. It is wise to request a sign that says either "Disabled child at play" or "Deaf child at play." The sign for deafness is the most efficient, as drivers will then be aware of a child that is unaware of them. A sign that says "Autistic child at play," although accurate, can be less than helpful due to the lack of knowledge among the general public regarding autism.

 ESSENTIAL

Children with autism usually outgrow the elopement problem. There are children who never do leave elopement behind, but they are in the minority. It is unclear if they simply lose interest or if they realize the level of danger, but the important thing to remember is that this is probably not a life sentence.

One of the most frightening forms of elopement can occur in the car. Without the realization of danger, a child with autism may open a car door while the car is moving. Always have your child safety-belted and in a car seat if she is under sixty pounds.

Take your car to a mechanic or dealer to have the inside door handle removed *on one side only*. In the case of an accident or other emergency, it is important that the other side of the car can quickly be exited. Always have your child with autism seated next to the door without a handle. If you can't find anyone to remove the handle, remove it yourself with a wrench and hammer. The cost of the repair, if you wish to have it replaced, is insignificant compared to the tragedy of a child falling out of a moving car.

The Law

The laws provide for reasonable accommodation for a disabled person in rental housing. If you have a child who elopes, or escapes, it is your right to have locks installed on the inside of doorways that the child is unable to open. Consider slide bars placed out of reach for younger children, and request a keyed dead bolt if you've got an older child who elopes. One trick that works well with a slide bar is to put it slightly out of alignment; the door handle has to be lifted slightly and a younger child is unable to unlock it.

FACT

Even if a child cannot escape through a window, it is possible that things you own will escape quite easily. Children with autism are still children, and there seems to be great entertainment in throwing items out of windows. Be sure your screens are adequate to keep bugs out and appliances in!

If you live in rental housing, you may also ask your landlord to install window locks if your child attempts to elope through windows. In a pinch, a sliding window frame can have a nail hammered into it that will prevent the window from being opened any further than desired. Other window styles will have ways to jury-rig them, and until a permanent fix can be implemented, don't hesitate to do what you need to do to prevent an escape.

The law provides for reasonable accommodation for disabilities. You can't demand remodeling that is frivolous, unreasonable, or abusive of the disability laws, but safety and security are reasonable expectations. Asking the landlord to fence the entire yard so your child can play outside is unreasonable; but if you live in a rental with inadequate locks or other safety concerns, the landlord must immediately address and correct these issues without penalty of eviction.

CHAPTER 5

Communication

C OMMUNICATION IS, without a doubt, the most serious impairment that a person on the autism spectrum experiences. When a person—particularly a child—is unable to communicate, it is very difficult to understand and meet his or her needs. A child learns security and safety through having her needs met, so the lack of communication means more than not hearing those wonderful and exciting first words. Communication is the underpinning of our psychological makeup.

The Nonverbal Person

Communicating with a nonverbal child intimidates many people. If a child understands language, even if he is unable to speak, it is hard enough to communicate with a child. If a child doesn't understand that language, communication between that child and others is very difficult and emotionally trying for the family. However, what most people don't realize is that they are already very proficient in communicating with a nonverbal person.

And You Thought It Was Baby Talk!

When parents bring home their newborn, they begin communicating nonverbally. All the little cooing and babbling sounds that come from perfectly rational adults are the beginnings of communication without

words. Tunes hummed to baby are another form of communication. It is through the tone and the rhythm of the voice that messages are sent. Although a baby does not have the ability to understand the complex messages literally, she begins to learn about communication from these sounds and their cadence.

Parents learn as well how to understand nonverbal communication. Parents learn to recognize when their baby cries whether it is hunger, discomfort, pain, or any number of things that are being communicated. Those first cries, and the subsequent response by a parent, are the first forms of reciprocal communication.

If only communication stayed that simple. As a child matures, his needs include much more than just hunger or comfort. He needs to convey emotions, complex needs, and desires, and it is very difficult without language. To keep things in perspective, remember that you have already established communication with your child. Yes, it was at a very young age and, yes, it isn't a fully efficient language. But you have the basics and you know more about nonverbal communication than you realize.

 ESSENTIAL

Do you talk to your cat? Kitty comes into the kitchen meowing, and invariably someone will pick up the cat food and ask the cat if he is hungry. No one expects to hear the cat answer, but a method of communication has happened in that moment. Talking to a human being is vastly different from talking to a pet. However, there are some valuable lessons here for the parent of a child with autism—body language, tone of voice, and visual cues increase the stimuli of all of those behaviors and communicate a message very effectively.

Trust Yourself and Pull Out the Stops

Much of the success in communication is about trust. If you believe your child will not understand, can never understand, and doesn't want to understand, you will probably find that to be true.

But if you believe she can understand much more than anyone realizes and you continue to communicate with that belief, you will find that her abilities will increase.

Never assume that your words and sentences are not understood. Your child's receptive language may not be at 100 percent, but something, somewhere, will get through and that is all you need to build on. Talk to your child as you would any child. Don't talk down to him, and don't talk over his head. Work at getting eye contact so he can see your facial expressions. Stand in front of him so he can see your body language, even if he appears to be totally oblivious of it. Consider your tone of voice and use every visual clue you can think of.

As the light begins to dawn for your child, and she realizes language is a useful tool, she will begin to attempt to understand it. It is a long and hard road for both parent and child, without a doubt. As the foundation begins with very little, and seemingly unimportant, understanding of minor words, you will realize that more complex receptive language skills can and will develop. Trust yourself.

Lacking Conceptual Images

For people with normal speech development, it is very difficult to communicate without using concepts. Things are big or bigger, happy or joyous, under, over . . . the list is endless. The human mind is built on and works through the understanding of concepts. But for someone with autism, concepts are very difficult to deal with. Can effective communication happen without relying on the conceptual imagery everyone uses each day?

A Language of Concept

Language by its very nature is conceptual. We believe, because we have been taught and we have seen the result, that these words are truly representative of something. If you go into an ice cream shop and ask for a large cone, you have certain expectations that you believe the other person understands. Generally, people do understand, and if they don't, they may ask for additional information.

Concepts within language are an obstacle for children with autism. When a word is first learned, whether verbal or through another form of communication, the use of that word has a hard and fast rule: a dog is always a dog; a cat is always a cat. But red? That is very subjective. Ask someone to go buy you a red hat and you will learn how many shades of red there are. Concepts such as quiet, hungry, or tired are even harder to grasp. Only time and experience can teach these lessons. Speaking normally with your child and using visual clues will help the process along, but there is no definitive method to teach a concept.

Echolalia

As a child begins to learn speech, it is common to see what is known as echolalia in children with autism. Echolalia is the repeating of words without using those words with any meaning. For example, a child can have a shirt or toy held up to him and a parent might say, "Is this your shirt or your brother's?" The response may be "Brother's." This may not mean that your child has signed off on the property in question; he may simply be repeating the last word he heard. If you are in doubt, test by using the question again, but reversing the order of words. If he repeats a different word, you can be sure it is echolalia.

 ESSENTIAL

When talking to your child, use universal signs to help him understand. Spread your arms to indicate "big." Mock shiver for "cold." Use clues for your child to help him link the word with the object or action. As linkages occur, language will begin to make sense and communication will be more effective.

Echolalia is also seen with a child who is involved in activity. The child may repeat words she has heard during the day or words that are common to her routine. "Everyone sit down," "it's lunchtime," or "here kitty, kitty" are examples of phrases that might be said without meaning. Echolalia is frustrating to parents because they can see that the mechanics of language, such as the voice, are working fine, yet there is no spontaneous speech. When your child engages in echolalia in response to a question, try to guide her to the correct answer and gently correct her. If she is playing alone and you hear repeated phrases and words, ignore it. It is not helpful to try to stop a behavior that is harmless; she is unaware this is an inappropriate social behavior.

Receptive Speech

People who have normal speech abilities take the skill for granted. Speech is the exchanging of ideas from one mind to another in a meaningful way. Speech is what separates humankind from the animal world.

Receptive speech is the ability of the human mind to hear spoken language from another person and decipher it into a meaningful mental picture or thought pattern, which is understood and then used by the recipient. Speech is the vocal expression of language.

A Confusing World

When a person has a deficit in his receptive language skills, the entire world is a mystery. People with autism are often assumed to be like people with deafness. But the inability to relate to others shows the difference between the two conditions. People with deafness can't hear sound, but they can understand the language and all the conceptual images within the words and put those to use within their own minds. People with autism hear the words but they do not have the same meaning. They may understand a fair amount of communication in the framework of their own mental processes, or they may understand little. Either way, they are operating on a different wavelength.

During early intervention, you will have a good idea of how well your child's receptive speech is operating. Children who have learned the appropriate use of the words *mommy, daddy, hungry,* and the like are beginning to understand that these words have a use. They are learning to understand how that usage applies to them. A child such as this will understand "pick up your toys" and "don't touch that." If a child does not turn in response to hearing her own name, does not have the ability to name certain objects after seeing them, or disregards verbal commands, there is a receptive speech problem.

 **FACT**

Don't think that a child is ignoring what is said to him if he shows no reaction or withdraws into his own world. You are not being ignored. It is much like being in a crowd and hearing people speak to each other—you know when it applies to you. To this child, the voice has no meaning and does not apply to him.

Improving Understanding

A speech therapist will most likely be working with your child if he lacks the ability to understand language. Other therapists will also dovetail their therapy with the speech therapist's exercises with the common goal of showing your child that language is useful. Children do not resist speech when they are autistic, as was commonly thought years ago. It is to their advantage to understand and use speech; they just can't. It is as if there is a gap between the ears and the brain, almost as though a piece of electrical equipment has shorted out.

You, too, will be working with your child at home. In everything you and your family do, you will be showing her that language is something she can participate in. She will learn with your help. If your child is totally or essentially nonverbal, go slowly. Big picture books are helpful, as are flashcards. Avoid teaching conceptual words. If you try to explain "big" versus "small" with examples, your child may become confused. A big dog? So, is the word *dog* or *big* what is being taught? Stick with nouns until receptive language skills begin and you have a foundation. Pronouns are also very difficult to understand when receptive speech skills are poor. Use people's names or speak in the third person to help comprehension.

ESSENTIAL

Pronouns are conceptual and should not be used unless a child has advanced speaking abilities. Speaking in the third person will be less confusing and frustrating. It is hard for a child with autism to understand that others have their own thoughts, and it's even more confusing when pronouns are used.

Expressive Speech

Expressive speech is using words and language verbally to communicate a concept or thought. If a person has expressive speech, they have some degree of receptive speech. Children learn their expressive speech by imitation; by receiving receptively from their parents, they learn how to use language as a tool. The first words a baby says are actually a sign that receptive speech has been working effectively for quite some time.

As stated previously, it is to a child's advantage to use speech, so if a child does not, there is a reason. Encouraging a child to speak is good, but forcing him to talk is stressful and not wise. Many parents will say, "How do I encourage without forcing?" There is a fine line between the two, but after some time it will become second nature. Hold up a cookie or something your child loves to eat and say "cookie?" He will not repeat it right away, but eventually he will. When he does, give him the cookie and praise him. Some children respond well to applause; others do not like the noise. The phrase "good job" is soon recognized as praise. The important thing is not to withhold the cookie because he doesn't say the word. Remember, expressive and receptive speech are tied closely together and safety and security are learned through communication. Continue meeting his needs and wants as though he was speaking and he will begin to see the usefulness of language.

Many experts state that if a child is not speaking by the age of six, she is unlikely to speak at all. However, this is not true. Many parents will report that their child began speaking for no apparent reason at the age of puberty. Some children have startled their parents quite dramatically by being silent for over a decade and then suddenly communicating their first verbalization in a complete and appropriate sentence. Others will tentatively begin talking with a few words here and there before trying a phrase. It is possible that a child with autism will not speak at all, but don't give up. You may hear that voice yet.

Sign Language

Sign language is the preferred language for people who lack verbal communication ability. American Sign Language (ASL) is the third most commonly used language in the United States. Only English and Spanish are spoken more than sign language.

The beauty of sign language is that it is convenient, portable, doesn't require any special equipment, and is standard throughout the United States. The major disadvantage—and this is one that can and should be overcome—is that the language has to be learned by all family members, not just the child with autism.

American Sign Language

There are two major forms of sign language. The most widely known through the deaf community is ASL. ASL is a consistent language used to allow people with deafness to "hear" the same things the rest of the population can hear. Speeches, concerts, plays, and many other public events have an ASL interpreter present for translation. ASL is consistent all over the United States.

Many communities have sign language classes. If you decide to use sign language in your family, it is very helpful to have classes to teach you in an orderly way so that you can pass this along to your children and work with your autistic child with ease. There are also many books, videotapes, and computer programs that can help. These are very handy for parents and siblings of the child learning sign language.

Exact English

The other sign language, usually preferred by the autistic community, is Exact English. Exact English is based on ASL but has some important differences that make this the preferred method. The learning curve is a little easier than ASL, but the difference is not significant. If you know ASL, you can work with Exact English very easily. Learning ASL will only make Exact English easier, so don't hesitate to get instruction on ASL. A book with the Exact English signs will show the differences and should be all the extra help, beyond learning ASL, that you might need.

 FACT

Check on the Internet for books on sign language. Some excellent books have large drawings of each sign and have signs arranged in alphabetical order. This is a quick way to reference a sign if you have forgotten it. It is also a good way to learn new signs.

The primary difference between Exact English and ASL is the use of conceptual thinking. Keeping in mind that sign language was developed for a community that had full receptive speech, the motions and gestures of ASL were created to say as much as possible quickly and economically. Entire phrases are often one single sign, and many of these phrases include words that are conceptual in nature. "I love you," for example, can be said three different ways: spelling out the letters of each of the three words (eight signs), signing one sign per word (three signs), or by using one sign that represents the entire phrase. ASL uses one sign for the entire phrase whereas Exact English uses one sign per word. This is helpful for children with autism as they learn about conceptual ideas. Love is not something we can photograph or demonstrate; it is an idea that we understand, and it is an idea that takes a long time to understand for a child with autism.

Another advantage to Exact English for parents is the gradual learning of the signs. As a child learns a new sign, parents can also learn the same sign. The alphabet can easily be learned by the entire family and can be used to spell out words if a child is prone to understanding words specifically by reading. This is a way to bring words off the paper and into everyday usage.

It is very common for a child to learn a sign and then verbalize the word that the sign represents. However, this is not always the case, and the goal of sign language should not be for the child to achieve spoken language. But, if this is the case with your child, this will be an opportunity to develop more language skills. It is doubtful that your child will be able to leave signing behind altogether, but as verbalization accompanies the signs, your child's skills in receptive communication improve along with expressive speech.

Communication Boards

Many styles of communication boards are helpful for a person with autism. The options range from complex, computer-run programs that are used to communicate to systems as simple to operate as a set of flashcards. There are systems you can purchase and systems you can make at home. Each child will have his own needs, and the most important issue is to personalize the board to meet those needs.

Picture Exchange Communication System (PECS)

It is common for children on the autism spectrum who have limited or no verbal ability to learn communication with a communication board. This is a form of augmentative and alternative communication (AAC). The beauty of this tool is that the learning curve is very low, and it can be used immediately. They say that a picture is worth a thousand words, and without a doubt, this is true for this form of communication.

Also known as picture communication system (PCS), this is the most widely used form of communication board used for children and adults with autism. All that is necessary are photographs or drawings that represent people and things (nouns), actions (verbs), and concepts such as size and color (adjectives). This system is favored because of its ease of use. One downside is that as a person's vocabulary grows, more and more cards are added to the collection and they can become unwieldy. However, there are systems that organize cards into categories, which make utilization of many cards very easy. It can also be difficult for a child to learn concepts from cards; if a card has a blue circle, is he communicating the color or the shape?

Building a Communication Board

If you choose to use PECS, you can test it out very easily with your child. Take photographs, or cut pictures out of magazines, and laminate them. Home machines to laminate can be purchased for $20 to $30 and are always handy to have around. Laminate about ten to fifteen cards, each one just a few inches square. Attach the cards together with a loose-leaf ring (without the notebook—these rings can be purchased separately) and show them to your child. As she learns that pointing to the picture of the television tells you she wishes to watch a program, she will learn the value of these cards. Make the cards relevant to your child's life so they are uniquely her own. Put them in a fanny pack and have her wear it so she has constant access to the cards.

 ESSENTIAL

Be certain when you create a system that you have copies and records of the cards that your child uses. If a card is lost or if you upgrade to a more sophisticated system, you will want to maintain the consistency of the same picture. Building this on a computer will make your life easier; create a file that has all of the pictures that are being used. Back it up on a floppy or CD, and put it somewhere safe.

If this is a comfortable method that works well for your child, there are more sophisticated systems available (see Appendix B). There are many ways to use PECS and they will open your child's world in a remarkable way. You are limited only by your own creativity and how you develop it for your child's needs.

Other Communication Methods

One method of communication that is very effective for accuracy is the keyboard. Many people with autism who cannot speak are very efficient readers and writers. They may not be able to say that they are thirsty and need a drink of water, but they are able to type it out on a simple word-processing program. Even a simple text file on a desktop computer, a laptop, or handheld computer device will work. If your child seems to understand language (receptive speech) and reads, try typing a simple question. "What is your name?" is a good one to start with. He may look at you, unsure of what you want. Say the question while you point to the words on the screen and then point to the keyboard. If he understands how to communicate through writing, he will attempt to provide the answer. Coach him a bit as you begin. If your child can use this as a tool, you will know very quickly.

If you elect to use keyboard communication, consider a handheld computer device. They are portable and have small word-processing programs that can operate either with a small keyboard on the device or with handwriting-recognition programs using a stylus. There is an added benefit of having a calendar on the small computer; most people with autism instinctively understand calendars and clocks and will use them to maintain their schedule and routine. It is also possible to play games on a handheld computer, which can be a great deal of fun and a good distraction for times when a child might be bored.

A very controversial communication tool is the method of facilitated communication (FC). This technique operates by another person assisting a nonverbal person's efforts in communication. The support may be as simple as providing encouragement to boost the self-confidence of someone who is unable to speak. It can also involve steadying or guiding a hand to pictures or words if necessary; people with tremors, nerve damage, or poor muscle control may require some physical assistance. The point of contention with FC is whether a facilitator may influence what is being communicated. Opinions vary widely and parents who are considering this form of communication would be wise to research it thoroughly to reassure themselves on their choice.

 ALERT!

Unfortunately, it is common for special education professionals to have only one communication system set up for children in their school district. A wise teacher or speech therapist will know that there are many nonverbal methods of communication and will work hard to find whatever it takes to establish effective communication. However, if you feel that the system that is being taught to your child is not the best system for him and your family, you have every right to have this changed. Talk with your child's teachers about other possibilities.

The most important thing any parent, caretaker, family member, teacher, or medical professional can remember about communication is that there is no one right way that works for every child. Children with autism are just like any other children; each is unique and will respond to different styles of learning and working. If one child works well with keyboard communication and another just can't figure it out, but is a whiz with PECS, it doesn't mean one child is more advanced than the other. It simply means they are two distinct personalities.

CHAPTER 6

Meltdowns

PERHAPS THE TRUE INITIATION of parenting a child with autism is the baptism by fire of the meltdown. Once just a scientific term in nuclear physics, the autism community has adopted the word. Seeing and experiencing the meltdown makes it quite clear why only this term would do. Dealing with meltdowns is a bit like dealing with a tornado: You have very little warning; about all you can do is ride it out.

Autistic Meltdowns Vs. Temper Tantrums

If you need to explain a meltdown to someone who doesn't have a child with autism, just define it as a bad temper tantrum, and let the topic go. It is unlikely that the finer points of a meltdown will be understood. But, if you mention the word to parents who have children with autism, you will get knowing and sympathetic looks. Rest assured, your child is not the only one who has these rather unique behavioral issues.

Temper Tantrums

A temper tantrum is very straightforward. A child does not get his or her own way and, as grandma would say, "pitches a fit." This is not to discount the temper tantrum. They are not fun for anyone.

Tantrums have several qualities that distinguish them from meltdowns.

- A child having a tantrum will look occasionally to see if his or her behavior is getting a reaction.
- A child in the middle of a tantrum will take precautions to be sure they won't get hurt.
- A child who throws a tantrum will attempt to use the social situation to his or her benefit.
- When the situation is resolved, the tantrum will end as suddenly as it began.
- A tantrum will give you the feeling that the child is in control, although he would like you to think he is not.
- A tantrum is thrown to achieve a specific goal and once the goal is met, things return to normal.

 **FACT**

If you feel like you are being manipulated by a tantrum, you are right. You are. A tantrum is nothing more than a power play by a person not mature enough to play a subtle game of internal politics. Hold your ground and remember who is in charge.

A temper tantrum in a child who is not autistic is simple to handle. Parents simply ignore the behavior and refuse to give the child what he is demanding. Tantrums usually result when a child makes a request to have or do something that the parent denies. Upon hearing the parent's "no," the tantrum is used as a last-ditch effort.

The qualities of a temper tantrum vary from child to child. When children decide this is the way they are going to handle a given situation, each child's style will dictate how the tantrum appears. Some children will throw themselves on the floor, screaming and kicking. Others will hold their breath, thinking that this "threat" on their life will cause parents to bend. Some children will be extremely vocal and repeatedly yell, "I hate you," for the world to hear. A few children will attempt bribery or blackmail, and although these are quieter methods, this is just as much of a tantrum as screaming. Of course, there are the very few children who pull out all the stops and use all the methods in a tantrum.

Effective parenting, whether a child has autism or not, is learning that *you* are in control, not the child. This is not a popularity contest. You are not there to wait on your child and indulge her every whim. Buying her every toy she wants isn't going to make her any happier than if you say no. There is no easy way out of this parenting experience. Sometimes you just have to dig in and let the tantrum roar.

Meltdowns

If the tantrum is straightforward, the meltdown is every known form of manipulation, anger, and loss of control that the child can muster up to demonstrate. The problem is that the loss of control soon overtakes the child. He needs you to recognize this behavior and rein him back in, as he is unable to do so. A child with autism in the middle of a meltdown desperately needs help to gain control.

- During a meltdown, a child with autism does not look, nor care, if those around him are reacting to his behavior.
- A child in the middle of a meltdown does not consider her own safety.
- A child in a meltdown has no interest or involvement in the social situation.
- Meltdowns will usually continue as though they are moving under their own power and wind down slowly.
- A meltdown conveys the feeling that no one is in control.
- A meltdown usually occurs because a specific want has not been permitted and after that point has been reached, nothing can satisfy the child until the situation is over.

Unlike tantrums, meltdowns can leave even experienced parents at their wit's end, unsure of what to do. When you think of a tantrum, the classic image of a child lying on the floor with kicking feet, swinging arms, and a lot of screaming is probably what comes to mind. This is not even close to a meltdown. A meltdown is best defined by saying it is a total loss of behavioral control. It is loud, risky at times, frustrating, and exhausting.

Meltdowns may be preceded by "silent seizures." This is not always the case, so don't panic, but observe your child after she begins experiencing meltdowns. Does the meltdown have a brief period before onset where your child "spaces out"? Does she seem like she had a few minutes of time when she was totally uninvolved with her environment? If you notice this trend, speak to your physician. This may be the only manifestation of a seizure that you will be aware of.

 ESSENTIAL

When your child launches into a meltdown, remove him from any areas that could harm him or he could harm. Glass shelving and doors may become the target of an angry foot, and avoiding injury is the top priority during a meltdown.

Another cause of a meltdown can be other health issues. One example is a child who suffers from migraines. A migraine may hit a child suddenly, and the pain is so totally debilitating that his behavior may spiral downward quickly, resulting in a meltdown. Watch for telltale signs such as sensitivity to light, holding the head, and being unusually sensitive to sound. If a child has other health conditions, and having autism does not preclude this possibility, behavior will be affected.

Handling a Meltdown in Public

Any parent who is raising a child with autism will tell you that meltdowns are most common in public locations. Stores, malls, fairs—anywhere there are a lot of people, activity, and noise raises the odds of a meltdown. It is common enough that many parents will do anything they can to avoid being in those environments with their child.

To Market, To Market

Inevitably, your child will experience a meltdown in a large, brightly lit variety store. Every parent knows about these stores—the one-stop shopping that turns into an ordeal and fiasco. A parent related the following story about her son, and any parent of a child with autism will laugh and cry at the same time; they all know what this is like.

"We went in for groceries and various items. It was a big shopping trip and I couldn't find a babysitter that day. I also couldn't put it off any longer. We did okay until we went by the home gardening section. A big, and I mean very big, lawn sprinkler was on display— a sprinkler that was a dead ringer for the tractor that my little boy loves, all bright green and yellow and just about the right size for him to sit on. At first he quietly asked 'tractor,' or, should I say, demanded it. I could see the look. I knew he had decided the tractor was coming home with us. And I knew it wasn't. His tone of voice raised and raised until you could hear the word *tractor* being screeched all over the store! We made our way to the checkout line, but by then, he was in complete meltdown. I am sure that they thought I was the meanest mom in the world for not buying my little boy a toy tractor. The meltdown continued into the parking lot and into the car; he was sweating, crying, screaming, and attempting to hit anything or anyone he could. He totally lost it. I was exhausted and so was he." She added, "I now make an extra effort to find a babysitter and have my radar up to scope out the aisles around us to avoid any more tractors."

 **FACT**

> If your child begins a meltdown by putting his hands over his ears or eyes, you can be sure he is experiencing sensory overload. He might even cover your mouth with his hand to prevent another sound. The best thing is to move him to a low-sensory environment; a dark, quiet, and cool place will help.

This mom handled this situation well. She had shopping that had to be done; this wasn't an optional trip to the store. And once the meltdown was in full swing, she was almost done. It wouldn't have been convenient for her to leave the store and return later to redo an enormous shopping trip. She kept her cool, didn't give in, and didn't worry about the opinions of others while her son spun totally out of control.

The Rudeness of Others

The little boy with, or in this case without, the tractor had a real advantage that day. His mother was not threatened or concerned about the opinions of others. It has been said that parents of kids with special needs develop thicker skins, and it must be true. But regardless of how thick-skinned you are, an insult to your child cuts, and cuts deeply.

For some reason, in public, many people feel it is their duty to point out (usually loudly) all of the mistakes they believe you are making in raising your child. This is even more common if your child is mentally challenged or if the child "expert" has no children. Just remember: You can't change the world; you can only change your little corner of it. How your child feels and how you affect his or her life are far more important.

Keep in mind that some people are receptive to learning and you may have a chance to educate someone about autism. There are also subtle clues you can use to notify people without saying a word that you have a child with some special needs. The tractor incident brought out a creative action by the mom mentioned previously. She said that she liberally used sign language, even signs her son didn't know, as a way to communicate to observers that there was an issue with her son.

 **QUESTION?**

Someone called my child a cruel name. Best advice?
If they called your child a goat, it wouldn't make him one. However, it is hurtful and it shows the lack of knowledge by the general public. A simple explanation is wise if you feel the person is receptive. Otherwise, ignore it. They will move on to be miserable somewhere else.

It is very common for people in environments such as the store with the tractor to stare and make comments that are very critical of a child in the middle of a meltdown. People will say things about you not controlling your child (or use unflattering words toward your child), and as much as you would like to throttle them in the heat of the moment, resist the urge. Excuse your child's behavior politely with the brief explanation of "he is disabled," and drop it. If a person persists in making comments and it is clear they are not interested in educating themselves, move yourself and your child to another location. If, on the other hand, it is staff at the establishment you are visiting who are making such snide comments, ask to speak with a manager. He or she needs to know that the staff is not equipped to understand a disabled child and steps can then be taken to educate personnel.

Defusing a Meltdown

Although it sounds like a cliché, the best way to handle a meltdown in progress is to defuse it. Sometimes that is much easier said than done, but it comes down to one simple sentence: Choose your battles. How you choose them will depend on your personality and your child's personality.

When Your Child Understands

When a child understands and manipulates a meltdown to get her own way, you are dealing with an intelligent child who can stop the behavior if it is caught in time. Keep in mind that a child with autism, regardless of how well she understands that her meltdown is not wanted, will not be able to control it once it reaches a certain point. The goal is to not reach that point if your child is cognizant of her behavior.

1. Recognize the signs that a meltdown is impending.
2. There is a certain trigger before the meltdown—determine what the trigger is.
3. If the trigger is fairly insignificant, such as him wanting to hold the red ball in the store, decide if it is worth it. A red ball is a small price to pay for a quiet shopping trip.
4. If the trigger is something that is not possible to resolve, such as the one in the tractor story, try to distract your child by moving to another location in the store and finding a reasonable substitute that will divert her attention.
5. If you are in a restaurant and a meltdown is approaching, reach for a new or very special toy you have hidden in your purse. Something complex, like a handheld puzzle, can work well.
6. As you are working to distract your child, speak softly to him about his behavior and let him know that it needs to stop. Don't dwell on what he can't have at that moment, but reiterate that he needs to slow down and stay in control. Stay calm so he has no idea you are panicking over the thought that he might lose it.
7. Persist in any calming techniques that work for your child. Some children will respond to a hug while others will not want to be touched; this is a matter of "whatever works."

You will not always be able to defuse a child bent on having a meltdown. If the cycle progresses and he reaches the point-of-no-return, you have two options. You can decide to ride it out or you can leave the environment. Keeping in mind that this child understands that he entered into this situation of his own free will and that you asked him to stop, it is often more of a learning experience to ride it out. It is not the easiest thing to do, but the goal is to help your child acquire long-term acceptable behavior patterns.

Much of riding it out depends on where you are. Right in the middle of a wedding may not be the best location to try to work with behavior modification. Other people, and those in certain locations, do have the right to have an undisturbed environment. However, in the real world, the everyday world, your child has to learn to operate in society, and society has to learn to deal with autistic children. It is more prudent to leave an area if others are being disturbed unfairly or the situation could become dangerous.

When Your Child Does Not Understand

A child who does not understand what type of behavior is wanted or expected of her is more challenging to deal with when a meltdown is about to occur. Parents will have the same warnings that they have with a child who does understand, but there is less they can do to stop the cycle. It is important to remain calm. Your child is already on a sensory overload and if you are upset, you will only aggravate that. Keep your voice even, quiet, and calm no matter what happens.

The primary tool a parent has with a child in this position is distraction. It is useless to try to reason with a child who does not understand that what he is doing is not acceptable. Molding a child's behavior through distraction and positive reinforcement will be a much more effective tool to stop the current problem and prevent future ones as well.

Distraction is 50 percent preparation and 50 percent creativity. Preparation is the easy part. Mom or dad can put items they will use to distract their child in a backpack or tote bag to have on hand when the meltdown begins. When it becomes apparent that the fuse is just about burned out and the explosion is about to begin, being able to pull "the rabbit out of the hat" is your best bet. Comforting toys, such as a favorite stuffed animal, are wise choices, as are toys that are so fascinating that they just can't be ignored.

 **QUESTION?**

Will I know if the distraction has things under control?
There will be no question in your mind. Your child will either become engrossed in the distraction and the meltdown will fade away or she will use the distraction as part of the meltdown. If the child throws the "distraction" toy back at you, it is a sign that you need to get creative.

Creativity is a bit more challenging. Think of toys your child enjoys and finds pleasure in. Every child is different; there is no "stop-the-meltdown-toy" available. Use the knowledge you have of your child and let his reactions guide you as you consider helpful distractions.

Behavior Modification

What is easier than handling a meltdown or defusing one? Avoiding it altogether. You may feel right now that you have little control over the tantrums and meltdowns, and it's true that you don't have total control of them. However, there are things you can do to minimize the frequency and severity of the outbursts.

Working with a child's behavior is always the first step a parent should take. If you can modify the behavior that is undesirable, your child will be happier and those around him will be as well. Don't ever think you are being cruel by working to alter unacceptable behaviors. You will be met with resistance; no one likes to change, least of all a child with autism. But at times, change is necessary, and when a child has a predilection to tantrums, the behavior must be changed.

Applied Behavioral Analysis (ABA)

ABA is one of the most widely used methods to treat children with autism. Dr. Ivar Lovaas, the founder of the Lovaas Institute, is the creator of ABA. His goal in working with children with autism has been to modify behaviors that are inappropriate and replace them with appropriate behaviors.

As Lovaas developed his theories of behavior in people, the foundation of his work centered on how people treated one another—was it environment or genetics that caused people to act a certain way? By a twist of fate, he began working with children with autism and observed that modifying behaviors was not the difficult part. The hard part was keeping those behaviors solidly in place after the behavior had been successfully changed.

Lovaas realized that the main difference in behaviors between children with and without autism was based on the way that children learn. Children who do not have autism are constantly learning. Even beyond school, every moment of every day is a learning experience for a child. Learning is a constant and dynamic process. However, a child with autism goes to school and for a prescribed number of hours each day, he learns things. When he returns home, the structured learning is over for the day and he retreats into his own world.

Continuing ABA Therapy

The key to modifying behavioral problems in a child with autism suddenly became obvious to Dr. Lovaas. A child could not come to the Institute, work on ABA, and then just return home after successful therapy was completed; the newly acquired behaviors broke down and everyone was back to square one. It may seem obvious now, but at the time, this was quite a breakthrough. Parents were taught how to continue the ABA therapy at home and permanent changes in behaviors were seen.

If behavioral issues have had a profound impact on your child's life, and subsequently your family's life, behavior modification might be appropriate to investigate. See Appendix B for resources to learn more about this technique. Meltdowns and tantrums, if your child is inclined to them, will not disappear entirely, but with training and therapy, there is an excellent chance these outbursts can be reduced dramatically.

Discipline

Children must be guided into the proper way to behave. Discipline does not need to be an angry or negative experience. If handled properly, it can be positive and motivating for everyone.

- Remember that positive reinforcement is much more effective than negative.
- Make the discipline fit the severity of the unacceptable behavior.
- Parents must be in agreement on what behaviors are to be disciplined and what is to be overlooked.
- Each parent must share in discipline and not put the work on one parent exclusively.
- Parents must have a policy on spanking, recognizing that to a child with autism it is just more violence. If spanking is used, it should only be when the child, another person, or pet is at risk of being harmed.
- Verbal and physical abuse is not an option. Ever.

It is a good idea for parents to have a talk about how they feel about discipline. If a child throws a tantrum or has a meltdown and these decisions have not been made, it can be difficult to know how to handle it. When a child is midmeltdown is not the optimum time to be discussing child-rearing philosophies.

Medications

When a child is young and her behavior is unpredictable, it is miserable for her as well as everyone around her. Children with autism will often lash out physically, kicking, hitting, and/or biting, when they become angry. And, unfortunately, anger seems to be an emotion that they easily display. If your child does this, take heart; you are not alone. It is a common behavior seen in children with autism.

There are several medications used to help in the control of unpredictable behaviors that children with autism will display. Parents are often reluctant to use medication, which is a prudent decision in most cases; however, there are times when medication is appropriate and even necessary. It is vital to remember that an out-of-control child is not a happy child, and that child needs your help. You have not failed as a parent if you and your physician decide medications are appropriate for your child.

ALERT!

A common medication used for aggression is risperidone. If your child is on this treatment, watch for excessive weight gain and facial tics. If either of these occurs, visit your physician to decide if the dosage needs to be adjusted.

If medications are prescribed for your child, and you are concerned about side effects or long-term use, talk to a pharmacist at length about your concerns. A pharmacist is one of the best resources available for a discussion of these issues as well as for advice on what over-the-counter medications are safe for your child to use. In a support group meeting, ask other parents what medications they have used and how they feel about them; a support group can be very helpful as a medication becomes part of the routine.

CHAPTER 7

ASD and Effects on the Parents' Marriage

IT IS ESTIMATED THAT 50 TO 75 PERCENT of marriages fail if a disabled child is in the family. Exact statistics vary widely depending on the source, but the numbers are always high. It is a fact: Having a child with autism is hard on a marriage and a family. It is difficult for a couple, particularly when they are young, to remain a couple and have a child who is so far from what they had anticipated.

Further, other people become so involved with your life, such as doctors, therapists, teachers, and social workers, that it feels they have become part of your marriage. It is hard to remember that you are still the same two people who fell in love, married, and planned to live happily ever after.

How Mom Is Affected

Pregnancy is an exciting time for a woman. The growing child within her—as it begins to move and kick and then show a silhouette on an ultrasound—is the person she most anticipates meeting. It doesn't matter if it is a first child or the second or the tenth. This baby is the focus of all her thoughts.

When the baby is born and the doctor announces whether it is a boy or girl, invariably the first question heard is, "Is everything alright?" And what a relief it is when all ten fingers and toes are present and there are no disabilities. A healthy child has come into the world.

A Child Regressing

It is a shock to a mom when she sees the developmental progress made by her child beginning to slip away slowly. Her beautiful baby, now approaching the toddler stage, with his few words and joyful reactions to the world around him, is changing. The words are fewer and fewer until they are heard no more. The interactive baby, who chuckled and had sparkling eyes just looking at Mom, now seems enclosed in a world of darkness where no one else can go.

Her child will no longer look at her, no longer try to learn new words or even use the already learned ones, and doesn't seem to hear her. *What have I done wrong?* is a very likely thought.

The Five Stages

There are usually five stages in a child's life. But the stages are different when your child has autism.

- **Infant**—The hopes, dreams, and visions of a new life are shattered with the realization that something has gone wrong.
- **Toddler**—The realization begins to sink in that what was wrong isn't going away and must be coped with.
- **Young school age**—More dreams are lost as a child enters school and Mom can see the contrast between her child and other children.
- **Older school age**—Progress is made but concerns begin over challenges brought by puberty, adolescence, and the beginning of young adulthood.
- **Adult**—As the child becomes an adult, Mom becomes aware that she, too, is aging and she begins to worry what will happen to her child when she is gone.

This is a lot for a young mother to absorb. And moms do think through all five stages within a few months of the diagnosis. Considering most children are diagnosed with autism before they are two, a mom lives an entire child's lifetime around the time two candles are on a birthday cake. Stress, fear, denial, anxiety, confusion, anger, depression, and sadness are inevitable. It may be one of the hardest times in a mother's life.

Diagnosis and Adjustment

Mothers are deeply affected when the process to diagnose their child begins. The protective and maternal instincts within a mother are natural, so her resentment toward all the "experts" who have suddenly intruded right into the middle of her family's life is normal.

 ESSENTIAL

Mothers may feel especially frustrated when the experts can't give a diagnosis within a day or two. The testing for autism and the other related conditions can take quite some time, and frustration with medical personnel is also normal. The acceptance that will eventually come is at this point a long time off, and it is a tumultuous time.

Eventually all of the emotions that run amok within a mom will settle down, and although none of them ever disappear entirely, they become manageable and a sense of acceptance occurs. Mom will begin to accept that this is the situation and will begin to reset goals and plans, accommodating her child's needs and abilities within that framework. There will always be times when she feels sad or depressed; she will have spikes of anger at the situation when a problem arises that isn't easily solved, but she will have learned to accept and do what moms do best: Love.

How Dad Is Affected

Dads are also affected by the realization that their child has been diagnosed on the autism spectrum, but the reactions of a father are different than those of a mother. A mom needs to be aware that the reactions of her husband, although different, are normal.

- **Infant**—When a dad has a new infant, his pride and delight are unparalleled. When something goes wrong, it is hard for fathers to come to terms with the disability and they may take a long time to accept it. Usually a father grapples with acceptance longer than a mother.
- **Toddler**—Realization begins to force its way into a father's mind. Fathers will either react with acceptance of the problem and begin to find ways to solve it, or they will deny the problem exists and look to place blame with someone. Denial is a common reaction for men because they feel responsible for the events that occur within their family.
- **Young school age**—As a child enters school, fathers begin to see the deficits and often have trouble seeing the progress. It is important for therapists, physicians, and the child's mother to point out the progress being made so that the father can see the glass as half full. This stage is normal, and it will pass. Again, dads feel responsible and frustrated that they can't fix the problem.
- **Older school age**—This is a time where fathers really shine if they have come to acceptance, which most have by this stage. The progress is evident and now the issues are ones that men handle well. There are specific challenges to be met and problem solving is the needed skill. Dad will find his problem-solving skills to be very useful and he will feel less like a failure and more like a dad.
- **Adult**—Like Mom, Dad becomes aware that his child has become an adult and that he will not always be there to protect his son or daughter. Most likely, he has started estate and financial planning to protect his child, but he will work on solving the issues that will face his child even after mom and he are gone.

Learning to Cope

Dad has a lot to absorb, just as Mom does. Men have different coping mechanisms than women do, so they will process and absorb all of this differently. It is important for Mom to remember that Dad's method of dealing with the diagnosis of their child is no less valid than her method. It may seem that a man isn't handling the situation well, and perhaps there is some denial involved, but given time the acceptance will occur.

It is hard for parents to adapt to the loss of the dreams they had for their child, and there is a period of adjustment as Mom and Dad establish new goals. Men, as problem solvers, want to fix it. They want to fix it quickly and when they learn that they can't, they have to understand that they have not failed. It is not their fault the child has autism any more than it is the mother's fault. Women can do a lot to help their husbands adjust by understanding the psychology of wanting to "make it okay" that is often inherent to a male's nature.

 ALERT!

A strong family is the key. For a father it is vital to maintain strong bonds with your spouse and your other children. Fathers need to provide the emotional and spiritual leadership, so that each family member does not have too great a burden.

Eventually acceptance will occur and a routine will be established. As these processes are happening, both Mom and Dad need to remember that their marriage is their first priority. Taking care of each other will enable them to take care of the rest of their family, and that includes their child with autism.

Keeping ASD from Affecting the Marriage

The strongest piece of advice most therapists will give a couple that has a child with autism is "Do not allow autism to become your entire life." It is so easy to begin to eat, breathe, and sleep autism, but it will do no good—not for you, not for your spouse, and not even for your child. There is enough stress within a marriage to begin with, and adding autism to the mix only ratchets up that level of stress.

What can be the results of stress in a marriage? Short tempers, communication difficulties, allowing your lives as a couple to drift apart, and the worst possible situation, turning to others rather than each other for companionship and support. Turning away from the marriage is not the solution.

 **QUESTION?**

Autism has come between us. Now what do I do?
When you are speaking with someone, you shouldn't say the words "you never" or "you always." Your spouse has different thoughts and approaching a conversation with "I feel" is the way to begin. It is possible your spouse is unaware of the problem and gentle communication will solve the problem.

Although your child has autism or another disorder on the spectrum, you still have control of your life. If you allow ASD to become your entire life, you will socially isolate yourself. Turn to each other for support and go to events, support groups, and other activities as a couple to strengthen your bond. You can become stronger because of autism and not allow it to unravel your marriage. It just takes a little time, effort, and a lot of love.

Maintaining and Creating Intimacy

One of the most difficult things in a marriage, let alone a marriage with a disabled child, is maintaining the intimacy that is unique to marriage. When a couple goes from being a man and a woman to being a mom and a dad, they often find it hard to remember they are still a man and a woman! The special intimacy that you knew before you had a child is just as important, perhaps even more important, than it was before. Sexuality is not the most important thing in a marriage, but it is the glue that holds marriage together and it is also important to remember that intimacy is not always about sex. So how do you keep intimacy alive when you have children, and especially a child with special needs?

- **Go out on a date with each other.** Schedule an actual date, go out, and talk about anything *but* autism.
- **Celebrate every occasion you can think of.** Anniversaries of the first date, first kiss, first anything—just celebrate!
- **Splurge on gifts for each other.** You don't have to have a reason other than the fact that you love each other.
- **Buy books on intimacy and sexuality.** Have grandma watch the kids and go to a hotel for an evening. Enjoy each other like it was the first time.
- **Give each other massages with no sexuality expected.** Just make the other person relax and feel good.
- **Plan a picnic and lie on the ground looking at the clouds.** Tell each other what you see in the clouds.
- **Whether or not you believe it, pretend.** If you reincarnate into another life, what will each of you be?
- **Remember, you are still the same woman and the same man who fell in love and got married.** ASD has not changed that.

It isn't that hard to keep the spark alive or to relight it if the years have allowed the flame to go out. Remember, the child who has brought some extra challenges, and, yes, some stress as well, into your lives is a product of the love you have for each other. This child can only benefit from the closeness that you as a couple will have by the efforts you make to keep your intimate life alive.

The Importance of Faith

Knowing that couples with a special-needs child have a higher rate of divorce is the first defense to protect your marriage.

Knowledge is the best defense, and the second best defense is a strong offense. It is important that both partners in the marriage put their relationship as one of their highest priorities in their lives.

 **FACT**

> It's all about priorities. First is your faith, second is your marriage, and third are your children. The fourth is your extended family. Then it is work, friends, hobbies, and whatever else is important. If you keep those priorities straight, life just seems to fall into place.

The priorities of your life are what will keep your marriage together. Keeping them in the proper alignment and place within your life will make life with an autistic child much easier to cope with and help keep your marriage healthy.

Everyone has a faith they follow. It may be Christianity, Judaism, Hinduism, Buddhism, or any number of faiths that people around the world believe. If you are agnostic or atheist, that, too, is a faith, because it is a belief structure about the world around you. Regardless of what you believe, it is important that it be the highest priority in your life. This is the foundation of who you are, how you make decisions, and how you interact with everyone and everything in your life.

The risk in allowing your belief system to fall to a secondary placement in your life is that you can lose yourself. This doesn't mean going to a place of worship every week or conducting any particular rituals. It means keeping that relationship between yourself and the universe intact and doing what you need to do to keep that relationship healthy. It may be prayer, it may be meditation, or it may be a social service that you do to improve the human condition. Whatever it is, don't neglect it, because it is who you are. It is impossible to be part of any relationship if you are on shaky ground with your own identity.

Making Your Spouse a Priority

After your belief system, the most important priority in your life is your spouse. People, and especially mothers, tend to let this priority slip from its proper placement, putting their children above their marriage. Although it sounds noble to not put anything above your children, in reality it is harmful for everyone, including the children. If anything is more important to you than your marriage, your marriage is at risk of failing. It is the foundation of the family.

 ALERT!

> One of the best things you can do for yourself, for your marriage, and for your children is to take a few minutes each day to pray, meditate, or have a quiet time. It will rebalance and refresh your spirit. Everything will seem easier to manage.

Many people feel that statements such as these are a sign of poor parenting and state they would feel guilty putting another adult, even a spouse, above their children. However, it is not a matter of viewing one person as more important than another. It is an understanding of how we need to attend to the obligations and responsibilities of our lives. A child cannot feel secure and grow up to the best of his ability if the family's foundation is insecure.

If a child's parents love each other and work hard to create the best relationship they possibly can, the child will feel that security within her own life. It has been said that there is no greater gift a father can give his children than to love their mother. It is also true that a mother can show nothing greater to her children than to love their father.

Children as a Priority

Most parents have no difficulty with this one! Children become the lights of our lives, and it doesn't take long for that to happen.

Regardless if they have autism or not, these children are still the hope of our future. Children are the gift that brings joy, happiness, frustration, irritation, laughter, tears, and every emotion there is right into the center of our lives.

Many times, it is hard, particularly for dads, to remember that they must keep their children above their work. Careers are a life-long project, and an occupation doesn't always understand that a child's needs are more important than a deadline at the office. It is so easy to be caught up in the mentality of "it has to be done right now." In reality, the only jobs that have to be done "right now" are those of trauma surgeons and the like. So, if you are a physician, paramedic, firefighter, or have a career along those lines, you have to make some extra efforts to keep your job in its proper perspective without ignoring the needs of those who depend on you.

For the bulk of people, most career obligations can fit into a normal workday. There is nothing that should keep you from your child's soccer games, concerts, or other activities that are part of the growing-up process. There will be many activities that your child with autism will participate in, and it is important you be there.

Yes, there will be times you can't attend an activity or be at a doctor's appointment without risking your job, and in those situations all you can do is do your best. Ask yourself if what you are doing at work is truly something you can't leave or if it is a self-imposed deadline. And if it is something you are putting on yourself, take some time to analyze your priorities.

Valuing Extended Family

Most people are part of a larger family unit; there are grandparents, in-laws, cousins, and other people who are part of your life. Those family members are important to you, your spouse, and your child. Growing up within an extended family is a wonderful privilege and provides another layer to a secure foundation for children. Extended family can be there to help you, just as you help them, and be part of very special relationships and memories.

However, it is important to not let the extended family relationships take over your life. This is where your priority system really can actively come into play and assist you in how you conduct your life. In any family, there are social occasions to attend. Parties, showers, weddings, and other celebrations are part of the family experience. Most of these are good for the family and very good for children, but don't let them dictate your own family's schedule.

 ESSENTIAL

> Many times during the year, particularly during the Christmas holidays, families find themselves going in fifty directions at once to do everything they want and what is expected of them. This year create a quieter holiday, and see if the sensory overload on your child is lessened.

Pacing your family's schedule is important. If your child is easily overstimulated by too much activity, chose family occasions that are the least stressful on your child. If you are involved in activities two or three times a week, you and your children might become too exhausted to attend to your own family. Saying "no" occasionally to various get-togethers is sometimes the best decision. Explain to your extended family the situation with your child and involve them in the life of your child, and they will learn about him.

Involve grandparents in the life of your child with autism. This can be a difficult and touchy relationship at times, but understanding a few things about how they may be thinking can save many hurt feelings. (More will be explained about that in Chapter 10.) Families have been created from love and for love, and although we can't choose our families, we can choose how to interact with them.

Handling Your Work

If you already have a career established when you learn that your child has autism, it would be wise to schedule a meeting with your immediate supervisor and explain the situation. Have with you a few printouts about autism that you can leave with your boss if she is unfamiliar with the condition. Don't put a scientific journal in front of her, but provide some basic information about autism that explains exactly what is unique about the autism spectrum. Remember, knowledge is power, and your supervisor's understanding about what is going on will prevent misunderstandings in the future should you require time away from work due to your child's condition.

 **FACT**

Many doctors now have at least one evening a week that they see patients. Try to find therapists and physicians who are available after you leave work to help relieve some of the stress of scheduling appointments. If you don't know of a doctor with convenient hours, ask at a support group meeting.

When you explain to your employer that your child has autism, emphasize this will not affect your work performance. Keep in mind that your employer, as nice as she may be, is there to run a business and her priority is to make that business function as perfectly as possible. Reassure your supervisor that your job performance will remain the same and that you hope to continue to advance in your work over the coming years. The only factor that might be an issue will be physician appointments, school meetings, and other meetings relative to planning your child's future. Also, volunteer to make up any missed time.

If you work for a large company, ask if there is a way that your company can become involved with autism awareness causes. Many companies will rally behind an employee who has a child on the spectrum and donate money to various fundraising campaigns.

Friends, Hobbies, and Everything Else

Life is good. It is a bit overwhelming at times, particularly when you have just learned your child has autism. But it is good and full and there is no reason it will not continue to be that way. Never allow yourself to think that because autism is now part of your life that all of the people and interests you have had over the years will no longer be something you can enjoy. You have a child with autism— the world has not ended.

Friends are a link to sanity. Meeting with them on a regular basis is part of our mental health. It reminds us there is a world out there, and conversations beyond how to take care of children are a welcome escape. The thing to be careful of is reliance on friends more than on a spouse, if you are married, or being with friends so much that other parts of your life are neglected. Visit with friends and make plans to do things that have nothing to do with autism, but keep those relationships in their proper perspective.

Hobbies, sports, and activities of any kind are healthy for a person, both mentally and physically. If you enjoyed certain hobbies before, there is no reason you should not continue to do so. Again, keep them in the proper perspective. You may be used to going skiing every weekend; perhaps now you need to plan to go once a month or work it into a schedule that keeps your other priorities in order. If you and your spouse love world travel, like cruises for example, don't think you will never go on another cruise again because you have a child with autism.

Yes, you will have to make some adjustments, but you will be able to do all the things that are important to you and your family. You will learn the skills to integrate autism into your life. Your experience will grow and you will become more confident in your understanding of ASD.

CHAPTER 8

The Single Parent and the ASD Child

ONE OF THE MOST DIFFICULT ROLES a parent will ever assume is that of the single parent. It doesn't matter how a parent arrived at that state: Divorced, widowed, or single by choice, it is a daily challenge. When a mom or dad is a single parent and there is a child with autism to care for, the challenges can make life feel like a true burden. But it can be done. It just takes a little more effort, organization, and, of course, a lot of love.

Unique Challenges

Although parenting always has challenges, parenting alone has some unique "solutions-in-progress." Think of them as solutions rather than problems, because you just haven't found the answer to the questions yet. Knowing that the problems can be solved is the first step toward keeping you from feeling overwhelmed. Every problem has a solution.

Many of the solutions you will need to develop are related to work, which will be addressed in the next section. Other challenges are about you—the single mom or dad. The real trick to success as a parent, whether single or married, is not losing *you* in the parenting process. There are some issues that every single parent needs to be aware of; working on the solutions before they become problems can reduce stress immensely.

The Difficulty of a Social Life

Everyone needs social interaction. But a parent who is parenting an autistic child alone works a full week, takes care of a special-needs child, perhaps meets the needs of other children as well, and takes care of a home. There may be other obligations, too, such as school or community activities. Exhaustion takes on a new meaning and the social life is so far on the back shelf that it is hard to even remember what it was like to have one.

Even so, it is important to carve out time in your schedule for social activities. This can be whatever type of activity you enjoy—hiking, biking, dancing, card games, movies, eating out . . . whatever you may enjoy doing with other people. The key is interaction with friends. Adults who do not spend time with friends begin to resent their schedule, their lives, and possibly their children. It is normal to feel that way and the best way to avoid the problem is to schedule times to socialize.

No Partner to Commiserate with Daily

One major advantage that parents who are married to each other have is companionship. Yes, there are many other advantages as well, but nothing is quite like being with a person who is living the same life with you. Having someone with whom you can collapse in the living room each evening and pour out your frustrations and victories of the day is always a relief. It is human nature to want to share.

If you don't have anyone in your life that you can share with on a daily basis, work at developing friendships in which you have a true give-and-take relationship. A local support group might be helpful in that regard, as there will most likely be other single parents included. Some support groups have a network of parents who are on "phone duty" and you can call them at any time when you need to talk or vent some emotions.

Potential Difficulties with Ex-Spouse and In-Laws

If you are single by divorce or made the choice not to marry your child's other parent, hopefully you have been able to create a good working relationship for the benefit of the child. If not, and every time you see each other the sparks fly, it would be wise to consult a counselor. Even if this marriage had no chance in the world, there needs to be a peaceful environment for the child.

 ESSENTIAL

Often in the case of separated parents, the child shows behavioral problems to the noncustodial parent when he or she first has the child for a long weekend. Questions about the ability of either parent to care for the child arise, when really the change in routine is to blame.

Children with autism may seem to be unaware of the environment around them, but they usually are much more in tune with the emotions of others than it appears. If the parents are arguing or fighting, the child is apt to act out aggressive and belligerent behaviors. The adults in the situation, by keeping their own tempers, can prevent this. Remember that although the relationship is over, neither parent's relationship with the child is over, or ever will be.

In-laws, or the parents of the ex-spouse, can be a problem for the custodial parent. This situation needs to be discussed with the child's other parent, as any other approach to the child's grandparents will be difficult. If you find this relationship extremely difficult and your former spouse will not cooperate to help you in this matter, limit exposure as much as possible. The grandparents have every right to see the child, and this should not be limited, but you can limit your own exposure for your own peace of mind.

A Multitude of Challenges

Every single-parent family with an ASD child will find its own challenges and obstacles. Some will require solutions unique to the individual family.

- Preventing elopement (escape) when the parent is temporarily unavailable is a high priority.
- Having safety measures in place within the household, especially if upper stories or decks are accessible to the child, will help prevent accidents.
- Protect younger children if there is an older ASD sibling as the older sibling's curiosity might put the younger child at risk.
- If you have a four-door car, be sure that the back doors cannot be opened while the car is moving.
- Financially providing for a family is difficult for a single parent and careful budgeting is necessary to meet the needs of each person.

Working and Caring for an ASD Child

Do you feel you are working full-time at everything? You are. There are never enough hours in the day to do it all. Society tells us we can have it all if we are just a little more organized, so people continually try to be all, do all, and accomplish all.

ALERT!

Attempting to do everything alone is just setting yourself up for failure. Do not hesitate to ask friends and family for help. Consider hiring a local teenager to mow the lawn and help with outside chores to ease the burden. You need to protect your own health!

The reality is that no one person can do everything. A single parent has the jobs of parenting, career, and maintaining a home, and these are all full-time jobs! How can anyone do all of these things and still find time to sleep? The answer is simple: They can't, and you can't either.

Priority One Is Your Children

The first priority is your child or children. Nothing is more important than being a mom or dad. Meeting the needs of a child who is autistic is going to take a lot of your time, and everything else can wait. You will be working in your everyday life to integrate sign language or speech therapy, sensory skills, behavioral management, and other things a child with autism has to learn. You may be using a special diet or physical therapies as well to coordinate with the therapists your child sees regularly.

Make your life easier by setting up a schedule that is realistic. Set up times for baths, medications, stories, and all of the daily and weekly activities you and your child engage in. If you know what time you do certain things, you will not feel the stress of trying to remember what needs to be done. It is hard to concentrate on reading your child a story if you are simultaneously trying to remember what else needs to be done. Putting up a poster board with drawings of the activities that need to be done with the corresponding times will help you stay on schedule and help your child know what to expect.

 **QUESTION?**

How do I make a schedule my child can interpret?
One easy way is to get a piece of poster board and mount it on the wall. Take photos of activities, such as your child brushing her teeth or making her bed, and put those on the poster board in order. Your child can reference this to stay on top of things.

Priority Two Is Your Job

Your second priority has to be your job. You have responsibilities to your job. It is very hard to mesh the single parenting of a disabled child with work, but it can be done. The way to ease the stress of working with having a disabled child is to find the most dependable day care possible. It may be a family member or friend—someone in whom you have the utmost confidence.

Talk to your employer about the responsibilities you have for your child that could infringe on your work hours. Don't be overly dramatic or appear as though you are seeking sympathy. Be matter-of-fact and businesslike. Emphasize that there will be as little interference with your work as possible and give an honest estimate of what kind of time you think you may miss each month or week. It is possible that a job-sharing option is available or that your employer will work with you to solve the problem in some other way.

When you are at work, give your job everything you have. Although it is difficult when you are tired, worried, or stressed to put your personal life out of your mind, force yourself to do it, and perform your job functions the best you can. If you excel as an employee, your employer will be more likely to work with you when things come up that force you to take time away from the job.

 **FACT**

Employers want people who are willing to work hard and deliver quality work. You may find your company is willing to make allowances for employees who have special needs. Split shifts, working from home, and flexible schedules are some of the options that may be available.

It is also a good idea to look into different options such as different shifts, different locations, or alternative ideas for income. If you have a skill or trade that you could be successful with at home, this would be a possibility worth investigating. Perhaps your existing employer would consider letting you telecommute. Keep in mind that once your child is in school, it will be much easier to work on a schedule that meets everyone's needs. No problem is permanent; some are just more persistent than others and require creative thinking.

Priority Three Is Your Home

You have to accept that there will be times when the house is more of a mess than you would like. *House Beautiful* isn't coming over to photograph, so just relax. No parent has ever been graded on how immaculate a house is; so don't even try to compete on that level. It is so easy to be caught up in the trap that the house reflects how good you are doing as a mom or a dad, and it simply isn't true.

Tend to the issues that keep the family safe. A clean bathroom and kitchen are important, but if all the towels aren't folded and you need to fetch one from the laundry basket, life will go on. Organize your schedule so that you aren't overwhelmed with a huge mess at the end of the week. Doing a little each night is much easier than trying to do everything on a Saturday.

Some simple timesavers can make your life much easier. There are many sources available, such as magazines and books, for tips on how to save time in the house. Research different ideas and use the ones that work for you.

- **Lighten up the kitchen chores.** Use paper plates except on weekends.
- **Make mealtime preparation faster.** Buy single-serving, ready-to-serve grocery products for your child.
- **Create less laundry from the kitchen.** Use a vinyl tablecloth, as it is easier to clean than a cloth, and use paper towels instead of dishtowels.
- **Eliminate the missing sock mystery.** Pin socks together as soon as people take them off so sorting is a quicker job.
- **Prevent unexpected laundry late at night.** Have at least two weeks' worth of clean underwear, pants, and pajamas for your child.
- **If you have a cat, buy a covered litter box.** Children with an ASD are often intrigued with the cat box.
- **Invest in a new laundry basket.** One with three compartments to separate laundry during the week will prevent having to sort it all at the same time.

- **Give yourself a night off once a week**. Visit the local fast-food restaurant. It may have a playground where your child can burn off some extra energy in a safe environment.
- **If a dog may become a part of the family, plan ahead.** If you don't have a fenced yard, consider who will walk the dog or who will watch your child when that chore is necessary.

 ESSENTIAL

One great timesaver can be setting up your bills to pay them online. You can create automatic payments of many of your bills on your credit card and then just pay your credit card each month. Many banks also have online services that have bill-paying features.

The Parent and Child Team

Enlist your child as soon as he is old enough to help. Teach him how to use a feather duster. The job won't be done perfectly, but he will thoroughly enjoy the process and it will save some work. Children love to help empty wastebaskets and children with autism are no exception. Teach your child how to make his bed and pick up his own toys.

Many little chores will help keep the house clean. It will allow you and your child to work on something together. It is also a good time for a child with autism to learn some basic life skills that he will use forever.

Finding Reliable Day Care

For the parent of a child with autism, this can be the most difficult obstacle to overcome. There is no question that day care for a disabled child is hard to find and parents are at an extreme disadvantage when they don't have a "normal" child. All too often, inquiries into a day care will be met with an answer of "I'm sorry, we are not equipped to handle an autistic child's needs." It can be incredibly frustrating.

There are no easy answers. Sometimes a family member can help. Grandparents, aunts, uncles, cousins, siblings, or extended family members are your best option. Talk to members in your support group, call your doctor's office, talk to the special education department at a local school, and contact various churches. There are options, but they can be difficult to find. Be persistent.

 ESSENTIAL

Schedule an appointment with the Health and Human Services Office in your area. They may have resources available for you that may be of great help to you in finding day care for your child.

Do not ever place your child in an environment that you feel uncomfortable with. Word-of-mouth continues to be the best recommendation, so don't hesitate to ask people you know and trust. When you do get a referral, visit the day care center several times, or meet with the person who will be caring for your child. If possible, arrive at the day care unannounced so you can see how things are run without an advance warning. Ask for references and contact them.

Future Relationships

Many single parents, particularly single moms, are unsure how to approach dating, or even if they should date at all. They are concerned how a potential serious relationship would affect their child with autism. They are equally concerned how another adult who is not the parent will feel about a child with autism.

Dating?

Dating after you have been divorced or widowed is difficult even for a person who has no children, but is a whole new experience when you have a child who is on the autism spectrum. The whole process of setting up a babysitter, getting ready for a date, and wondering what you will talk about is almost enough to make you cancel the whole thing. It seems easier to crawl back into a sweatsuit and spend the evening with the kids. After all, isn't that what VCRs are for? Is it easier to stay at home and watch cartoon films on the VCR instead of venturing out on a date? Yes, of course. Is it the best thing for you? Absolutely not!

Many single parents justify a life of solitude by saying that it is for the kids. They shouldn't bring a stranger into their life just to have them leave again, the time away isn't good considering how many work hours keep them away already—the list of reasons goes on and on. But it is usually a false front to cover what one woman honestly admitted: "Who would want me? An over-thirty woman with an autistic son? What kind of catch am I?" Men feel the same way; it is not an emotion exclusive to women.

You Are Worth It

This is where you sit down in front of a mirror and say out loud 100 times, or as many times as it takes, that you are an individual worth knowing and loving. Autism is part of your family's life, but autism does not define you. Your child is not autism, and you are not autism. Your child has an ASD but he is much, much more than that.

When you begin to see your own self worth, then someone else will be able to see it, too. Every person you meet has issues in his or her life. Your issue happens to be a child on the autism spectrum.

The Possibility of a Stepparent

When a relationship turns serious, marriage may very well become a possibility. For all practical purposes, whether a couple decides to live together or legally marry, the result is the same. A commitment will be made for two adults to bring their lives together, and this is going to involve any children in the relationship. It will be of special concern to the parent of the child with autism.

There is another person who will be apprehensive. If the one marrying the parent of the child with autism has no experience with special-needs children, it can be intimidating. Many men worry greatly that they will not know what to do or how to handle this child. They are concerned about whether they can be an adequate parent to a child that they are not entirely sure they understand.

 **FACT**

Some statistics report a 50 percent failure rate in second marriages. To keep that statistic from including you, have your future spouse attend support group meetings with you. At a meeting, it is possible for your new partner to ask questions that he or she may not otherwise feel comfortable asking, and information will remove fears.

When adults commit to a second marriage and there are children involved, it is wise to talk to a counselor. Many times issues that are lurking in the background can come to the surface in a discussion with an objective third party, and fears can be put to rest. You can get advice and discuss concerns that either of you may have. It is also a good idea to bring the stepparent-to-be to the child's primary care physician to talk.

The biggest mistake people make is to visualize all the potential problems and situations that could ever possibly come up in an entire lifetime, and imagine them occurring all at once. Remember: One step at a time. You don't have to solve it all in one day. This is where a counselor or the child's physician can be helpful. Once worries are stated aloud, they can be seen in the proper perspective.

Concerns of Women

It is very likely you are the custodial parent of your child with autism or perhaps you have joint custody with your ex-husband. Regardless, it is the nature of the mom to feel that as far as her children are concerned, "the buck stops here." The responsibility of these children is not something any parent, mom or dad, takes lightly, but to mothers it is of critical importance.

If you have joint custody, you have the advantage of the time that your child is with his father. That will enable you to have a social life without involving your child until you feel it is appropriate. Many mothers feel it is best not to involve a man you are dating with your children unless the relationship becomes serious. It is uncomfortable for everyone if a child asks in front of your date, "Is this my new daddy?" Schedule your social life and dates around the times your child is with her father until you feel introductions are appropriate.

If you have sole custody of your child, or if you are widowed, it is a bit more complicated, but you can't deny yourself a dating life if that is what you want. It is still best to hold off introducing a man you are dating to your child until you feel it is appropriate, so enlist the help of family and friends. Your support group may be able to help here as well. Many support groups set up rotating schedules for moms to care for one another's children to solve this very problem.

In many ways, a child with autism quickly sorts out the kind of men you will date. A woman commented in an interview that if her child who was autistic turned off a man, she knew he had some inherent flaws. This is very true, so if someone rejects a relationship because of your child, he wasn't worth it to begin with. Your child is a treasure and any man you develop a relationship with will be lucky to know him.

Concerns of Men

Women always say that men have it easier in the dating department, and it is true. Although we live in a liberated society, it is usually a man who asks a woman out. The advantage is that men are afraid of rejection. That sounds like a contradiction, but when you have a child with autism, it truly is an advantage. A man can be fairly sure if a woman would be receptive to a child with autism before he takes the risk of dating her.

The other advantage men have is that the biological mother of the child usually has custody. A single dad's schedule is typically more available and at his control than a single mom's is.

But it isn't all unfair advantages. Men who are single fathers have some definite disadvantages. Women might perceive them as "mom-shopping" to care for their children. A woman might also see a man with children, particularly a special-needs child, as blocking her opportunity to have her own children due to the responsibility issues and therefore not wish to build a relationship with him. She also may not wish to have to deal with the presence of his ex-wife, a woman that she will have to interact with even after the child becomes an adult.

It sounds trite and clichéd, but it is true: Love can conquer many things. No one has perfect parenting skills. No one will always do the right thing with any child. We all make mistakes. The important thing is the love within a family, and that is something that can never be wrong if it is given unconditionally.

CHAPTER 9

ASD and the Effects on Siblings

AUTISM AFFECTS EVERYONE in the family. Perhaps no one feels this effect more than the siblings of the ASD child. Parents of the child on the spectrum are often so wrapped up in the issues surrounding autism, and understandably so, that they overlook the ways autism is affecting their other children. It isn't bad parenting; it is human nature. Raising children is a balancing act for parents as they try to meet everyone's needs and provide a complete childhood for each of their children.

Older Siblings

When an older child or a teenager has a new sibling, it is enough of an adjustment. Adding autism into the mixture a couple of years later makes this adjustment even more challenging. A child who is ten years older (or more) than the new arrival will view the family dynamics differently than a younger child.

New Considerations

If there are a significant number of years separating the older sibling from the child with autism, the younger child may not have much impact on the daily life of the older child. This is especially true if the older child is in high school, for example, and nearly ready to move out of the house to live on her own or to go to college. The older child may not be much involved with the daily trials of living with a child with autism.

However, the older sibling may have some concerns that other children don't think of. The older child likely recognizes fairly quickly that autism is going to be around for the rest of her life, and she may already be concerned about her role in taking care of an autistic adult in several years. This will impact not only her life but the life of her future spouse and any children they may have as well. Autism affects everyone in a family.

Slightly Older Siblings

When a child has a sibling that is two to eight years younger and that child is diagnosed with autism or another spectrum disorder, it can affect the sibling(s) in several different ways. Children have their own personalities and how they react in a given situation will depend on their personality. There is no blanket way children handle issues in their lives, but there are some generalizations that can be made. Understanding the mechanisms behind observed behaviors can assist you in helping your other children. Typical reactions can include the following:

- A sibling acts as another parent.
- A sibling pulls away from the family.
- A sibling attempts to "make up" for autism by being a "model" child.
- A sibling establishes his or her own identity through flamboyant behavior.
- A sibling struggles with anxiety or depression.
- A sibling feels resentment toward the child with autism.

Although this list is by no means all-inclusive, most siblings of children with ASD will fall into one of these categories. Just when autism itself seems overwhelming and more than any person can emotionally handle, the realization that the other children have developed needs because of their younger sibling can overwhelm the most patient of parents. But it is, in reality, a simple process of identifying the issues and addressing them one by one; tackling the entire situation at once isn't going to work. Dealing with one issue, one crisis, one dilemma at a time will work with a little practice. And it's okay to make mistakes.

 ALERT!

Children who are used to their sibling with autism not participating in games are thrilled when interaction and participation begins. They also can become jealous because of the attention focused on the child with autism. Don't forget to praise your other children for their skills and achievements.

Parents will often report that they observe two of the behaviors in the previous list more commonly than other behaviors. Most of the siblings of a child who is on the spectrum will take one of two roles. They will either fall into the role of an "alternative" parent or isolate themselves from the family and autism as far as humanly possible.

The Parental Sibling

Children who begin to act as another parent have both positive and negative issues to deal with. The positive side is the child's acceptance and involvement in the family. As that child matures into an adult, he will have a compassion for people with disabilities; it is not something that is foreign to him as it is to so many people. The downside is that the parents might rely on such a child heavily, and it is possible for that child to lose his own childhood in the process.

Parents need to be aware of a child who becomes parental. It isn't a behavior to be discouraged, as families should work together and look out for each other. But it is important not to let a child take on so much responsibility that he becomes overwhelmed and loses himself in the process. A child who observes her younger sibling about to poke a fork in an electrical outlet and stops him is a good thing. A child who feels she is responsible for everything that the child with autism does, and carries the guilt of an accident or problem, is a bad thing.

Younger Siblings

When a child is born to a family that already has a child with autism, there are different issues to deal with. There is no adjustment period for the nonautistic child—he has never known his sibling as being anything other than autistic. The element of adjustment is removed, but other challenges remain.

Most children who have a sibling that is one or two years younger have much of the same issues as any siblings that are close in age, but magnified. A child with autism, because of the very nature of ASD, demands more time, patience, and tolerance than a child without the disorder would ever have. The major problem? A child without the disorder can "get lost." It is so easy to postpone the needs of a "normal" child because of the heavy demands of an ASD child.

 FACT

Negative attention is better than no attention—or so a child thinks. It is especially true for the sibling of a child with autism. If your other children begin having behavior problems, review how much individualized time they get from you. Negative behavior can be changed into a positive outcome.

Jealousy and Resentment

It is important that parents go the extra mile to avoid jealousy and resentment from the child who is not autistic. Jealousy is a problem that begins subtly, but when the children reach their teenage years, it becomes a serious problem. Resentment is the result of jealousy, and a resentful teenager is a problem waiting to happen. The teenage years are challenge enough without having undesirable behaviors surface as attempts to gain attention occur. You can watch for signs in your children indicating that jealousy and resentment may be becoming an issue. A child may:

- Request that Mom and Dad attend school functions alone (without the child with autism attending)
- Feel concern or embarrassment about having his or her friends visit for sleepovers or other activities
- Become more in need of physical contact with one or both parents, wanting closeness such as cuddling
- Express jealousy overtly (the phrase "But he gets to . . ." is a definite sign of jealousy)
- Excessively argue about chores and responsibilities
- Show behavior that indicates an obsession with his or her health

Competitiveness

It is also important to watch for competitive behavior. Competitiveness may be the first sign of jealousy. A child who goes out of her way to show the parents accomplishments and skills may be feeling that the child with autism is getting a lot of positive feedback for reaching what is perceived to be very small goals. A child without autism does not understand that finally speaking one or two words is an enormous victory and will not understand why such a fuss isn't made over his normal or above normal accomplishments. It is important to take the time to praise all of your children for each milestone or goal they accomplish throughout their childhood.

Other behaviors will surface that are unique to each child, and the parents are the best gauges of those actions. A little common sense, a deep breath, and some thinking the problem through will usually guide a parent into a proper course of action. Contrary to what children think, moms and dads love their children equally, and it is the job of the parents to display that through their behavior. As the child with autism demands more and more attention in order to raise them into the best they can possibly be, no parent intends to leave the other children behind. Don't hesitate to check yourself to be sure you are conveying the correct message to your family, and remember that it is never too late to change.

Growing Up Too Fast

The baby boomer generation is dovetailing careers and family. Because of this, it is common to have age gaps of ten years or more between children. If there is a child with autism in the family and another baby comes along ten years later, there are some unique issues to be faced by the family.

When a sibling is much younger than the child with autism, the younger child will never know of any adjustment that had to be made in the family. This is simply life, the way it has always been, and the way it will always be. The main risk to a sibling of a disabled child is through the maturing years.

 ALERT!

> Safety is an issue for parents with a newborn. If a child with autism is not totally self-involved, he will be very interested in the new baby. His curiosity, which is unlikely to be tempered with caution, could inadvertently cause harm. Parents should take extra safety measures to avoid accidents.

It is very easy to inadvertently cause a child to "grow up" too quickly. The younger child starts watching out for the older because it is the natural thing to do. The burden of that responsibility is too much for a child to bear, and it may be sowing the seeds of resentment that will fully bloom later in life.

Most children realize as they approach their young adult years that this sibling with autism will be a part of their life forever. Realization strikes that someday this may be their responsibility. It isn't necessary to bring up this topic; it will arise on its own when the time is right. And it is very possible that a child with autism will eventually live in a supervised group home or even live independently.

When a child is much younger than his or her sibling with autism, it is less likely there will be interference in the activities of childhood. The family will have adjusted and found their own routine that the younger child will fit into. It would be wise to find respite care so that the younger child will have time with parents alone. Involving extended family is an option that is not only helpful but also supportive. As the family pulls together, a family life is created that is secure and comfortable for all members.

The Isolated Sibling

Some children will not form a parental type of attachment to their sibling with autism. This happens more commonly in children who are more introverted. They attempt to put as much distance between them and their sibling and family as possible. Often, the cause is quite simple: They are tired of autism.

It is important that a child who withdraws from the family because of autism be allowed to flourish on his or her own. These children are often susceptible to depression, and it is often helpful to have a therapist address the issues of this one child alone, without any mention of autism. It is very important that the parents spend time with that child alone to enjoy activities and projects that are totally unrelated to autism. Parents also need to be clear, verbally and through their actions, that they do not feel the sibling is responsible for his brother or sister. The less the child with autism impacts his sibling, the better the chances for both children to evolve a healthy relationship over time.

 ESSENTIAL

Support groups for parents of children with autism can provide information on locating a support group for siblings. Check with your local chapter of the Autism Society of America or other organizations that have support groups. Your child needs to realize she is not alone.

It is common for parents of several children, when one or more is autistic, to make provisions they might never have considered otherwise. For example, one mother said she would have never allowed a television in a child's bedroom until autism joined their family. However, the reality was that the nonautistic child could never watch his favorite programs without the child with ASD constantly changing the channel and throwing a tantrum when his own television shows were switched. Making that one adjustment increased the peace in the family. As this mother said, "Choose your battles. It just wasn't worth it. My other child deserved to watch his own shows and I just take a little extra time to monitor how much and what he is watching."

The Social Impact of Having an ASD Sibling

Children who have a sibling with ASD have mixed feelings about their brother or sister. At times, it affects their social life, and at other times, it is totally irrelevant. Like any brother and sister combination, it can be a rocky road laced with arguments and love, all at the same time. The sibling of the child with autism will claim his brother or sister as his worst enemy or best friend, depending on the day. One thing is certain: It is always an adventure!

Peers

Some of the biggest problems siblings of ASD children face are issues within their own peer group. Your child, having the experience of a sibling with a disability, has a different outlook on the world than many children have. It is not unusual for children, particularly in the middle and elementary school years, to hear other children tease or outright ridicule their sibling with autism. Parents should address this immediately, as the problem will only escalate and eventually alienate a child from her own peer group.

If a child is being singled out because of her sibling, it is important for the parents to contact the school system. In this case, it isn't enough to tell your child to ignore the teasing, for two reasons. Your child will generally rise to the occasion to defend her sibling with autism and be on the defensive whenever interacting with her peer group. Additionally, the children doing the teasing will continue to be intolerant of people who are different from them and the cycle will continue. Do not hesitate to schedule a conference with counselors, teachers, or other school staff to address and put an end to the problem.

Family Events

Of course, you don't always have to keep your children free from each other. Your nonautistic children may find that their friends are more accepting than they expected, and they may be worried for no reason. One child, who has a brother with autism just a year younger than she is, had a band concert at her school. She had recently taken some verbal harassment over her brother being autistic and although she wanted her brother to attend the concert, she was worried at what might happen. Her solution was to have the entire family attend, but she asked her father to sit with her brother right next to the exit just in case things got out of control. A hasty exit prevented anyone from knowing about the tantrum that occurred twenty minutes into the concert.

Don't hesitate to ask your child what he or she might suggest as a way to solve situations that could arise during a social occasion. The goal is to make the sibling who is not autistic feel comfortable without leaving out the child with autism. Sometimes it is not appropriate to bring a child with autism to certain events, just as it is not appropriate to bring any children to some events, and a babysitter is the best option. But other situations, with some family brainstorming, can usually be worked around.

Considering Future Children

It is difficult, if not impossible, to advise a couple on whether or not they should consider having more children if they have a child on the autism spectrum. So many factors are involved and it is a very personal decision. It is not a decision a couple can rush into or let others make for them.

Genetics or Unknown

If the disorder your child with ASD has is a proven genetic disorder, such as Rett syndrome or fragile X syndrome, genetic testing is in order to determine what the risk factors are for a future pregnancy. If one child has been born with a genetic disorder, the odds are high another will be as well. This is a decision that requires a genetic counselor and perhaps family counseling to reach a difficult decision.

The cause of other disorders within the autism spectrum is unknown. They could be caused by genetics, the result of unknown disease processes, vaccine damage—the bottom line is no one knows. No matter what testing is done, there is no way to know if another child would develop the symptoms of autism.

Many parents with one child with autism have several children with other disorders on the spectrum. Parents will receive the diagnosis of autism in one child, then as time goes by, they will suspect another child is on the spectrum. Testing will often show Asperger's or PDD-NOS. There are also many cases of a family with a child with autism and a child with another developmental disability. ADD/ADHD is common in the siblings of a child on the autism spectrum.

Mental, Emotional, and Financial Impacts

Not only should a couple consider the mental and emotional impact of having a special-needs child, they should also consider the financial and long-term issues involved with raising children on the spectrum. It is rare for private insurance companies to cover any treatment that is needed for autism and related disorders. There are a few, but generally, insurance companies have an exclusion for autism. This boosts the costs of medical care and therapies that are needed over the years that parents must bear.

There are alternatives to help parents who meet certain guidelines. SSI, or Supplemental Security Income, is a program managed by the Social Security Administration. It was put in place to assist blind, aged, or disabled individuals who meet certain financial criteria. Benefits are paid directly to families to help with the expenses of daily living. Autism is an automatic allowance for benefits if your family meets certain qualifications such as income level and value of assets.

 **FACT**

If your child has private insurance and sees his doctor for a condition unrelated to autism, be *certain* that the insurance forms do not indicate the diagnosis of autism. If a child is seen for an ear infection, it is not necessary to include the autism diagnosis, which may block benefits.

Be certain before you apply for SSI that you are able to thoroughly document the diagnosis of an autism spectrum disorder by physicians, therapists, and even school personnel. Regardless of a child's age, the school system can become involved to help with the diagnosis and early intervention. Even if your child is under school age, contact the school district to find out what programs and resources are available.

It is also important to remember that financial planning must be in place to protect and provide for any special-needs children in case of the death of the parents. Life insurance, trust funds, and wills that provide for guardianship of a child are not luxuries. They are necessary and must be kept up-to-date at all times.

It's Your Decision

There are many well-meaning people, such as extended family, friends, and in-laws, who often feel it is their place to advise a couple on their family planning. Although it is difficult, you must stress, very kindly, that this is a personal decision and let the matter drop. If people persist in advising you against your wishes, be firm but polite in asserting your right to privacy.

If you decide to not have any more children, be at peace with that and do not allow others to make you feel guilty or inadequate. Many people feel it is their business to advise other people on childbearing and raising those children. It is no one's business but yours; just politely thank them for their interest and change the subject. If you decide you do want more children, again do not let others spoil your joy. These decisions are yours; you and your spouse will make the best decision for your family.

CHAPTER 10

ASD and the Extended Family

AUTISM AND ITS RELATED conditions are often not understood by the extended family. Many of your relatives may have never heard of autism. There are various responses by family members as they attempt to advise the parents and educate themselves in the process. Regardless of whether or not the family relationships are close, remember that even a close family can be torn apart by ASD. Understanding common reactions and how to handle them can prevent misunderstandings from occurring that are harmful to family relationships.

Grandparents

Grandparents can be the easiest or the hardest family members to deal with when a child is diagnosed with autism. Most of the time they are a blessing, as they assist and provide moral support through the early years of a child's life. Grandparents have wisdom gained from years of experience that have taught them what is important.

Those Who Are Helpful

There are no official statistics on how grandparents respond to autism, but most parents say they wouldn't know what to do without their parents. Grandma seems to come through and shine when mom herself

is falling apart over the diagnosis. Grandpa will usually do what dads do best—try to solve all the problems.

Often the grandparents put up the first alert that there is something wrong. A grandparent will question whether the child can hear properly. Grandparents are close enough to love and care deeply for their grandchild, but they are not there day in and day out, so they spot the lack of development more quickly than do the people in the household who see the child every day. It is common for the grandparent who suspected something was wrong to be very close to the child as the years go by. It has been said that the generation gap exists between parents and children, but not at all between grandparents and grandchildren.

Your parents can be your best advocate and stress reducers. If your parents are not near or you just don't relate well with them, perhaps you have developed closeness with your spouse's parents.

 ESSENTIAL

Grandparents may never have heard of autism. They need to be educated, but books can be overwhelming in the beginning. Create your own list of "frequently asked questions" along with answers and give this to them. A copy of this will help your parents understand what you are dealing with and save you from answering the same questions repeatedly.

Those Who Are Difficult

Although this is not the most common scenario, it is extremely hard on families when the grandparents of a disabled child are difficult. It is important to remember that this is not a common reaction of grandparents, so if there are problems it is wise to look for the cause of the problem; most likely, it is something that can be worked through. If there is a true conflict, you, as the parents of the autistic child, need to determine what the source of the problem is. Generally, one of two issues is at the center.

The most common reason grandparents relate poorly, or not at all, to a grandchild who is disabled is simply that they are baffled. They just don't have the vaguest notion of how they should act, what they should do, if they should make allowances and, if so, what kind and how much. They want to interact with the child but don't know how to get from here to there. It appears as though they are ignoring their grandchild, but the reality is that they are at a loss, trying to handle a situation they have never been prepared for.

If you have a parent who appears to be ignoring your child, try to determine if it is because they are unsure of what to do. If that appears to be the cause, you can help them become involved with their grandchild again by guiding the way. Give them a copy of this book and other books you have found helpful. Gather current magazine articles covering autism. Above all, show them how to act with your child; if they see that autism isn't the worst thing in the world, they will learn how to interact and become more confident in that relationship.

Less commonly, and much more difficult to handle, is the grandparent who chooses not accept a disabled child as being a "legitimate" grandchild. This attitude paves the road to an extremely rocky journey through autism and in family relationships. Resentment builds between the adults in the family because of the grandparent's feelings about the child who is autistic and can be a volatile trigger for arguments and disharmony. Other children, who are treated normally, receive a distorted message and sense the dissension in the family; they can become tense and insecure of their own self-worth. After all, they may wonder, would they be rejected, too, if something happened to make them "less than perfect"?

Solutions for Difficult Situations

Suggesting the grandparents see a counselor will only make things worse; it's bad enough, in the grandparents' eyes, that the child isn't perfect, but to suggest *they* have a problem will only create anger and bitterness. Most parents who have struggled with this have said that only some distance makes the situation bearable. Distance can help everyone cope.

If putting some distance between you and the situation is not possible, limit contact as much as possible. Your other children can still see their grandparents, but explain to the children that the activity or location they are going to visit is not appropriate for your child with autism. Although it is tempting to argue the point with the grandparents, you are not going to reach a solution; it is less stressful and, in the long run, better for all parties concerned to avoid the situation.

 ESSENTIAL

Dealing with grandparents who don't want to confront autism directly can be painful and upsetting, but the situation needs to be kept from the children as much as possible to prevent them from experiencing undue guilt and stress. If you know you aren't going to be able to change the situation, there is no need to make others—namely your other children—feel uncomfortable or awkward.

The Unique In-Law Problem

In this case, a problem doesn't exist between the in-laws and the child with autism, but rather between the parents and the in-laws. There are no hard and fast rules on when this problem occurs, but there are some definite trends.

Mom and Her Mother-in-Law

When family relationships are difficult, the most common problem is that between the mother of a child with autism and her husband's mother. This relationship can be touchy even if there is no disabled child involved. This, of course, is not always the case and sometimes this is a very special and precious relationship. But when it is not a good relationship, the entire family can feel tremendous stress.

When a woman and her son's wife do not get along, and a child is diagnosed with autism, a bad situation is exacerbated.

Mom may find every decision or treatment being questioned by her mother-in-law. Raising a child with autism is challenging enough without having to defend every decision to your husband's mother.

If you have a problem with your mother-in-law, ask your husband to talk with her, or both of his parents together, to work toward a solution. If he won't, or it does no good, handle the situation with as much grace as possible and avoid as many interactions as possible. It is not good for you to feel stressed and resentful with your mother-in-law at every encounter. It is also not good for your children; if you are being questioned on decisions and choices you make for your family, it undermines your authority as a parent.

 ALERT!

If either set of parents question every decision you make regarding your child, you need to assert your independence as a parent. When questions are asked, assume they are from concern, but if you are being doubted, stand your ground. Thank them for their help. But don't allow anyone, including your or your partner's parents, to cause you to doubt yourself.

Dad and His Mother-in-Law

The old jokes about in-laws have always centered on a man's mother-in-law, which is usually an unfair commentary on a woman's mother, but when it is a difficult relationship, the jokes ring all too true. This is only magnified when a child is disabled with a condition and the cause is unknown. Couple that with the lack of any definitive treatment and a tense situation can be the result. The mother may blame autism on genetics, even when there is no definitive cause established—and, of course, it will be the fault of the father of the child because of his bad genes. This is also sometimes used as a justification for saying, "I told you marrying him was a mistake."

When a dad has this problem, his wife needs to talk to her parents. A father has his own issues to deal with when his child is autistic, plus he is juggling career, kids, and other activities. Again, like the woman with a difficult mother-in-law relationship, it is stressful for everyone involved.

Other Family Members

Mothers-in-law are not the only family members that can make relationships uncomfortable. There are aunts, uncles, cousins, nieces, nephews, and even grandchildren involved in an extended family. And if a family is very large, there will be a great number of people related only by marriage who are involved as well. It can bring to mind the old film *The Good, the Bad and the Ugly*.

The Good

Fortunately, this is the most common situation for parents of children with autism and their extended family. Every family has its trials and tribulations, but when a family can work together for common goals, everyone benefits. If your extended family enjoys a good relationship, it will only help your child with social and interpersonal skills.

If your family is supportive and helpful, involve them in activities as much as you can. They can help with autism awareness functions you may be involved in. They are an extra set of eyes at a picnic to ensure your child's safety. Above all, they are a wonderful support system for the immediate family of a child with autism.

The Bad

Usually when a situation with extended family is not ideal, it is because of lack of involvement. This is a two-way street. Parents may decide not to participate in family events because they haven't figured out how to manage autism easily or because they feel unwelcome. Either way, the result is the same. The family with the affected child becomes isolated from the extended family.

If you consider your extended family ties to be less than ideal, try to figure out why. Is it a self-imposed exile, and is it possible that no one knows what to say or how to act with your child? A little education about autism can make the unknown less intimidating. Most people in a family want to get along and be together; they may need your help to achieve that with your child. Ignoring the issues won't change or make them go away, but addressing them directly can improve the situation.

The Ugly

Situations between family members can become very ugly when people in families have negative feelings toward one another and feel a need to express those feelings. This is especially true when autism is used as the vehicle. And it does happen.

If the relationships in your family are hostile or so saturated with bad memories, you may not be able to work through the situation. Using autism as a pawn in interpersonal relationships is not good for you or your child and must not be allowed to continue. Your first priorities are your own family and you have to do what is necessary to protect them.

Celebrating Family Holidays

Just about the time you have an established routine that works, a holiday comes along. Some are more disruptive than others, but all are something different than the normal day. Learning how to cope with various holidays can make them more fun for your family, and all you need to do is a little thinking ahead. When you know a routine is going to go out the window, make a Plan B so you, at least, are prepared.

Spring and Summer Holidays

Several holidays during the warmer weather are enjoyed by families and should continue to be enjoyed even after autism is a part of your life. Having a child with autism should not change this.

Planning and being aware of issues that may overstimulate your child can ward off many potential problems.

Mother's Day and Father's Day are two dates that parents can use to teach a child about giving to others. This is also an opportunity for a couple to demonstrate to the children their mutual respect and love. Dad giving Mom a Mother's Day gift—one that isn't a toaster or pancake griddle—teaches the children that Mom is a person, too. This is an important lesson for a child with autism to learn. As these children tend to "use" other people as tools, any opportunity to show that people are individuals to be respected and loved is an opportunity to not be missed.

Autumn Holidays

For a child, there is only one holiday in the fall that matters: Halloween. October 31 is a day to dress up and collect enough candy to give them tummy-aches until the next trick-or-treat date comes along. For the parent of a child with autism, this holiday presents some extra challenges.

 ESSENTIAL

Put reflective tape on your child's costume or clothing so you can spot her easily should she get away from you. Bright-colored costumes are helpful in finding your child in a group of costumed children; avoid the most popular costume of the year, as there will be many of those worn by children and it can be confusing.

How does a parent explain to a child who is struggling with communication and conceptual skills not to take candy from a stranger, but then allow them to march up to a strange doorway and ask for candy? If a child is on a special diet to treat autism, how do you explain to that child that all the other children get candy, but he doesn't? And how do you ever keep your own little goblin straight in a swarm of ghosts, bogeymen, and skeletons?

Unfortunately, there are no easy answers. Some parents only take their children trick-or-treating in a controlled environment, such as a shopping mall. Others go only to the homes of people they know.

Regardless of how you handle this holiday, be consistent year to year. Although it seems like a big gap between the dates, your child will learn rather quickly that Halloween is a dress-up day, and a routine will be established. Expect the Halloween costume to be worn for about a month, but for the fun they have that is a small price to pay.

Winter Holidays

Although many holidays change our daily routines, there are none quite like those from Thanksgiving to New Year's. The activities that the holidays bring can turn a child's world topsy-turvy. Most children adapt well to this, as they are just as caught up in the excitement as the adults. But for a child with autism, the change in routine is not only unwanted, it is upsetting and can cause behavioral issues.

Some of the events that arise during the holiday season are predictable—so predictable that most parents don't even think of them as being upsetting.

- Parents may go to parties, meaning a babysitter will be needed.
- A visit to Santa for photographs each year is a common activity.
- Friends and family may "pop in" for a visit unannounced.
- Carolers outside your front door are a total mystery to a child with autism.
- Shopping increases as families buy presents and the time in stores and shopping malls is greatly increased.
- Regularly watched television shows are often pre-empted for Christmas programs.
- Winter vacation may mean school is out of session for up to two weeks.
- There is a sudden influx of gifts, a decorated tree, and holiday baking.

All of these and many more holiday events individual to each family are enough to upset anyone's routine. But for the child with autism, this can cause total upheaval and overstimulation. Although the old saying "If you can't beat them, join them" is not good advice for moral choices, it is wonderful advice to a parent of a child with autism at Christmas. Involve the child in decorating the tree; it may be the most unique (and perhaps bizarre) tree you will ever see, but it is a delightful and memorable way to celebrate.

 **FACT**

As the holidays get into full swing, remember that children with autism have their own special talents and abilities to contribute, and even though their creations may not be traditional in nature, they are things of beauty, things to be treasured, and remembered for a lifetime.

When overstimulation becomes an issue, and it will if your family is busy during the holidays, the best advice a parent can follow is to "go with the flow." Use common sense—don't visit Santa during the busiest part of the weekend. Find a way to do your holiday shopping without having to take your child to the busy mall—buy all your gifts over the Internet or from catalogs.

Christmas is a holiday that all children figure out very quickly. Like Halloween, they will build a new routine, as they will understand that a Christmas tree means presents, and presents mean fun. Some adjustments will have to be made, but Christmas will be just as fun, or even more fun, than ever. Trust yourself and follow your instincts; if your child appears to be overstimulated or agitated, slow things down.

Special Occasions

One challenge every family faces is the normal interaction and activities of social events and occasions. The following is not a complete list, of course, as every family is unique and has its own special activities. But many of these events are common to most families and can be problematic for a child with autism.

- Weddings
- Bridal showers
- Baby showers
- Graduation ceremonies
- Family picnics
- Family reunions
- Camping trips
- Birthday parties
- Anniversary parties

These events can be stressful for the entire family when a child with autism is having behavioral issues. And as typical for stressful events, when the pressure is anticipated, the entire situation becomes even more stressful. Fun events become dreaded, and important gatherings are often missed.

 ESSENTIAL

If a family member has passed away, particularly one who was close to your child, alert your child's teacher and therapists. Behaviors may begin that will surprise everyone if they are not aware of the situation. Children with autism may not directly express their grief, but it is present.

If at all possible, continue attending family events. For both the immediate family and the farther-flung relatives, interacting with the child with autism at these events will help them feel involved and ultimately more comfortable with the situation.

A death in the family can present unique concerns. Because concepts are difficult to understand for people with autism, and death is a difficult concept for anyone to understand, your autistic child may be troubled by a funeral. Acting-out behaviors are common in these situations. Children with Asperger's or high-functioning autism may have a grasp on the situation, and in that case, parents should follow their instincts.

Having autism in the family may change your interactions with your extended family, but if you plan ahead and prepare, those changes can be positive for everyone involved.

CHAPTER 11

Dealing with Society

P ARENTS OF CHILDREN with autism become very used to the behaviors of their child. Society, however, is still not accustomed to this disorder. The number of children affected with ASD is increasing, but many people have not interacted directly with a child who is autistic. And the majority of children appear to be perfectly fine, as their appearance is no different than that of any other child. When an apparently "normal" child begins to exhibit bizarre or out-of-control behaviors, challenges, which are victories waiting to happen, can't be far away.

Shopping

One of the biggest challenges a family faces is the shopping trip. The weekly grocery shopping is hard enough, but a trip to a shopping mall is often considered more trouble than it is worth. Variety stores are also an environment that can be difficult for not only the parents but for the child with autism as well.

The Grocery Store

It is always an adventure to go grocery shopping with children and this is especially true with autistic children. Although Saturday morning cartoon advertising for 800 varieties of breakfast cereals does not sway

them, kids with ASD know what they like. And what they like, they want. And when they want it, they want it now!

The easiest way to avoid the grocery store trauma (and it is a trauma most of the time) is to avoid taking your child at all. Have your spouse watch him or get a babysitter during the time you need to shop. But there is a practical side to taking your child grocery shopping, even though it is harder for you. Shopping is a basic skill that needs to be learned. It often takes years for a child with autism to learn how to shop, and it is a skill that will help your child with independence in her adult years.

 ALERT!

If a child with autism wants something, he will simply put it in the cart. He may not even know what it is, but the colors or shapes could attract him. Keep an eye out while your groceries are being checked out so that you don't accidentally buy merchandise you don't want.

Involving your child in shopping is one way to prevent battles over what goes into the grocery cart. For example if you are going to buy a dozen apples, have your child select them and put them into a bag. As he is choosing the apples, guide him and show him if one has a bruise or isn't what you want, so he can learn. As he fills the cart, keep an eye on items such as bread that might get squished and help him arrange the cart. He may not seem to be listening, but he is, and he will learn each time he visits the store with you.

One useful trick a parent can use to keep a shopping trip under control, particularly if it is a young child sitting in the child seat in the cart, is to find a small, inexpensive toy for the child to play with while a parent shops. Handheld puzzles, travel toys, and action figures are good choices. Avoid noisy toys or those with many parts. And unless you want to be running all over the store, don't choose a ball. Children learn very quickly how to teach their parents to chase a ball.

The Variety Store

Shopping in variety stores—those huge one-stop shops—is a particular challenge for parents with children who are autistic. When everything you could want is under one roof, it takes little time for a child to realize that fact. Coupled with the sensory stimulation that a busy variety store supplies, it is a recipe for autistic meltdowns and frazzled parents.

If you are taking your child with autism into this type of store, keep in mind the sensory overload that is likely to occur. The lights are fluorescent, and it is not unusual for people with ASD to see the blinking and flashing that most people cannot perceive. There are also many bright and colorful items within the store, and this will come rushing into your child's visual processing center all at once. There is a great deal of noise from intercom systems, other children, and crowd chatter—these sounds are painful for autistic ears. Don't be surprised if your child covers his ears in an environment such as this. All of this sensory input occurs within seconds of entering the store, so before the shopping even begins, as a parent, you are already set up for a problem.

As with grocery shopping, if you can avoid taking your child into this kind of store, it is much easier. Although shopping for clothes and household items is an important skill to learn, it is also important to keep your household running smoothly. Once every few months is fine, but weekly can be a very stressful experience. You are not depriving your children by leaving them at home, so you don't need to feel guilty for calling in a babysitter.

The Shopping Mall

Shopping malls are a mixture of good news and bad news. The good news is that there is enough to keep a child entertained, and the bad news is that, like other kinds of shopping, overstimulation is very apt to happen. Going from store to store to store is enough to confuse anyone, but for a child with autism it can be far too much.

ESSENTIAL

If your child has a service dog, that dog is legally entitled to go anywhere. If you are denied access, speak with a manager. Be certain that the dog is trained well; he helps your child and you have become an ambassador for the benefits of a service animal.

Religious Services

Most parents think that attending church or other religious services will be the easiest environment to deal with and are quite surprised to find out it is one of the more difficult situations for the family of a child with autism. Church is intended to be a time of worship and quiet reflection. However, when a child on the spectrum attends church, it can be anything but quiet.

Regular Services

For many families, Sunday morning worship (or whatever day is set aside) is a part of life. Sunday school, worship service, and brunch are something that starts the week off properly and establishes the foundation of the spiritual life of the family. There is no reason this should change, but church does present some unique challenges.

If you go to a church that includes the entire family in its worship service, rather than one that has a children's church, go to church armed and ready to keep your child entertained and happy for the duration of the service. There can be a lot of sensory stimulation in a church service; as quiet as adults think it is, it is not a quiet environment on a sensory level. Organ music can be so loud that people can feel the vibration in their chest, which would be a very disconcerting feeling for a child with autism. Singing is also a tremendous amount of sensory input when trained and untrained voices join enthusiastically in a hymn. Add to that stained glass windows, candles, flowers, and possibly incense and just about every sense is being overloaded.

Few people consider the number of senses that are involved in a worship experience. It is a "whole-body" experience, and as such, it can be a lot for a child with autism to cope with. Bringing along a personal stereo with headphones to block out extraneous sounds and to give your child his own music to listen to can be a tremendous help. Providing coloring books and (washable) crayons is a way to keep visual stimulation to a minimum. If your child has a specific toy or stuffed animal that provides comfort when the world seems crazy to him, bring it along.

 FACT

If your church has children's church, carefully consider whether or not it is a good idea to leave your child with the other children for the worship service. Many children with autism can become aggressive with no advance warning and unless you have adults familiar with autism caring for your child, it can be very difficult for everyone.

Sunday School

Sunday school, like regular school, is geared toward children who read, write, and participate in discussions. For a child with autism, this is difficult due to the verbal and social deficits. If your child is not aware of what is going on in the class, and why, acting-out behaviors are almost certain to occur. This will not only disturb the classroom environment, but will make the teacher and other students uncomfortable as well. It isn't because they dislike your child; they just don't know how to respond or what they should do. It also is very difficult for the siblings of your child, as they will suddenly feel they are different because of their brother or sister.

School Functions

There are two types of school functions parents have to deal with when they have a child on the autism spectrum: those that involve the child and those that involve the child's siblings. Each presents difficulties and each has accomplishments. Either can make a parent wonder who ever invented after-school functions.

In the Spotlight

If your child is in special education, he may not be involved in many school functions such as concerts and plays. But if your child is in inclusive education, meaning he has classes with the rest of his nonautistic classmates, and some special-ed classes for specific needs, there will be more occasions for after-school functions. Many children with autism have an aptitude for music and do well in school band. If your child participates in band and is able to function as part of the greater whole, it will be tremendously rewarding for your child as well as for you. The steps of progress in autism are often slow and greatly delayed, but the victory felt as each new accomplishment is made is a feeling like no other.

In the Audience

Much more commonly, your child will attend his sibling's school functions with you. Concerts, plays, band recitals, and athletic events are only some of the events you will attend over the years. Sometimes your child with autism will enjoy them, and it will be a pleasurable experience for everyone. Other times, it will feel like *Nightmare on Elm Street,* and although it may still be worth it in the end, it can be very stressful at the time.

Following much of the advice for worship services will be helpful for school functions. There is a lot of noise whenever school-age children get together and sensory overload is more apt to happen than not. Centering your child's mind on his music and coloring, or on whatever he finds of interest, will provide a better experience for all concerned. If the activity is something that your child enjoys, you will find him watching with great interest, and so much the better. This may become an interest for him to pursue as well. "I would have never considered bowling for my son," a mother said. "It seemed boring for an autistic boy, but my daughter had an after-school bowling party, and we needed to go watch her team play. My son was intrigued! We tried it later in the week and he loved it!" Had they not attended the bowling party with their son, they may have never known of his interest.

 ESSENTIAL

Consider bringing a babysitter to school functions to be in charge of handling any situations that arise with your child with autism, in case she must be taken out of the audience quickly. This will allow you not to miss any of the performance of your other children.

If the situation is not a warm and fuzzy, positive experience, don't throw in the towel. Sit near the exit, and be prepared to make a quick dash in case the experience is less than interesting for your child. Never let your other children feel embarrassed by the actions of their sibling; it is hard enough to cope with school and child-hood without having to explain a brother or sister's actions.

Restaurants

Eating out in restaurants with a child who is autistic presents some of its own challenges. Parents of children with autism sometimes become so involved with autism that the disorder becomes another member of their family. The most important thing you can remember is that your child *has* autism; he *is not* autism. All of the activities you have enjoyed as a family, or dreamed of enjoying, can still happen; you will have to make modifications, but you haven't lost everything you love to do. You can still eat out at restaurants— you just have to be prepared (as with everything else).

Eating-Out Behaviors

It is important to teach your children appropriate eating habits; they need to eat well-rounded and balanced meals. They need to learn this at home; a restaurant is not the place to enforce rules about eating that are likely to be met with resistance. If a child with autism refuses to eat anything round—and this is a common obsession with autism—it is not a good time to try peas as a side dish. A child with an aversion to round things, when presented with meatballs, melon balls, and round slices of carrots is more likely than not to decide his dinner would make adequate apparel for his parents. And throwing a plate of food at a parent is a sure way to get a lot of the kind of attention you don't want.

 **FACT**

Spending time outside your home with your child is another chance to educate people about autism. A father laughed about an experience in a restaurant, when a waiter heard wrong and thought the child was artistic. They all saw the humor and it afforded the family a chance to teach about autism.

Just order what your child loves and what you know she will eat. Grilled cheese and fries are a sure hit with a child. Chocolate milk can also make many things better and is very useful for calming an unhappy child. Cheeseburgers are always a success, as is spaghetti or macaroni. Eat in ethnic restaurants as often as you like, but for your own sanity, be sure they have a basic children's menu. Sushi is not going to be on the list of favorites for your child, and experimenting with new food is best done at home.

Go Out for Dinner!

Keep in mind some basic strategies for dining out. Don't let autism keep you from the things and places you enjoy. You can easily adapt and have a great time with your family.

- Choose a booth whenever possible, and have your child take an inside seat to prevent him from bolting.
- Unless your child is a water drinker, request that no extra glasses of water be on the table to prevent spillage.

- Have plenty of napkins available in case something is spilled.
- Remove salt, pepper, and all other condiments from your child's reach.
- If your child is exceptionally hungry, his behavior may become irrational before the meal is served. Request a side dish of mashed potatoes and gravy, or some other favorite, to be served immediately to raise his blood sugar.
- Don't let dessert items be brought to the table until everyone, including your child, has finished their meal.
- Don't worry about food spilled on your child's clothes; in the scheme of things, it is a small thing.

Vacations

Most families vacation once every year or two. Because of the infrequency of a big family vacation, it is something anticipated. Unfortunately, it is often something not adequately planned in advance. However, there is one thing worse than a poorly organized vacation—not going on one at all. Many parents of children with autism think that autism precludes them from taking a week or two away from home, but that simply isn't true.

Vacations, although for relaxation and fun, can pose difficult issues. However, these issues can be confronted and the problems solved. Remember, you want to protect your child, not become so panicked that no one can enjoy his or her vacation. There are two things to remember as you work to maintain the routine of your child. The first is that you want to maintain this routine as closely as possible, and the second is that maintaining the routine is impossible. Although that sounds like a contradiction, it is mentioned to remind parents that it is not possible to accomplish everything.

The Importance of Routine

People with autism thrive on, and depend on, their routine. Schedules are seldom veered from, the order things are done in is consistent, and the way the day unfolds is predictable. Some children adapt well to a disruption in their routine; other children will not adapt at all, and behavioral problems can be the result.

As you plan your vacation, consider your child's routine each day. If possible, keep as much of that routine the same as you can. Getting up and having breakfast at normal times will start the day off on a better foot when the family is away from home. If your child is used to watching television in the morning, and you are in a motel or hotel with a TV, turn it on and find her favorite programs. If you are camping, find an activity that will distract your child from dwelling on her routine.

 **QUESTION?**

How can I keep some semblance of a normal routine on vacation?
One of the biggest things a parent can do to keep things flowing along smoothly is to keep meals consistent with what the child is used to. Eating is one big sensory experience and meals are pivotal parts of the day for a child with autism. If your child is used to having a grilled cheese sandwich or a hamburger and fries at lunch, your vacation is not a good time to introduce the possibility of fish and chips at noon.

Another tip all parents who have been on this road will pass along is to keep your child's sleep schedule the same. All people tend to burn the candle at both ends on vacation, packing as much fun and activity as possible into their time. Children who do not have autism can handle this temporary adjustment in their schedule, but autism does not lend itself well to this change. If your child is exhausted, difficult behaviors will be hard to control, and the entire family will feel the stress of the ordeal. If you are able to analyze the daily routine your child has come to expect, your vacation will be fun and restful, not only for your child but for the entire family as well.

Using a Vacation as a Sensory Therapy

Although a vacation is a time to "get away from it all," your child will still have autism. Incorporating different activities can provide a sensory therapy for your child that he might not have otherwise experienced. Don't burden yourself with the idea of therapy; consider it part of the fun that you will have with your child.

Textures, sounds, sights, colors, and music are just some of the examples. Going to the beach and playing with sand is sensory therapy and so is walking through a forest and feeling the different varieties of leaves. Museums provide opportunities to identify colors and shapes. Your entire vacation is one big sensory supply package and can be used to learn and experience with a lot of fun.

A Special Memory Scrapbook

One idea that will keep a child occupied and busy, as well as create a special memory, is the creation of a vacation scrapbook. Purchase a scrapbook with heavy pages and nontoxic glue. It is also helpful to have clear tape, double-sided tape, glitter, stickers, and colorful markers. On the cover put your child's name and a photograph of the vacation spot you are going to visit.

 ESSENTIAL

Take photographs of the family during the vacation, then put them into the book with everyone's names written next to the pictures. A child with autism is self-involved and photographs can show him interacting with others.

During your vacation, help your child collect leaves, flowers, brochures, wrappers, photos, and other items of interest. Pasting or taping them into the scrapbook is a tactile experience and will journal the vacation. If your child is nonverbal, he can point to the mementos to let you know what he is thinking about, and this can also be used to add to the use of sign language. Starting the scrapbook before you leave is also helpful for communication; having photographs of things a child would need to ask for can prevent frustration for everyone. If your child can point to a picture of a bathroom, an accident can be avoided, and he will have learned another way to manipulate his environment.

Bringing the Vacation Home

It is also fun on an outdoor vacation to bring along an empty coffee can to collect pebbles and rocks. Different rocks have different colors and feel quite different. It is a sensory exercise to feel the textures. This is also fun at the ocean, where a collection of shells can be gathered. No matter where you go, it is likely that something can be collected and used for a sensory exercise that is a lot of fun.

Collecting postcards is another way to integrate therapy into your child's life. The visual element will help him to remember the places the family visited on vacation. Punching a hole in the upper corner of each card and attaching them together with a ring or key chain makes these cards easy to view and talk about. This will allow you and your child to look at the cards and remember your vacation together.

CHAPTER 12

Starting School

T HE FIRST DAY OF SCHOOL is always exciting for both parents and children. For the parent of a child with autism, daily trips to school have been occurring for quite some time; they don't begin at kindergarten. In the United States, all fifty states are mandated to have early intervention programs and special education available to children. For children with autism, early intervention will most likely begin around the child's second birthday. Special education starts for children at the age of three.

What You Need to Know about the Law

The special education maze is complicated at times, and you may find yourself feeling like you're in an adversarial relationship with the school system. But never forget that *you* are your child's best advocate. Staying informed about political and legal issues that affect children with autism is critical to your child's successful school career.

IDEA

In the mid-1970s, a new law was enacted called the Education for All Handicapped Children Act of 1975. The federal government had finally recognized that inadequate education for children with disabilities was costing American society a great deal. In 1997, the law was given a major facelift and was renamed the Individuals with Disabilities Education Act. Revisions to the law are planned in 2003 that will overhaul various issues within IDEA.

Title I is a federal funding program for public schools above a certain population count. IDEA requires public schools receiving Title I funding to follow two standards: All students must have available to them a free appropriate public education (FAPE), and that education must be within the least restrictive environment (LRE). This education is to be provided from ages three to twenty-two, but may have variances by individual state laws.

The Legalese of Special Education

Although it may feel as though you need to be an attorney or political science expert at times to understand the technicalities of the government's involvement with special education, it isn't all that difficult. Laws will come and go, change and modify, and evolve to better (hopefully) serve our children. What is important is that the basic principles of special education laws are understood so that when changes do occur, you as parents will understand the effect they may have on your child.

In 2003 proposed changes to IDEA, the primary law regarding disabled students, went to congressional review. The changes that could affect students with autism center on behavioral issues related to the condition; often children with autism will have violent outbursts that make it difficult for them to get along in a group setting such as a classroom. If a child is prone to aggression, even if it is caused by his condition, he may or may not be able to continue in school depending on the outcome of the revisions to IDEA. Parents should be aware of any changes to IDEA due to its effects on the autism community.

There are many newsletters and Web sites that provide current and up-to-date information on issues in the government that can affect special education. It isn't so important that you understand and are aware of every little detail but that you know how to handle the laws should you have problems with your child's education. No one can be an expert on everything, but anyone can be an expert on finding any piece of information they may need. Avail yourself of all of the experts to stay current on congressional issues that affect the rights of disabled students.

Integration and Special Education

When a student is disabled, education includes much more than the three R's. Beyond academic learning, students in special education programs also learn much about managing the needs of their daily life. Daily skills, such as dressing appropriately, toileting, self-feeding, and other hygiene needs are also taught. The needs of a student in special education are the same in some ways as what nondisabled students need, and also very different at the same time. Thus a multifaceted program, coordinated by teachers, administrators, therapists, and parents, is planned out annually. This plan is known as the Individual Education Program (IEP), which is discussed in more detail in the next section.

Least Restrictive Environments, Mainstreaming, and Inclusion

IDEA establishes that students must have access to an education in the Least Restrictive Environment (LRE). In practice, what this means is that a student must be placed in the same classroom she would attend if she were not disabled. Supplementary services, such as aids, support systems, and communication equipment, should be used to achieve this goal. If a student's IEP clearly shows that the regular classroom is not suitable, after thoroughly researching the use of various supports, aids, and paraprofessionals, other arrangements can be made. *Inclusion, mainstreaming,* and *LRE* all refer to the same thing.

However, IDEA has recognized that the regular classroom is not suitable for all students. A "continuum of alternative placement" is to be in place to answer to the needs of each child. This includes special education classrooms, special schools, instruction in the home environment, and in group homes or institutions.

Achieving Free Appropriate Public Education (FAPE)

FAPE is something every child in the United States is entitled to and it is a phrase very few parents know. Every child is entitled to have the best education possible, to have it be easily accessible, and with no attached fees. This includes services such as special education and "related services" necessary to fulfill the IEP goals. This mandate applies to all Title I schools and encompasses academics, physical education, and speech therapy.

 FACT

> If a school claims a lack of personnel to provide related services, remind them of their obligation to provide FAPE. The law says that no child shall be denied services needed because of inconveniences to the school district. Your state department of education can assist you in resolving the problem.

Related services include hearing evaluations, speech therapy, psychological counseling, physical and occupational therapy, recreational therapy, vocational counseling, and health care counseling. This is not an all-inclusive list, as any service that is necessary for a child's success is included in this category. These are not luxuries; they are essential to acquiring the free and appropriate public education that every child is entitled to, by law, in the United States.

A free and appropriate public education means that every child with a disability is in essentially the same environment as he would be were he not disabled. Least restrictive environments are part of this education and related services are as well. FAPE and LRE (or inclusion, as it is commonly known) are the tangible manifestations of IDEA.

Individual Educational Program

Individual Educational Program (IEP) is a term that you will become quite familiar with. Think of it as the road map that runs from early intervention through graduation. This plan describes in detail all special education services that will be called upon to meet the needs of your child with autism. Each IEP is different, as each student is different. It outlines goals and expectations for your child and gives you an idea of what to expect for the school year.

The IEP is a fluid plan, meaning it changes from year to year and sometimes even within the same year as different accomplishments and problems occur. It can also be thought of as a sort of contract, as it commits the school to using resources to achieve the goals the team sets. A well-done IEP also serves to eliminate misunderstandings by all of the members of the educational team. Without an IEP, there is no special education; therefore, think of this document as the single most important part of your child's education.

 QUESTION?

Can a parent ask for a meeting to discuss the IEP at any time?
Yes. A parent has the right to call for an IEP meeting anytime he or she feels that there are needs to be addressed or revisions that should be made. Children change over a twelve-month period and the IEP may need to change as well.

Traditionally short-term goals have been a part of every IEP but the ever-evolving laws may change that at some time in the future. Long-term or annual goals in the IEP—the heart of the document— will be the baseline on which a child's education is planned. The goals that are to unfold over a twelve-month period must be reasonable, practical, and designed to strengthen a weak area that is of educational concern. It is important that these goals match well with the student's current level of performance; they should not reach too high or too low. Parents and teachers need to consider a child's abilities and how they can best enhance those for progress and maturity.

The IEP Team

The IEP team is made up of a group of people who work with you and your child to create the best education plan possible. Certain people are required to be involved. Other experts may be involved as well.

- **The student**—In reality, it is unlikely that your child will be included in an IEP meeting, so it is your job as the child's parent to address his desires and concerns if he has expressed them.
- **The special education teacher**—This individual will be the one to oversee the plan that is established in the meeting.
- **A school administrator**—This will be either a principal or special education director.
- **An adult service agency representative**—This is only required if transition services are being planned that would involve an outside agency. If it is physically impossible for someone to attend, a phone conference will suffice.
- **An interpreter**—This is a requirement if the parents are deaf or do not speak English.

Other teachers and therapists may be asked to join the meeting if appropriate. Parents may also request an advocate of their choosing if they wish. It is very helpful to have an advocate, particularly if you are new to the IEP process. Parents must be notified of an IEP meeting reasonably ahead of time and if the date cannot be arranged with their schedules, the IEP must be rescheduled. If a parent is unable to attend—for instance, because she is serving in the military—the school is to make alternative arrangements through phone conference or another satisfactory method that will include the parent.

ESSENTIAL

The IEP meeting can take place without the parent present. This is a last resort option. Parents need to be involved and the school district must go out of its way to include parents. If the parents are not in attendance, adequate documentation of efforts to include them must be recorded.

The IEP Process

The first time you meet for an IEP may be intimidating. A conference is usually called by the school, but can be called by anyone who feels a meeting is necessary. This includes parents, teachers, administrators, and anyone involved (even a member of the lunchroom staff isn't out of the question if a child has dietary issues). The entire process can be unsettling to a parent, as this large and structured of a meeting can emphasize the severity of their child's disorder. But remember that this team has been created to help your child acquire the best education possible, and you are a member of that team with equal ranking and qualification.

IDEA states that an IEP must be conducted within thirty days of when teachers and you determine that special education and other related services are necessary. IEP meetings take place at the school or a school district office and will include the entire IEP team. Paperwork will be signed by all parties to acknowledge the meeting date and time for permanent records and you will sign a form that acknowledges you have a copy of the special education laws and that you know the rights of you and your child.

The meeting itself involves covering all of the team's goals and expectations for your child. You and the team will go through various categories of his education, such as communication skills, and rate his current levels of performance. Goals will then be established to work on for the next twelve months. This process will continue for each category of your child's education.

ALERT!

Schools may say they are testing your child to determine her disability, but only a physician can diagnosis a medical problem. Their documentation can only support the diagnosis. If you do not have an official diagnosis and intervention at school is being delayed, consult with a pediatric neurologist who is familiar with ASD.

It is helpful for parents to have a list when they attend the IEP meeting. If you feel that the school should provide particular services, this is the place to discuss it. Even if the school district does not agree with what you want, if you feel strongly enough about it, it needs to be addressed. For example, a school that will not provide the instruction of sign language at the parent's request needs to have a very good reason for not doing so. Lack of personnel or schedule concerns are not good enough reasons.

The IEP meeting can be held at any time of the school year for convenience. As it comes time to reconvene to plan the next years' IEP, parents should think about the progress their child has made over the past twelve months. Step back and observe your child's behavior, speech, and social skills. Be as objective as possible. If you feel she is progressing at the rate expected, you know the IEP is working. If she isn't progressing, the IEP needs to be revisited with changes made to help your child.

Further Education

At the age of fourteen, your child with autism reaches a transition stage. The first half of transition is to determine what your child's goals will be. If your child is able to communicate his hopes for his future, his opinions should be part of the transition process. The second half addresses how the school will provide an education that will assist your child in meeting those goals.

Identifying Your Child's Interests

After puberty, children start expanding their horizons to include special interests. This can also be true for children with autism, as long as they have direction and supervision in their exploration of the possibilities. Direction is essential, as most people with autism suffer from a lack of hobbies and downtime. It's important that parents spark interests and talents in their child to discover what role the child will play in the future. Choosing a "default" future with little opportunity for fulfillment is not a desirable option.

How do you determine the interests and talents that may be hidden in your child? If you don't have a computer at home, get one and load it with drawing, reading, and math software as well as other software of interest to children her age. Avoid the video game model where a child seems to be in a trance with repetitive activity; autism has enough of that without adding more. But games and activities that will stretch your child's mind are valuable.

 **FACT**

When your child turns fourteen, transition services must be included in the IEP. Watch for two things: the student's goals for his adult life and how the educational plan of the next year relates to those goals. Outside agencies involved with transition must attend the IEP as well.

You may discover that your child has a talent in graphic arts, or that math is second nature to her. You may find she knows more about computers than you do! Many people with autism are finding their way into technology fields because of the home computer. This is an especially strong field for people with Asperger's syndrome.

Another option to find the abilities that are within your child is the time-honored tradition of "bringing your child to work" day. It doesn't have to be your place of employment; any activities you are involved in may be of interest to your child. He can garden with you, file movies and books away, help you paint a wall, or wash the car. Anything you do is something your child might be interested in, and it will give him more than just a window to watch the world through; it will also provide your child with a doorway to walk into the world.

The Traditional Educational Path

Some children with autism continue with traditional education throughout their school career. They may go on to college and become very successful at a chosen field. Being autistic does not preclude a college education and a career. Some people with autism have progressed to earn their doctorate and become a leader in their line of work.

There are two primary methods used to instruct children with autism: applied behavioral analysis (ABA) and Treatment and Education of Autistic and Related Communication Handicapped Children (TEACCH). There are supporters and detractors of each method; neither method is right or wrong, as what will work for one child may not be suitable for another child. Parents need to understand both methods and decide which is best for their child.

The TEACCH Method

TEACCH is the most commonly used method for the instruction of students with autism. Your school system may not use the term *TEACCH* for the structure they have in the classroom, but it is easily identified. It can be less intensive and therefore less stressful, especially for younger children.

 ESSENTIAL

Some critics of the TEACCH method feel that it does not emphasize socialization and verbalization skills enough. Additionally, no long-term studies have been done to determine the program's value.

The basis of TEACCH is visual learning and structure. The traits of autism are thus used to the instructor's advantage as well as to the student's benefit. Visualization is a powerful tool for people with autism and can be used in a child's learning. TEACCH uses schedules that are posted in various locations to help a child associate a picture with an activity; this helps with learning the usefulness of words as well as in creating a routine that can be relied on.

The ABA Method

ABA was developed from the principle of positive reinforcement techniques. Skills are taught to a child and when the skill is performed correctly, the child is rewarded, reinforcing the desired behavior, skill, or activity. Chapter 17 covers ABA therapy in more detail. Behaviors that are desirable for a child with autism to learn are taught at first, such as eye contact, imitative behavior, and language. When these skills have been mastered, they are used to build on, and skills that are more complex are then taught.

Parents' Expectations

If you can get through an entire school career without at least one major battle each year, you will have the respect and envy of every parent of a child with autism on the planet. Keeping your goals and expectations positive and realistic can minimize those battles, and if you have to engage in one, at least you know you can win. More importantly, your child can win.

There is a new PTA for you to join. Not the one at your child's school but the one that stands for:

Parent   Teacher   Advocate

You are now all three in one package. You know you are a parent, and you may have figured out that you are your child's first and best teacher as well. You are also your child's best, and sometimes only, advocate. Running interference is just part of being a parent and it may be the first line appearing in your job description: Parent of a child with autism.

CHAPTER 13

Child to Teenager

*P*UBERTY, TEENAGERS, ADOLESCENTS. These are all words a parent dreads, and it is no different for the parent of a child with autism. Many of the issues that arise during those years bring up questions and concerns that are difficult to solve. With the increase in autism, many affected children are now in their teens and people are beginning to collect information to make this time in a family's life easier. Teenage years can be fun and this is true for teens with autism as well.

Physical Changes of Puberty

Puberty! That word can put chills up and down the backs of even experienced parents of neuro-typical (NT) children. It is a time of changes, of testing the boundaries; it is a time of becoming mature, but acting immature; and it is a time of testing the world. For a child with autism it is all those things and more. Many changes happen to a child with autism when puberty arrives. Some are physical and others are emotional and mental.

Autism-Related Changes

If a child is prone to seizures, this time in his life will likely indicate the role seizures will play in his future. If he has not had seizures previously, he may begin them at puberty. If he already has them, they may increase

or possibly cease. If your child's conditions as related to seizures changes, consult with your physician. He or she may wish to make medication changes.

Another physical change can be related to bowel problems. A child who has had encopresis may suddenly be "cured." Bowel habits may become more regular and comfortable for your child. Be sure to discuss any concerns with your physician. If your child continues to have problems with bowel function, stool softeners can be most helpful.

 **FACT**

> The term *NT* or *neuro-typical* is used to refer to children who do not have autism. This avoids having to use the term *normal,* which is relative and which can suggest that being different is bad.

Dealing with Other Changes

Most new issues you'll face when your child hits puberty are the same ones that any parent of a child in adolescence faces, but they can be harder to deal with if your child has autism. Acne is often an indicator of the hormonal changes in puberty, and it is difficult to get children to care for their skin. It is important, however, that this be done, as a child with severe skin eruptions is only that much more isolated from his peers. Establish a routine that keeps your child's skin clean and free of oil and bacteria; cleansing pads are good for this purpose.

If you haven't seen the reality of "growing pains," you may become aware of them now. When a child grows very quickly, the bones grow faster than the muscles, tendons, and ligaments can keep up with. The result is a very lanky child who has extremely painful limbs and joints. If your child seems irritable or tends to absently rub his arms and legs, be suspicious that this may be the problem. Try to relieve the discomfort with the over-the-counter pain reliever your doctor recommends. Plenty of calcium is important at this stage in a child's life, so if your child does not drink milk, consider orange juice with added calcium.

Other physical changes are normal and natural but may confuse your child. Body hair begins to appear, boys' voices crack, girls develop breasts—your child wakes up in a new and unfamiliar body. If you find your child analyzing his or her body, ignore it. The novelty will go away and if you draw attention to it, you will inadvertently reinforce the behavior.

Emotional Changes of Puberty

Even more dramatic than the physical changes are the emotional and mental changes that a child experiences as he abandons childhood for adolescence. It is important for parents to fill in the gaps for their child to prevent further social isolation. Autism is isolating enough without puberty complicating the situation.

It is the job of the parents to be certain the things we assume our teenagers will do for themselves are still done. It is true that a child with autism may not be interested in the latest fashions at her school, but Mom and Dad need to be certain that their child is following sensible guidelines when choosing clothing. Your child may not care about the latest haircut or even whether she has taken a shower, but you need to care for her. A teenager's world turns on social acceptance and since children with autism struggle with social interaction, they need all of the help they can get.

Other emotional changes can include fragile emotions, willfulness, belligerence—your child may experience all of the emotions that any adolescent has when he enters puberty. If your child is inclined toward aggression or anger outbursts, do not be surprised if the nature of those outbursts changes. Some children have fewer outbursts while other children have more than they did before puberty. It is common for a child to have fewer but more intense outbursts.

Sexuality

It is difficult for parents when any child grows from the relative innocence of childhood to adulthood; sexuality is a topic that requires education, explanation, and understanding. It can be bewildering and even frightening for a child. But when the child has autism, the problem is magnified. How does a person with autism express her sexuality when her social skills are challenged?

Mom and Dad, You Need to Talk

This is the most important thing you can do for your child. Both parents need to sit down together and talk about how they feel about puberty, adolescence, sexuality, and the role of sexuality for your children. It is important that you agree on issues of such importance. Individuals with autism will have problems with sexuality that are as unique and diverse as they are with the only common thread being all people on the autism spectrum have social issues that affect their behavior. How those behaviors are expressed is a snowflake; you will never see two alike.

 ESSENTIAL

Many adults are uncomfortable about dealing with the sexuality of their children. Parents need to put those feelings aside so that they can have a dialogue about this topic. If the conversation is delayed, you may find yourself facing an even more uncomfortable conversation after a bad situation arises that could have been prevented.

Experiencing sexuality may not be appropriate for a child who has autism. Coming to terms with the fact that a child might not marry or have children someday is another loss for a parent struggling with the diagnosis of autism. When parents realize this part of their child's life may be diminished or nonexistent, it becomes another loss—another item on the list of things their child will not experience.

Some people with autism do not have a sexual drive at all, and if that is the case, there is no reason to try to change this. Some medications can cause a loss of libido; other times the cause is unknown. Given the problems a person with autism encounters with sexuality, a lack of sexual drive can be a blessing in disguise.

Understanding Sexuality

A person who is autistic and has a functioning libido will have difficulties expressing his or her sexuality in an appropriate manner. Matters of disease prevention, sexual abuse, birth control, and behavior management are difficult to explain to a young person, or an adult, who struggles with understanding concepts. As with the other things in your child's life that you have had to take control of, if his autism is severe enough to limit his judgment, you must take control of his sexuality as well. If it is any consolation, it will be harder on you as a parent than it will be on your child. No one wants to deny their child a life full of love and experiences, but sometimes it is the only choice available.

"Informed consent" between two adults is the generally accepted measure of whether a sexual activity is appropriate. Understanding what informed consent is will help you as a parent to assist your child as he grows up. Informed consent cannot happen unless an individual has several qualities:

- A person must be able to communicate to another person the word or the meaning of the word *no*.
- If a person is given different choices, she must demonstrate her ability to make a choice based on the information she has.
- A person must understand that there are appropriate places and times for sexual behavior.
- A person must be able to understand and detect danger and threats in order to react properly.
- A person must understand the word *no* and be able to cease an activity if told to do so.

There are many more factors involved in determining a person's ability to make an informed choice, but if these are not skills a child has, he is not capable of making sexual decisions for himself. And even if a child communicates well and clearly, social interactions may still be beyond his grasp. Saying "no" does a person little good if they don't know when to say it.

 FACT

> It is wise when parents are working with the school on an IEP to include these issues. It is important that the school's personnel know you are aware of the potential problem with your child's sexuality. It is also helpful for the teachers and aides to work on helping your child to understand when saying "no" is appropriate.

Unwanted Sexual Advances

Primarily parents need to consider the risk factors as they make decisions. HIV/AIDS is a risk for any kind of unprotected sexual contact that involves body fluids. Children with autism are also easy targets for sexual abuse, as they do not always understand dangerous, threatening, or inappropriate situations. Parents should not let themselves be ruled by fear, but they need to become proactive in the protection of their children.

Children and adults with autism have every right to have friendships and relationships. If parents are in charge of their child's sexuality, their goal should be to help the child understand her sexuality as much as possible to prevent their child from becoming a victim of unwanted sexual activity.

When a child has a sexual experience against his will, or without his understanding, it is very hard on the entire family. Preventing sexual activity through behavior modification is the ideal role for families to take *before* a problem occurs.

Menstruation

Since 75 percent of children with autism are boys, there is not a lot of information available for dealing with menstruation in girls with autism. Considering what a monumental step this is for any girl, it can be frightening for a girl who has communication deficits. It may be natural, but it is still blood, and it is alarming. It is reassuring to know that few girls with autism are unable to learn how to deal with their periods, and although the transition can be difficult, it can be done.

Indications of Menarche

The best way to deal with a girl beginning her menstrual cycle is to be prepared for it ahead of time. Watching for the signs that show parents a young girl is entering into menarche will allow you to prepare and teach your daughter. You will be able to observe discreetly, and when you know that it is imminent, you can begin preparing your daughter for this new stage of her life.

When girls enter puberty, their behavior may be the first indication. In NT children, this is obvious. Parents, particularly dads, will notice the irritability in their daughter; things that were once loved by her are now a source of embarrassment. It takes little to provoke a bad mood in a prepubescent girl and anger outbursts are common as well. But how do you recognize the arrival of puberty when irritability and outbursts are part of the daily routine?

 ESSENTIAL

Children with autism are notoriously immodest. If you permitted your children to run around without clothing when they were young, puberty is time to teach them modesty. Children with autism do not understand that different environments require different clothing, and you don't want your teen stripping in the grocery store.

It is important for parents to be attuned with their daughter's behavior. Routines can now be your best friend; even though you may feel a slave to them, use them to be aware of what is going on with your daughter. If things are upsetting her that didn't six or twelve months ago, and you see a hair-trigger temper, that is a warning sign for you.

Breast development is usually the first physical sign that puberty has arrived. Her figure will start changing; she will develop hips and a waistline. She may develop quickly or slowly, as each girl is individual in her growth. These are changes she may or may not acknowledge; it entirely depends on how aware of her own body she is. At this point, it is time to start preparing her for the start of her menstrual cycle. The rule of thumb is that within one year of the development of breasts, her period will begin.

Preparing Your Daughter

Visualization is your primary tool in teaching about menstruation. Begin a role-playing project that will mimic what happens during your daughter's period. Buy an easy-to-read calendar and put it in the bathroom. Purchase supplies and select several different brands for your daughter to see. She may have a sensory reaction to one product and prefer another one based on criteria that do not apply to you. The color of the package, the shape of the pad, or an odor associated with the packaging will be some of her determining variables.

 FACT

One beautiful aspect of the menstrual cycle is that it can be charted. People with autism will generally use a calendar, loving the structure of the routine, and if a girl's cycle is regular, the groundwork has been laid for a smooth transition.

Begin by showing your daughter the calendar and the pads. Talk to her as though she understands each word you say even if she is totally nonverbal. Take a red pen, circle the date on the calendar, and then place some red food coloring on the pad. The goal is to imitate in a nonthreatening way what she will see when her periods begin. Handle the situation in a matter-of-fact manner. Dispose of the "used" pad, replace it in her clothing, and repeat this every two to three hours. Continue this practice for about five days. Twenty-eight days later, repeat the process.

Theory into Practice

When you begin teaching your daughter how to handle the hygiene issues of having a period, it is important that a woman be part of the instructional process. If you are a single dad, you need to find some help. *A girl should never believe that it is appropriate and acceptable for any male, of any age or relationship to her, be in any kind of intimate contact with her.* That is a rule that can never be broken. Single fathers can rely on their own mother, sister, a school nurse, or another trusted female. It is impossible to teach a girl what is appropriate for her own body if that rule is not adhered to closely.

 ESSENTIAL

If the menstrual cycle is extremely difficult and hygiene is a constant battle, discuss your options with your daughter's doctor. Some physicians put girls with autism on medication to suppress their periods. This may be an option if medically appropriate.

When the big day arrives, and remember, you will have no warning of the actual date, fall back on your planning techniques. Keep in stride as you circle the day on the calendar and attend to hygiene. Remember to teach her proper disposal of the pads and be sure you keep a supply of her preferred brand.

There are no guarantees this will be the magic bullet and that your daughter's periods will begin and continue uneventfully. There are likely to be trying times for the entire family. Hygiene may be a continual problem or it may go smoothly, without any problems at all. Every child is different and there is no way to know how she will feel about any of this. If you can convey calmness and avoid a production over the situation, the chances are greater she will take it in stride.

Birth Control

It is easier for parents to make decisions regarding their child's sexuality if they proceed with a philosophy of discretion being the better part of valor. Sexuality is always a matter of informed consent between two adults. Factoring in the mental age of your child and his or her social abilities is essential. Unfortunately, no policy can exclude the possibility of sexual conduct that is unplanned, and for girls on the autism spectrum, this is a problem.

Most states do not allow permanent methods of birth control to be used on a child, even if he or she is over the age of majority. There are no exceptions to those laws for children with disabilities. If your child is impaired enough that having children is out of the question, check with the laws in your state to find out what can and cannot be done.

So how do parents prevent an unplanned pregnancy that is the result of their child engaging in sexual contact without understanding the implications of the activity? Many physicians will prescribe a birth control method for girls with autism or other spectrum disorders that can be taken daily in a pill form, injected every few weeks (frequency depending on the patient), or implanted. The advantage to the injections or implants is that the concern is removed without the daily use of a pill. The disadvantage can be the possible side effects of these methods of birth control, including weight gain, headaches, and problems that may be associated with long-term use of these medications.

It may be unfair that parents of boys with autism do not have as much to be concerned about in this area, but the reality is that girls are at a much higher risk for the consequences of sexual activity. It is not important, at this point, to make a point regarding the responsibility of sexual behavior; the important issue is to protect your daughter.

Inappropriate Behaviors

Although there are many behaviors that can be considered inappropriate, none upset people quite like those behaviors that are sexual in nature. Because of inappropriate behaviors, the deficit in social skills is even more evident and isolating for the person with autism. Children become aware at very young ages that it is inappropriate to touch other people in certain places; a child with autism does not have that built in control and if curious may reach out to touch a body part of someone out of curiosity. This is particularly common in adolescent boys attempting to touch a woman's breast. Dealing with these behaviors when a child is young is important so that they are not a problem when a child becomes an adult.

Self-Stimulating Behaviors

This is a difficult subject for parents. When they discover their child with autism actively masturbating with not the least hint of discretion, they wonder how to handle the situation. To keep a proper perspective on this activity, remember that all children masturbate. NT children just aren't caught doing it. Children with autism have no inhibitions, because they are unaware of the social taboo against masturbating in public.

 ALERT!

If your child engages in this behavior excessively, genital irritation can result. A quick (and very discreet) check when your child showers will let you know if this is a problem. Some medications used for autism, notably SSRIs, will also slow down the libido and may be appropriate if this behavior is out of control; your physician can best advise you on this.

The mistake that parents will often make—and it is an easy one to make—is when they find their child masturbating in a public area. Their goal is to stop the behavior immediately, and they will usually shout or sharply pull their child's hand away. That does stop the behavior, but it also sends a message that sexuality and the human body are bad or dirty.

Your goal should not be to stop the behavior, but rather to redirect it to an appropriate time and location. Masturbating in the middle of the living room is not appropriate, and redirecting your child to his or her bedroom (with a closed door) will solve most of those public displays. Keep in mind that people with autism are dictated by the structure of their routine. If they are taught that their bedroom is the only acceptable location for self-stimulating behavior, they will adhere to that routine.

Inappropriate Touching of Others

The majority of paraprofessionals that work with students with autism are female. Females are also still in a majority as caregivers, whether it be at home, day care, or in other environments that care for children. A young boy with autism who has raging hormones in his system may not understand that touching others in a sexual manner is not acceptable. Do not be surprised if you find out that your son has tried this. You may get a note from school that says, "Your son copped a feel today," which is a quote from an actual school note received by one parent.

This behavior is not malicious or intended to degrade. Your child has no idea that it is unacceptable to touch another person inappropriately. The behavior must be stopped. It may be somewhat humorous when a ten-year-old child does it, but if it's allowed to continue, it will not be nearly so funny when he is a thirty-year-old man.

Generally, the situation will resolve itself. A girl is less inclined to engage in this behavior. And when a boy crosses the line, a woman's natural reaction when touched inappropriately will generally solve the problem; most males do not enjoy a slap across the face. The most important thing that parents and school personnel can do is teach your child that this is not allowed in any circumstances so that the behavior is not a problem when the child is too big to redirect him. It is much easier to modify behaviors in a child than it is to change those same behaviors in an adult.

Teaching your children about inappropriate sexual behavior is difficult because obviously you are not going to demonstrate. There are books for very young children that have drawings geared toward children who might not understand the language, which might be helpful. The goal is to help your child with autism learn to control his sexual behavior in a way that will keep him safe.

CHAPTER 14

Life as an ASD Adult

W HEN PEOPLE BEGIN having children, they have expectations and goals for their life and their children's lives. One of those goals is watching a child grow to independence. Parents are truly satisfied when they know their adult child is equipped to face and handle the world. But having a child with autism causes parents to have to re-evaluate that goal and determine what the future will be for their child as he or she becomes an adult.

Living Independently

In a perfect world, children with autism would mature and acquire enough skills to live on their own. They would understand the things that are needed to live safely on their own: balancing checkbooks, turning off stoves, locking doors, and handling all the daily activities that most people never give a second thought to.

Activities of Daily Living (ADL)

Before the bigger issues of independent living can be addressed, parents and caretakers must be sure that a young adult with autism can be responsible for his own personal care and hygiene. A young adult must be able to:

- Bathe or shower daily.
- Independently use the bathroom.
- Use deodorant, skin care products, and other toiletries appropriately.
- Brush and floss her teeth.
- Brush his hair.
- Dress properly for weather conditions.
- Dress appropriately for work, leisure, and sleep.
- Determine which clothes need to be laundered.
- Take medications at the proper times in the proper dosages.

Most children with autism do learn all of these things and develop a routine that is seldom veered from. If you have a child who is six years old and he has not mastered all of these skills, don't worry. He may be behind but the odds are very good that he will catch up and have his own system to care for himself. Parents sometimes forget that children who are not autistic resist brushing their teeth and washing their hands, so it isn't always autism that is the culprit. Sometimes it is just being a kid.

Building the Daily Care Habits

As parents work with a child to build the habits and skills she will need as an adult, they learn that the trait of living by a routine can work in their favor. If your child heavily relies on a routine to make sense of her world, use that to teach her the skills she needs.

Making Lists

Before you begin building a routine to teach activities of daily living (ADLs), sit down with a piece of paper and pencil and outline all of the skills that are necessary for your child. All people have some common activities, such as bathing and using the bathroom, but there are many individual ones as well. Some children need to use certain skin care products to treat acne or eczema as well.

Make a list and divide it into three parts: morning, afternoon, and evening. In your three-part schedule, list out the activities that occur, or should occur, during those times. For instance, the morning list might include using the bathroom, brushing teeth, showering, medications, and so forth. Do this for all three sections, listing out all the activities you can think of. Keep the list handy for a few days and add in the things you overlooked so the list will be as complete as possible.

Creating a Communication Board

Now you can start teaching your child to make this list second nature. If your child is nonverbal, make a communication panel and put it in the bathroom where he will be able to reference it easily; above a sink is a good location for something of this nature. Attaching small drawings that represent the activity are good or you can use photographs (keeping in mind your child's privacy). Attach them with Velcro so you can adjust the order in which things are done if necessary.

The next step is simple. Start the routine each morning with your child. Explain to her as you go through it what she is to do and point to the picture on the communication board. If she is verbal, a cheat-sheet on the wall that she can read is another option. After three to four weeks, a new routine will have developed. Keep an eye on it until you are confident that she has mastered the skills. That is one less thing for you to worry about as your child learns to get herself ready each morning!

 **FACT**

An instant camera can make quick work of creating visual cues that help your child understand his life and routine. Take photos of him brushing his teeth, the bathtub, his clothes, and other items he uses. This will make your communication panel unique and specific to his needs.

Repeat this entire procedure for the afternoon and evening care. The most important part is following the schedule closely. Be certain your child follows it as well. As mentioned before, people with autism are ruled by their routine, and this self-care routine will be something that will help your child achieve independence.

Residential Living

Many parents have their children live at home after they reach adulthood. However, this is not always the best choice for an adult child or for the parents. There are other available options and there are no blanket answers as to what the best solution is for a given child. It isn't just the child's abilities that determine what is best for the family. It is also the family's needs, lifestyle, available emotional and physical resources, and finances.

Remaining at Home

This is one of the biggest topics discussed in support groups across the country. Someone will usually, and tentatively, ask the question, "What do I do when my child is grown?" The most important consideration in deciding where your child will live as an adult should be whether or not the environment is productive and interesting. Whether your child lives at home with you, lives in a group home, or needs to be institutionalized, the life she leads must be actively in touch with the world around her. As a child turns into a young adult, and then from a young adult into a mature adult, his happiness and satisfaction will hinge on his environment.

One of the most distinctive aspects of autism makes it impera-tive that an adult with autism has an environment full of variety and interest. It is too easy for many people with autism to retreat into their own world and if that is allowed to continue, they can retreat further and further from those around them. Couple that with the lack of conceptual understanding, and it is easy to see how someone with autism becomes a couch potato, staring at a televi-sion for hours on end.

If you wish to keep your adult child at home with you, be sure you have the physical and mental capacity to keep him busy. He will need to participate in various activities, have a schedule that keeps him interested (and whatever you do, stick to the schedule as much as possible), and he will need to be physically active. You will need to either keep up with that schedule yourself or have someone in the home that can. You will also need to plan ahead to make arrangements for someone to care for your child when age and health make it impossible for you to do so.

Group Homes

Group homes and assisted living are the options most parents choose for their children on the autism spectrum. Group homes are generally staffed with four to six residents. Two staff members are on the schedule at all times except during sleeping hours, when one is sufficient, and other personnel for special therapies come in and out. These homes are usually single-family residences in neighborhoods around the country.

Group homes are very popular for several reasons:

- People with autism see people without disabilities and thus have role models outside their immediate family members.
- People in the community are exposed to autism and learn they are people like anyone else.
- Group homes with several people give everyone a chance to continue a degree of socialization.
- Therapies and education are provided to the residents in group homes and life skills are taught by staff members or other qualified people.
- Activities are planned regularly such as swimming, bowling, and field trips that everyone enjoys.
- Group homes may be permanent but they can also teach a young adult with autism the skills necessary to live independently or return home to live with parents and other family members.

Assisted living is for people with high-functioning autism who need less supervision than those in a group home. Two people may share living arrangements and have a social services worker visit daily to be sure that their needs are being met. Each of these situations would vary depending on the people involved and their abilities.

Institutionalized Living

When you think of institutions, you may think of the horror stories that you've heard rumors about or seen in films. It is true that institutions in the past were the last stop for people with mental disabilities. It is also true that abuse and neglect were common problems for the people unfortunate enough to find themselves placed in an institution. Much of the problem came from a lack of understanding of the various disabilities and illnesses that affected people. The social isolation of an institution only added to the situation, as no one in a community really knew what was going on behind the closed doors.

 ESSENTIAL

The important thing to know is that no parent, whether she chooses an institution, group or assisted-living, or keeps her adult child at home, is wrong in her decision. This is a very individual choice. Don't let pressure from family, friends, or society make you feel bad for your decision. Many factors enter into the living situation of an adult child. You might seek the professional assistance of a counselor as various issues are considered.

Institutions in the modern era differ vastly from the creaky, ancient fortresses that were once common. They can be modern and have a homelike setting. They can be clean without looking like a hospital and be geared toward meeting the needs of the residents. Professionals who enjoy working with the mentally challenged population staff them. It *is* possible and those facilities *do* exist.

An institution is something that may be appropriate for a person with autism if he has behavioral disorders that can be a source of danger to himself or others. Group homes or assisted-living facilities do not have the close supervision that may be necessary for such a patient. Patients who have other physical complications requiring a great deal of therapy and/or medications may also be best suited for an institution.

Providing After You Are Gone

If you do not have a will, put down this book and call an attorney to have one drawn up immediately. After you have an appointment, begin reading again and make some notes about what pertains to you and your family. The worst thing that could possibly happen is for something to happen to you or your spouse when you have no provisions made for your child. Everyone asks what the worst-case scenario is when you have a child with autism—the death of parents who have not prepared for their child is the worst-case scenario.

Asset Protection

When a young couple marries and begins to build a life, they make plans for the future. Seldom do they think that the decisions they make in their twenties may affect their baby when he is a senior citizen. But it is important for parents of a child with autism to protect all of their assets to provide for their child when he is an adult.

In our highly mobile society, the average family moves at least every seven years. Many families move more often. Most of these families own a home and as the years go by; they sell, buy, and upgrade a little each time. They start with a small home, move to a moderately sized one, and have the goal of a certain kind of house that will be their last home purchase. As a result, there is no "family home" and no mortgage ever gets paid in full.

ALERT!

Although many states have made it legal for a person to write his or her own will, it is not advisable for the parent of a child with a disability to do so. If a parent has made his or her own will, it is more vulnerable to being successfully contested. Get the assistance of a licensed attorney.

If you have not yet bought a home, it would be wise to start working toward that goal. If you can stay in that house, perhaps improving or remodeling it, your house value will increase, your mortgage payments will be stable, and it will be paid in full in fifteen to thirty years. That is the most valuable asset your child could ever have. Although he would need someone to handle his finances, that house you are considering buying now, or may already own, will provide him with security for his entire life.

Cars, jewelry, paintings, stocks and bonds, and just about every other asset you have can go down in value. A house, on land that you own, is valuable security not only for you and your family now, but also in the distant future for your child with autism.

Trust Funds

A trust fund is often set up by a parent to provide for a child's needs. Because a child with autism is not likely to understand money management when she is an adult, preparations to protect her future are important. Although a will does declare where you wish your assets to go, a trust fund has funds and assets that can be distributed over a person's lifetime. As with guardianship, it is important to select a trusted friend or organization to oversee the trust fund. It is possible to select more than one trustee if you wish to have the responsibility shared.

Every state has different laws governing how trusts are set up and maintained, and it is important that you are aware of your state's regulations. Most states have two types of trust funds, one of which is of particular interest to the parents of a child who is disabled. An after-death trust is set up to protect the financial needs of a child when both parents are deceased. An estate attorney can best advise you concerning your specific needs, concerns, and state laws.

ESSENTIAL

When you appoint in your will someone to care for your child's finances, be absolutely certain of your confidence and trust in this person. It might be wise to consider a professional accountant, who is subject to audits, to protect your child's interests.

The trustee, or person(s) you appoint to oversee the trust, must be someone you trust implicitly. Trustees are held to a high accountability, both legally and morally, and although they may be paid a small fee for their services, the judgment they provide is beyond value. If you chose a family member or friend, be certain they understand financial management. If they can be trusted to fulfill your wishes and your child's needs, but lack some knowledge in the finer points of money, don't hesitate to also appoint an accountant or other professional to advise your primary trustee.

Guardians

If something happens to you or your spouse, do you know who will take care of your children—especially your child with autism? Most people feel confident that a family member would step in, but when a crisis such as this happens, it doesn't always work out that smoothly. It may be impossible for grandparents, due to age or health, to assume the responsibility for your child. It may also be more than another family member can handle if he or she is raising a family already. Do not assume anything.

A Serious Discussion

In choosing potential guardians, make a list of the people you feel would be the best to raise your child in the event you are unable to. Then talk to those people. Talk to them in a setting where you have their total attention and it isn't an "off the cuff" conversation. This is a serious decision for all parties concerned. Outline what your child's needs are now and what those needs are apt to be in the future. Explain what financial resources would be available, what health issues your child has, and what you would want done in his adult years.

As you compile this list of people, think about your child, his life, and the lives of the people you are considering asking. If it is a family member, perhaps your own brother or sister, does he or she have a career that might make this responsibility difficult? A career military officer may be stationed all over the world or called to active service with little advance notice, and he or she would then have the same problem of deciding who would step in. Also, consider the person's lifestyle and how he feels about his family life. One person who has eight children might easily handle another one, even one with autism, but another person with a large family might panic at the idea of another child.

 **FACT**

You may hope that your other children would step in to care for your child with autism if the need arose. But the older siblings of a child with autism may or may not feel up to this. Making a will with a sibling as the first choice and having four or five alternatives leaves everyone's options open.

When you approach people about assuming care of your child, they may have several reactions. One possibility is that they would want, or insist, on caring for your child. Another reaction is that they need to think it through and consider different options, and yet another reaction may be that they know this would not be the right decision for them or their family. There is no right or wrong answer in this. Your big sister who always bailed you out of a problem may have family issues you are unaware of that make this responsibility impossible. Your parents may have health concerns of their own that would prevent them from taking on this responsibility, even though they may wish they could step in.

A Controversial Choice

Sometimes parents make decisions about guardianship that are not understood by family members, and conflict can arise. It would be so easy to say that the only way to avoid a problem is not to tell anyone, reasoning that a conflict probably won't arise, but if one does, you won't have to hear about it anyway. Consider, though, the people you have chosen. If your family members do not know in advance what your wishes are, and yet you have made those choices official in your will, bad feelings could result at the best, and a custody battle could ensue at the worst.

Many parents do not choose a family member to assume the custody of their child in the event it is needed. Sometimes another family that has a child with autism is the best choice; they know exactly what they are getting into. Other couples are not close to family and it would not make sense to ask their families to raise their children. And it is common for people not to want their children raised as they were; this is particularly common with dysfunctional families. Whatever your reason, should you choose a nonrelative to care for your child in the event of your absence, do not feel guilty or pressured to change your arrangements. You and your spouse, or if you are single, you alone, know what is best.

 ESSENTIAL

Expect that you will have to revise your choice of a guardian every few years. Your child's needs will change and you will learn more about what his or her specific needs are. Other people's lives change as well. Plan ahead and be flexible to change when it is necessary.

When you have a list of people who would be willing to step in, have your will state those people by name as your choice to raise your children. It is wise to have several names in case something prevents one of them from stepping in. If you have more than one name on the list in your will, you can avoid having to rewrite your will every six months, and it will save attorney's fees. It will also give you peace of mind to know that you have done all you can to protect your child and his interests.

Financial Protection

Every family attempts to protect itself financially, but when there is a child with autism involved, this protection becomes much more critical. Mom and Dad find they are making decisions that affect the "here and now," as well as the distant future.

Insurance

When you are young, you think you will live forever. Everyone realizes his or her own mortality at a different age, but it doesn't usually happen when a person is in her twenties. However, that is the time when life insurance is incredibly inexpensive and easy to acquire.

A staggering number of parents find themselves widowed with small children, and out of those, a large number of them have no life insurance to fall back on. Imagine a woman who has lost her husband very unexpectedly who has been staying at home with the kids and has no financial resources available. It is as scary as it sounds. Social Security will pick up the burden for a time for the children, and she may qualify for Supplemental Security Insurance or another form of state aid, but these are not long-term solutions.

One of the smartest investments a couple can make when they have children, especially if a child is disabled, is to purchase life insurance—a lot of life insurance. As much as you can afford to buy. When you are young and healthy, the rates are much lower than if you wait until your late thirties or forties to purchase a policy.

IRAs and Other Funds

Parents can, through their employment, set up various financial plans that will protect and increase their money over the years. IRAs and other retirement plans can protect a family in many different ways. Tax benefits can be seen immediately, and funds will be available to provide for family members upon retirement or in the case of an unexpected death. IRAs supersede the will, so be certain you keep your beneficiary updated.

Every state differs in regulations regarding financial matters. Financial planning is a complex subject with many pitfalls for the uninformed. If you are planning to set up a portfolio for your family's security, consult with an accountant and estate-planning attorney for the best course of action. You will be preparing not just for your lifetime, but for your child's lifetime as well.

CHAPTER 15

Assistive Techniques and Technologies

ANY DEVICE OR ITEM that can help a person with autism compensate for his or her deficits is considered assistive. There are many forms of assistive devices—some are based on sophisticated technology and others are very basic and can be made at home. Others are not devices at all but are living, breathing animals that are "on the job" when their services are needed. Anything you use or adapt that helps your child function to the best of his or her ability is an assistive device.

A Mind Like a Computer

The 1990s saw more changes in the world than just the dramatic increase in autism. It also was the time of technological breakthroughs; once previously inaccessible, computers moved from the scientific world into the average American home. Home computers became as common as microwave ovens. And a computer is a tool for a child with autism to increase understanding, reduce undesirable behaviors, and learn independence to exist in an adult world.

Children with autism seem to have a natural flair for computers. It takes little time for them to understand how the computer operates. Their abilities on the computer are amazing; a child may be nonverbal and restricted by his own repetitive activities, but put that child in front of a computer and you are the one limited, not him.

Children with autism have the ability to understand computers better than they understand other human beings. Understanding how an autistic person's mind works, and how computers work, helps people without autism understand why this is and what it could mean for a child.

 **FACT**

If your child engages in self-stimulating and obsessive repetitive behaviors, consider getting him his own computer. This does not have to be a top-of-the-line model. A basic computer on which you can install programs and run CD-ROMs is enough. The unacceptable behaviors will likely be reduced, and he will be learning simultaneously.

Visual "Thinking"

Visualization is a very helpful tool for people with autism. The autistic mind processes things visually, so it is the strongest learning center an autistic person has. Think of the mind and its functions as being similar to a series of snapshots. Each photograph represents a memory or an understanding of something specific. The brain of a person with autism stores memories and knowledge in that format. One snapshot or picture of something tells them what they need to know.

It is a nonlinear style of thinking. Visual thinking is associative, and the memories and knowledge of a person with ASD are not filed in the brain the same way that they are in a person without autism.

Computers also "think" in that manner. Each file or "memory" can be brought up on the screen, intact and self-contained. If you can access that file, you can access everything you need to know about that memory. And carrying this a step further, associative links, tying together different parts of the computer, create the complete memory. Therefore, seemingly unrelated memories are linked together to make a whole picture. The computer sees the link and understands why, even if the typical person does not.

You can turn off the sound on a computer and it will still work. You may not understand why it works the way it does at times, but it is unrelenting in its way of doing things, and you have to modify your behavior; the computer will never change. A person with autism thinks in a similar manner, and what seems like techno-babble is in fact a logically ordered visual system used by both the autistic mind and the computer. Computers and people with autism think alike.

Daily Life with the Computer

Many people reserve the use of the home computer as a reward for children who have successfully completed their chores or homework. It is viewed as a recreational item, and like any privilege, it can be removed. But for a child with autism, a computer is an important part of everyday life and not just a privilege; it is a communication tool, learning aid, and social companion. Because of this, when you integrate a child's computer into everyday life, it should be viewed as a necessity and not a luxury.

 **QUESTION?**

Is there aid available to help my child get access to a computer?
It is acceptable to use SSI money to purchase a computer and programs for your child. This would be considered assistive. You just need to be able to show that the computer is for your child's needs and that it is not the family computer.

Children who have autism have realized many benefits from their use of a computer. Attention, motivation, and organizational skills have increased from computer usage in children with autism, as has the ability to independently handle skills for self-help. Socialization has also improved, and expressive language becomes more appropriate and useful for a child with autism. The computer, with its order, has helped to organize and order your child's disordered world.

Hardware That Helps

Various accessories to the computer have helped children with autism learn various programs, games, and activities. For children with deficits in fine motor skills, some of these devices can make the computer easier to use. Other devices can help a child who struggles with the understanding of concepts, bridging the gap between the abstract and the concrete.

 **FACT**

A QWERTY keyboard has the keys placed in the accustomed arrangement. The first letters in the top row spell out the word QWERTY. ABC keyboards are also available, which may or may not be suitable for your child. ABC keyboards will never replace QWERTY, and learning two keyboards is difficult for anyone. The QWERTY is not at all difficult for a child to learn and it will become second nature for your child to use one.

Monitor Devices

One of the most popular assistive devices on the market is the touch screen window. This allows the computer user to use the computer with limited or no use of the mouse. Schools and libraries often have a touch screen window because it reduces the risk of a mouse being lost or stolen, so if your child is older, she may have already used this device.

One of the major benefits of a touch screen is to children who have a conceptual problem understanding that the mouse controls movement on the screen. When a child can become involved "with" the computer, he will derive more benefit from its possibilities. Removing the mouse for a child that struggles with this issue will reduce frustration and the subsequent behaviors that may occur.

If your child has problems with overstimulation when she uses the computer, it could be caused by the glare from the computer. Some people are ultrasensitive to the light of a computer monitor, which will cause fatigue, eyestrain, and headaches. Many inexpensive filters are available that can be placed over the screen to reduce the glare and make the time on the computer less fatiguing. This will also ease overstimulation, if that is a concern.

Keyboard Devices

Some children with autism have problems with fine motor skills and have limited dexterity. An alternative keyboard can ease the problems encountered when attempting to type on the small standard-size keys. This is also good for preschool-age children who are learning hand-eye coordination.

When shopping for alternative keyboards, remember that you won't be able to find every feature on one keyboard. You need to prioritize your child's needs and then make a decision. If he has problems with dexterity, a keyboard with large keys would be helpful. If he has vision problems, a lighted keyboard would help. There are many sizes and shapes of keyboards; comparing what is available will help you make the best choice.

After the computer is set up, if your child has some problems with the operation of the keyboard, check in the operating system for accessibility options. You can program the keyboard to specialized function—for example, ignore rapidly repeating strokes if your child tends to rest his hands directly on the keys. Several options can personalize the computer and make it easier to operate.

Mouse Devices

The computer you bought came with a mouse that was the most basic mouse available. It left-clicks, right-clicks, and moves the cursor. It is small and probably not very efficient. Other options may work better for your child.

ALERT!

When choosing the peripheral equipment for your child's computer, cross off wireless mouse from your shopping list. There are few things more upsetting than an enraged child with autism who can't find his computer mouse. A corded mouse is also difficult to throw in an anger outburst.

Trackball mice are very popular, and with good reason. The mouse is stationary, solid, and versatile. The ball is in a fixed position within the mouse and is operated by either fingers or thumb. Left- and right-handed versions are available. The trackball is easy to get used to and will give your child more control of her activities on the computer.

Useful Software

Once your child's computer is set up, it is time to load it with programs and software. A trip to your local computer store will probably result in your finding more programs than your child could ever use. The trick is to find the programs that will help him and won't be a waste of time and money.

Look for programs that are educational but are also fun. No one can expect any child to stick with a program if it is boring and lifeless. Math programs based on popular cartoon characters are a great favorite and illustrate clearly the concepts necessary to understand the skills being taught in the program. Instead of just hearing that one plus one equals two, a computer program can show it. This will be helpful to the primary learning method of your child—the more visual the program, the better it will work for him.

Programs created for the child with ASD will be extremely useful but a little more difficult to find. Buying these programs on the Internet is the most convenient. These programs can address the problems children on the autism spectrum face regularly; speech (receptive and expressive), dexterity, and social interaction are some of the areas these programs address.

 ## ESSENTIAL

Many sources on the Internet sell computer software programs at reduced prices. Compare the prices before you purchase anything. If you are unfamiliar with a site, check its privacy and security policies, order one product, and if you are satisfied with the service, you can return for further purchases.

Service Dogs

The use of service dogs or other animals for assistance is a relatively new concept for people with autism. Dogs are the most commonly used animals and are worth considering for your child. A service dog can reduce the risk of elopement, aid in socialization, and protect in a public environment. If that sounds like your own private police department and hospitality host rolled into one, you're right. It is!

Before you get so enthusiastic that you run down to the local dog adoption center, several things must be considered. Anytime an animal is brought into your home, whether it is trained by an agency or you self-train, it is a decision that must carefully be weighed. Remember that a service dog is there to work, and work he will; whenever your child and her service dog are together, the dog is working. But a dog is still a dog; it has to be allowed to play, dig holes, torment the family cat, and do all the things dogs do. Your success will be determined by how well you integrate the needs of the child and the needs of the dog.

Family Considerations

It is vitally important that a child not be frightened of large dogs before you get a service dog. If your child is very young and you are considering this option for the future, expose your child to larger dogs that you know are comfortable with children. It can be alarming for a child who has never been around a large dog to suddenly have an animal at eye level. A hesitant or scared child will not bond with the dog, and no training in the world will allow them to perform as a good team.

 **FACT**

Children have a different body language than adults. When a child approaches a dog, they usually have open arms, totally unrestrained behavior, and tend to grab or pull on the dog. A child will understand better how to approach a dog if she is raised around one. If you are considering getting a service dog in the future, it would help to have a pet dog now.

Time is an important element. Regardless of whether the dog is trained by a service dog facility or is trained at home, this is an extraordinary time commitment. Selecting a dog from one of the facilities that specialize in training dogs to work with children with ASD will require one to two weeks at the facility with the dog and the child. Expect a year to two years of training if the dog will be self-trained at home. Regardless of where you get the dog, continued training and reinforcement will be a necessity.

One parent must be involved in the dog/child team. If there are many caretakers involved, this will be confusing for both the child and the dog. One adult who can supervise the team and provide the dog with direction as to what is expected at a given moment will help the dog perform to the best of its ability. Children best adapt to a service dog after they become toddlers and before they enter school for the first time. A rule of thumb is ages two or three to six, with exceptions, of course—a child this age will be more receptive to the concept of dog/child teamwork.

Canine Considerations

Dogs are still dogs, regardless of their occupation. It is important that a fenced yard be available to the dog so it can go outside for play and relaxation. Think of this dog as an employee as well as a family member and service animal. Everyone needs off-hours, and a service dog is no exception to this. Even the best-trained service dog is not above treeing a cat, burying a bone, or rolling in the mud. These activities also provide exercise that is essential to the physical and mental health of the dog.

Like any other animal, dogs can become ill or need preventative medical attention. Veterinary bills can be expensive. It is wise to have a bank account set up that you put funds into on a monthly basis to cover any expensive procedures or treatments that may be needed. Emergencies happen as well, and having that backup fund is akin to medical insurance for a dog.

Different breeds of dog require different grooming. A dog with a fuller coat will need frequent brushing to stay neat. Some children are interested in this, whereas others are not able or willing to perform this task. A parent can brush a dog regularly if they are willing to give the time required. Remember that nail clipping, dental care, and other grooming needs specific to a particular breed should be taken into account when a dog is being selected.

Different dogs have different dietary needs. Some dogs cannot tolerate certain foods, and high-grade dog foods are the best for a dog that is working full-time with a child. A working dog should not be allowed to become obese, and a child should be taught not to feed the dog table scraps.

 ESSENTIAL

The Department of Justice states that animals other than dogs may be used as a service animal. Cats, ferrets, and parrots are very helpful service animals with a child who has autism. Determining what your goal is will help you determine which animal is appropriate for your child.

Homemade Assistive Devices

You do not need a technological piece of equipment to provide an assistive device to your child. Many of the most efficient items are readily available at any variety store. If you think of a step stool as an assistive device for someone who is shorter than the top of the refrigerator, it is easy to understand how many things can be used to help your child compensate.

Next time you visit your local variety or office supply store, take a shopping cart and load it with things you think could be useful in helping your child. Some ideas to get you started are provided, but use your imagination:

- Dry erase boards, either formatted for scheduling or blank, or possibly both.
- Inexpensive photo albums.
- Notebook rings that are loose in the package.
- Plastic storage bins of varying sizes.
- Sidewalk chalk in various colors.
- Yarn or string.
- Magnetic letters and numbers.
- Personalized pens and pencils with your child's name on them.
- A laminator.

Consider your child's strengths and weaknesses and be a little creative in coming up with solutions. For example, small storage bins could hold laminated cards that show an activity or chore that has to be done. This would help a child who does not sequence daily activities well. As your child completes each activity—such as brushing his teeth—he can move the card to the "Job Completed" bin. This will assist with sequencing and will provide motivation because the task completion is easily seen.

Sidewalk chalk can be used to provide direction if a child tends to wander when she goes outside with you; it can also show the limits of an area she is allowed to explore. Personalized writing tools are a great way to teach ownership; if your child uses the entire family's belongings, having his name on things will help him understand what is his and what isn't. Magnetic letters and numbers can be used in many ways—to mark a special occasion or holiday or to put up a goal for the day. You are limited only by your imagination.

Learning Through Toys

All toys can be considered assistive devices if you consider what a child's job is, and what the purpose of a toy is. A child's job is to play; through playing, a child learns to maneuver successfully in the world as he matures. Toys are his tools and equipment, and sometimes they are even his teachers. Every toy has something within it that teaches a child.

Finding toys that assist is not very difficult. What can be difficult is understanding, as an adult, how a toy can help. Expanding your definition of what assistive means will help you think "outside the box" and see the potential in many different toys. Toys will not provide direct assistance for a particular task at a given moment. But they are still assistive in many ways because of the manner in which they aid a child and her functioning in an area in which she is deficient.

Although it is important to educate and assist a child as he is growing, it is also important not to overwhelm him. Too much therapy, too many exercises, and not enough time to just "hang out" are difficult for a child. Parents tend to worry if they are not enriching their child's mind every waking second, but the reality is that this will only teach them about stress. Children with autism have enough stress trying to cope with a world that makes little sense to them.

A child can be outside playing with dirt and water, and upon discovering that together they make mud, she has learned something. If nothing else, the child has learned that small quantities of water can be a wonderful thing! Yes, they are entertained, but the very nature of life is that it is a continually unfolding learning process that does not cease.

If you see a toy that really isn't an educational toy, but you know your child would love it, buy it. Let him enjoy it. No one goes to work (play for the child) without a break every so often. The day is full of activities to challenge and energize your child; sometimes it would be nice to just kick back with a teddy bear.

CHAPTER 16

Challenging Obstacles

HAVING TO DEAL with autism on a daily basis seems like challenge enough, but you aren't going to get through all of this that easily. Problems that are routine for NT children can present obstacles that produce opportunities for creative thinking. Every problem, hidden or obvious, is an opportunity for a developmental step to be taken. Approach each day as though victories are waiting to be made, and the problems will be less daunting. A problem is merely a solution in disguise.

Communicating Needs

One of the most important things you do for your child is to meet the needs she has. Many times, however, children with autism have trouble expressing their needs to you in a way that you can recognize immediately. This can be frustrating for you as well as for your child. It is a waste of time and very discouraging for everyone if you continue to offer one thing and then another to help your child, only to be rejected.

The Frustration of the ASD Child

Frustration is a terrible thing. It leads to impatience, irritability, anger, and tantrums. It can lead to meltdowns and the feeling that there is a serious lack of control by anyone and that any control you thought you

had was only an illusion. Remember how you felt the last time you were frustrated about something? Your child feels the same way but lacks the communication to express it and the maturity to understand that it is a temporary situation.

 ESSENTIAL

> When a child is upset, it is natural for a parent to reach out. But autism creates a sensory system that is always on red alert, so hugs and love may be met with resistance. This is not a sign of bad parenting, and do not let yourself feel bad if your child does not want to be touched when he is upset.

Chapter 6 has valuable information regarding frustration resulting in tantrums and meltdowns. Frustration can also betray its presence in other ways. Although anger is the most common manifestation of frustration, some children withdraw and display their frustration quietly. These children may begin an extreme display of repetitive behavior, such as rocking or head banging. Some children will shake all over or bite themselves on the arm. You can almost hear them shouting from deep inside, "Will you please figure out what I need!"

Telepathy Would Help!

Every mother and father of a child with autism will tell you that they would give anything to get into their child's head for a few hours. How the thought processes of an autistic mind work is not well understood. There are some documented papers and books written by people who have "come out" of autism to report what they experienced as a child. But it is doubtful that reading about those emotions and experiences is anything like actually experiencing them.

Until you can take a pill to read minds, you are going to have to attempt to anticipate what it is your child needs. Bottom line: You are going to have to guess. Most children with autism will try to communicate what they want, so as long as you can keep the effort to help him in motion, you can avert a tantrum. Giving up will only anger him more, so don't get so frustrated yourself that you give up. If you are using a communication board, you will be much better off, as your child will have a place to start his efforts at communication. If your child is still learning how to communicate, just do the best you can do; don't beat yourself up over the situation, and don't think you are a bad parent, because you aren't. Parenting is a creative experience. There is not a book written that could tell you everything you need to know to care for your own child. There are needs unique to her that you will discover as you wing it through this part of your life. This is true for all children, NT or autistic.

 **QUESTION?**

"I am going nuts! What does my child need?"
When a child is unable to communicate her needs, she is just as frustrated as you are. Communication works both ways and parents just want to understand. Try to step back for a moment, look at the scene objectively, and imagine what your child may be thinking. She wants to communicate as much as you do.

Illness

"I couldn't believe it. I didn't get him to the doctor for two days. I didn't even know he was sick." A mother spoke with all the guilt she was feeling. "I should have known. I don't think I am a very good mom." What this mom didn't realize is that there was no way she could have known. Contrary to what children think, parents do not have eyes in the back of their heads and are not able to read minds.

Objective and Subjective Symptoms

Some symptoms are obvious. A child who is vomiting is clearly ill and needs attention. A rash is an objective symptom. Objective symptoms are those symptoms that can be measured, seen, heard, or felt by another person. A rash can be seen and cultured if necessary. It is an actual proven fact. A subjective symptom, on the other hand, is a symptom that the patient perceives and experiences. A rash, felt subjectively by the patient, is experienced through itching and burning. It cannot be measured or even proven. Itching is subjective.

You will have no problems with objective symptoms, and as time passes, you will learn to spot those very quickly. You will develop a sixth sense that will alert you long before a parent of an NT child would notice. The clues are subtle but they show that illness has arrived. Elusive as they may seem right now, they are there in the very beginning, and you will learn to notice them.

 ESSENTIAL

Most children become cranky when they are ill, and this behavior intensifies if the child is autistic. Since autism causes behavioral difficulties anyway, imagine how those difficulties manifest themselves when illness intrudes. After all, inappropriate behaviors are a relative thing. How do you tell whether behavior is worse or just manifesting differently? This is the root of the problem for parents of an autistic child in trying to determine if their child may be ill.

The problem that parents have with their children who are not strong in communication is separating the objective symptoms from the subjective symptoms. Subjective symptoms are another matter entirely. And unfortunately those subjective feelings of illness are often what prevent a child from getting much sicker than necessary—he can tell his parents, and they can then start appropriate treatment at home or with a physician. An NT child will come home from school and announce she has a headache and feels rotten. Mom or Dad will feel her forehead, put her to bed to be on the safe side, and take preventative measures to keep the child from becoming sicker. It isn't that simple for your child with autism. He will come home from school with the same headache as the NT child, feel just as miserable, and you won't have a clue.

This is where guilt comes in. Big time guilt! The next morning your child awakens with a fever and rash, is very lethargic, has glassy eyes, and you nominate yourself for the "worst parent in the world" award. Then it's off to the doctor and you come back home with the frustrating diagnosis of "it's a virus," and everyone moves on. You are *not* the worst parent in the world. Not even close.

Is My Child Sick?

It is very difficult to determine if a child with autism is ill unless the objective symptoms jump out and announce themselves. Even experienced parents will not notice the clues that indicate illness. Watch for alterations in your child's routine. You know that your child has a routine and you are well familiar with it; your whole life is scheduled according to that routine. When it changes abruptly for no apparent reason, that is a red flag that something is wrong and it is time to investigate the possibility that your child is getting sick.

Behaviors are another indicator of illness. This is a bit tricky, as behaviors can change; waxing and waning behaviors are typical for children with autism. For example, a child may line up objects around the house and you expect this. It may be more prevalent on one day over another, but it is something you know will happen. But if suddenly, everything in your house is lined up and your child becomes very aggressive over keeping his lines in order, this is a new manifestation of a previously observed behavior. The exaggeration of the behavior is an objective symptom; it tells you that he is possibly experiencing a subjective symptom that he has been unable to relate.

Other clues can be found in activity levels. A child who suddenly curls up on the sofa, covers himself with a blanket, and stares at the television is probably not up to snuff. How does your child react to his siblings or pets? Is it typical or does he refuse to interact in his normal manner? If your child would never turn down a tussle with a sister and he rejects her baiting him, he is sick. If your child tends to reject physical closeness as a rule but suddenly shows a desire to be hugged and cuddled, feel his forehead and back while you are getting that snuggle—you may find that he has a fever. When activities that are part of the routine are ignored in favor of just lying down, you need to look into it.

 **FACT**

Eating habits are another way to determine if a child is feeling ill. If her favorite food is grilled cheese sandwiches but one day she pushes them away with a look of disinterest, it is time to look a little deeper. When a child with autism rejects her favorites, observe her behaviors closely. Do her eyes look flat or glassy? Does she rub her tummy or try to lie down? Imagine how you might feel if you were experiencing the subjective symptoms that would ruin your appetite and then look for the objective symptoms that you have learned about.

Trusting yourself isn't the easiest thing to do and it is the hardest thing to learn. But your child is tougher than you think, and if you miss a cold or flu that is beginning, both of you will be fine. As you and your child learn more and more about each other, you will be surprised how quickly you will tune into him when he isn't feeling well.

Running Away

Safety is a constant worry for the parents of a child with autism. The world seems fraught with perils that their child doesn't understand. One way to ease the worry is to establish a routine of your own. It will become part of the entire family's life, and although you will never stop feeling the concern and worry, you will know you are doing all you can to prevent an accident or tragedy.

Elopement is perhaps the single biggest cause of gray hair in parents. Elopement, or being "a runner," means that a child has a knack for escaping her home (or other environments, such as school) and wandering off, oblivious to her surroundings. The children who elope have skills that would make Houdini envious. It seems they can unlock any lock, get through any opening, take apart any mechanism that is a barrier, and do it quietly and quickly. The world is literally theirs, and they don't hesitate to wander off in it.

If you have a child who tends to elope—and most children with autism do—take every precaution to prevent your child from escaping without your knowledge. Extra locks on doors, a service dog, or a security system are all options that can make your life easier and safer. Remember, windows are a handy exit point for a child bent on leaving, and they need to be secured as well.

The goal is not to prevent your child from exploring his environment. This is normal and natural and should be done with your supervision. Children with autism are oblivious to danger. That is a concept they do not grasp, and they could walk right in front of a moving car without any sense of consequences. Protection with freedom is the best way to handle a child who elopes.

A Missing Child

When children go missing, it is frightening. However, it is important to keep things in perspective. Very few children are abducted by strangers, and they make the news because they are relatively uncommon. Having said that, however, a child who elopes is much more likely to be in an environment where the risk of abduction is higher. The first step to prevent the tragedy of a child gone missing is to prevent elopement from happening.

 ESSENTIAL

In public, do not use your child's name excessively. Children will go to an adult who knows their name almost without exception. Even if a child understands the concept of what a stranger is, that child will not consider a person who knows his or her name to be a stranger.

The second step is to be prepared if the unthinkable should happen. Keep current photographs of your child on hand, and give a set to a family member or neighbor to keep as well. Talk to your local police department and explain your child's autism so that they are aware of his disability and the potential issues. Be aware of people who enter your house for repairs and services and keep a list of their names and the company they are with. Have a cell phone with you at all times—a parent should be able to be reached at all times, and this is especially true if your child is disabled.

Your child should be wearing an identification bracelet that has his name, address, phone number, and any important medical information printed on it. Above all, it should have "nonverbal autistic" engraved on it, if this is the case. If emergency personnel are ever involved with your child, they need to know about the deficits in his communication skills.

Above all, if a child ever goes missing, contact the police immediately. Many police departments will not institute an immediate search for an older child because they assume it's likely to be a runaway. If you have already contacted the police department to make them aware of your child's disability, you will not have to explain about autism and elopement. If they are aware of your child's autism, they can begin to assist immediately.

Safety Concerns

Most other safety issues are the same ones all parents have with young children, only amplified because of the autism. Keep in mind the disregard for danger that most children with autism have. This list is by no means conclusive, but it can serve as a start for safety within the home.

- Stoves, refrigerators, microwave ovens, and irons are items that intrigue children and can cause serious injury.
- Electrical appliances (hair dryers, curling irons, shavers, etc.) in the bathroom are an accident waiting to happen.

- Water and a young child with autism are a dangerous combination. Be sure your child eventually learns to swim, but keep in mind how hazardous a bathtub can be.
- The family medications should be in a box that can be locked with a key, as an independent child may attempt to treat herself.
- Keep mirrors or glass doors out of your child's bedroom, and if a tantrum begins near glass, remove him immediately to a safer location.
- Electrical outlets are something "open" in the eyes of a child with compulsive tendencies; if she attempts to plug something into the outlet, she could be injured seriously.

 ALERT!

Teach your child the sign for "help" whether or not he uses sign language. Be sure everyone he is regularly in contact with also knows the sign so they can respond to him. This one sign can make all the difference in the world!!

Many things will become second nature to you as you go throughout your day. Washing machines and dryers can be hazardous for young children and for their pets. Cats do not enjoy the spin cycle—and, yes, it does happen. Scissors and children with autism can be disastrous. Most of the things that happen will be laughed about later, but it is worth the extra work to prevent a terrible accident from occurring.

Toilet Training

Facing a major developmental milestone such as toilet training is daunting to the most experienced of parents. Both the child and the parent can end up frustrated, exhausted, and no further ahead. Remember this one tip if you remember nothing else, and repeat it like a mantra: How does my child view this situation? If everything you attempt to teach is approached from that standpoint, everything will become easier . . . a lot easier.

The issues of training a child who has few or no receptive skills, a lack of conceptual thinking, and no understanding of imitative behavior are unique. Your child may have additional complicating factors related to sensory problems. A child who is oversensitive to sensory stimuli may panic at the feeling of something passing from her body. A child who is undersensitive may not even notice. And the routine that has been there forever is being shaken up, which is one of the hardest things to deal with during training, when a child is not totally reliant on either the bathroom or diapers.

The Social and Language Symptoms

One of the primary symptoms of autism is the impairment in socialization skills. NT children will learn toilet training because they understand that it will make their parents happy and that they may get a reward. It is a game of give and take, and they are happy to participate. However, a child with autism may not have that kind of incentive and will be disinterested in the social gain of using the bathroom.

 **FACT**

Motivation is necessary to learn a new behavior. Although a child with autism is not motivated to learn through imitative behavior, she does have one powerful motivator to use: the completion of an activity. A child with autism will be very pleased at her ability to complete something.

Language difficulties complicate the transition from diaper to bathroom. When you are unable to explain what you want, how to do it, and why it should be done, you are at a disadvantage. Children who have receptive abilities may understand a portion of what you are saying, but if a child has no receptive skills, it will be much more difficult. He may even wish to please but has no idea of what is expected of him.

Sensory Problems

Most people are in tune with their own bodies. They are aware of when their stomach growls, and they know when a sneeze is coming. They certainly are aware when their bladder or bowel signals the need to be emptied. Children with autism, however, may not be aware of this urgency or understand what they are to do about it.

If that weren't enough, the bathroom is a place of constant sensory stimuli. The water is running, the sounds of a fan may be heard, the toilet itself is cold, the flushing is a strange sound, and what may be the worst is that this activity requires the removal of clothing. All of those sensory triggers come rushing in all at once and if a child has problems with sensory overload, he may max out. If you have a half-bathroom in your house, consider using that for your training. There are no distracting elements that send the message of multiple uses for a bathroom. Bathtubs, hair dryers, and toothbrushes send a different message than what you are teaching right now.

The Power of Visualization

Visualization means to tie the weakest skill in a person with autism (language) with the strongest skill (seeing). Using visual clues is essential to toilet training your child.

If you can communicate the desired behavior, your child will be much more compliant. Nothing is worse for anyone, autistic or NT, than not understanding what is expected. This is exacerbated in a child with autism with the learning of a major new skill such as using the bathroom. It is essential that the sequence of activities is clearly explained by you and understood by your child.

Visually Assisting Sequencing

A small communication panel is very useful in communicating with your child. You will have something to show your child, and she will have something to reference. Simple paper with drawings or pictures that have been laminated is all that you need to create an effective system. She will see the pictures, hear your voice and the words you say, and learn what is expected of her, and when it is appropriate. The goal is to reduce the confrontation that occurs because of frustration.

A good visual sequencing communication board will have the following instructions on it:

1. Pull down pants.
2. Pull down underwear.
3. Sit on potty-chair or toilet.
4. Use toilet paper if appropriate (tailor the communication board to a boy or girl).
5. Place toilet paper in the toilet.
6. Flush toilet.
7. Pull up underwear.
8. Pull up pants.
9. Wash hands.
10. Return to normal activities.

You can tailor this list to meet your child's specific needs. Just remember you are establishing a routine. It is easier to start a routine now than it is to change one in the future. Adapt the communication board to fit your house, your routine, and your child's needs.

 **QUESTION?**

How often should I take my child to the bathroom?
Scheduling times is a very good way to begin. Every hour on the hour, or every thirty minutes for some children, is a good place to start. Your child will learn that certain times on the clock mean it is that time again. Make his routine work for you.

Visual Cues

One of the most important aids you can use is the cue that indicates a child needs to use the bathroom. This visual aid is something he may use all of his life if he does not have proficient speech. The use of a visual prop for this is also helpful in setting the "tone" and notifying your child of the activity. Many people use an object such as a rubber duck; picking up the rubber duck indicates the bathroom is the next stop. Your child can also use this cue once he is older to tell you that he needs to use the bathroom.

Even better than using a prop, which can get lost or misplaced, is to use the ASL sign for "bathroom." This can't be lost, is appropriate for all ages, is discreet, and can easily be understood.

Problems and Complications

Toilet training a child rarely goes without any problems. You won't get out of this without something that baffles you. If you are unable to think of a creative way to deal with a problem, speak to your child's occupational or sensory integration therapist. Some common problems and solutions are:

- **Refusing to use the toilet at all.** Increasing fluids and fiber is helpful but if the problem is severe, talk to your doctor, as severe constipation can result from refusing to have a bowel movement.
- **Refusing to use toilet paper.** This is a common problem and is often due to sensory issues. Trying different brands of tissue (without scents or colors) may be a solution. Be certain it is plumbing-safe if you try a different method, such as baby wipes.
- **Using too much toilet paper.** All children are guilty of this one. Some easy solutions are counting squares, measuring it against a line on the wall, or replacing it with facial tissue.
- **Inaccurate aim.** This is something boys have a tendency to do (either accidentally or deliberately) and can be helped by using a target in the toilet. Floating something in the water can give them something to aim for. Just be sure it is

safe for your plumbing. If all else fails, show him how to clean the seat with a baby wipe.

- **Flushing inappropriate items.** Do not ever let your child see you flush anything that doesn't belong there! You understand the goldfish went to fish heaven; your child may not understand that the cat shouldn't go as well.

This list is by no means complete. Your child will come up with his or her own unique difficulties and challenges. The good news is that you will come up with just as many unique solutions.

CHAPTER 17

Intervention for ASD Children

THE MOST IMPORTANT STEP a parent can take to help their child with autism is to begin early intervention. If various therapies and treatments can begin before the age of three, the development of a child with autism is greatly enhanced. Your child's potential abilities will be expanded as she matures, and she will learn to relate to others in a way that did not happen before early intervention became the norm. Early intervention involves physicians, therapists, and schools, as well as parents, of course.

Who's Who Among Physicians

Although everyone agrees that finding a good physician can make all the difference to a family stricken by autism, they will also agree that it is very difficult to find one who knows anything *about* autism. A smart doctor will admit it if she isn't well informed on the topic and will refer you to a specialist, or she will make an effort to learn all she can to benefit her patients. Throughout your child's growing years, you will likely have contact with several different physicians.

The Pediatrician
Pediatricians are specialists who care for the needs of children. They see children from birth to age twenty-one and beyond in certain circumstances.

Pediatrics is a specialty of medicine, as children are not just minia-ture adults—their health needs and issues are different and must be treated differently than an adult would be treated. Pediatricians have eleven years of college and training behind them: eight years of col-lege and medical school, one year in pediatric internship, and two years in pediatric residency.

A pediatrician should posses many qualities, but some of the most important for your family are a kind nature, gentleness, the ability to relate to nonverbal children, and a lot of patience. Pedia-tricians must be involved in keeping your child well, not just treating him when he is sick.

 **FACT**

> A good pediatrician will take the time to learn about your entire family. He or she will ask about your life, marriage, and health. It is not prying but rather it is a way to understand the environment in which your child lives and how it affects his health and well-being.

Selecting the right pediatrician for your child is important. It is important that you feel comfortable with this physician. Many par-ents feel that a team exists to raise their child and the pediatrician is one of the most valued members of that team. The pediatrician should feel the same way about your child. Begin by speaking with family and friends, and, of course your support group; collect a list of names and organize yourself to find the best physician you can.

The Pediatric Neurologist

Neurology is the study of brain and nervous system disorders. Pediatric neurologists are highly specialized in both neurology and pediatrics and have all of the training of both fields, plus specialty fel-lowship training. They treat conditions from headaches to brain tumors and are likely to be able to make the final diagnosis of autism.

A pediatric neurologist will not be the source of primary care for your child. In other words, don't call his office for a sore throat or rash. However, if your child has some coexisting conditions such as a seizure disorder, you will be working closely with this physician for many years. He or she should have a special interest in autism and have other patients with autism. A physician who is aggressively pursuing continuing education regarding autism would be your best choice, as information on autism changes daily.

The Child Psychiatrist or Psychologist

It is hard to not balk when you are advised to consult with a child psychiatrist or psychologist. To keep this in the proper light, remember that mental health professionals do more than work with mental illness; they have a unique understanding of how structural brain disorders affect behavior and how best to treat those problems. There is a definite relationship between the mind, body, and spirit, and a psychiatrist works in those somewhat nebulous areas.

A psychiatrist is a physician who has had additional training studying the brain and the mind. He or she will have twelve to sixteen years of training. The psychiatrist can prescribe medications, whereas other experts in mental health cannot. A child psychiatrist will work to determine how all aspects of a person's life are affecting his or her health; this includes physical, emotional, educational, developmental, and social issues, all of which will influence overall health. A child psychiatrist can also be helpful as a family adjusts to the diagnosis of autism.

A clinical psychologist will have either a master's or doctorate. They are not physicians but work closely with many physician specialties to coordinate the use of medication from the physician and counseling from the psychologist. They can make a recommendation to the child's physician that a particular medication be used. Psychologists will often work with an entire family to modify undesirable behaviors in a child with autism.

ESSENTIAL

All professionals in the mental health fields should be pursuing additional study on various issues in the ever-changing health care field. Look for a psychiatrist or psychologist with a special interest in autism. If the doctor regularly deals with autism, the condition will be familiar to her, which will result in better care for your child.

Selecting the Right Physician

The first thing to do is organize your list by geographical convenience; it matters little how good a particular physician may be if you can't get there. You don't need to be in your doctor's backyard, but in an emergency, it is nice to have a doctor a few minutes away. It is possible the physician may have more than one office if it is a large practice, in which case knowing what days the doctor is in is helpful. While you are mapping out locations, it is helpful to make a note of what hours the office is open. Many offices will be open in the evening one night a week to accommodate working parents.

Next, decide if you prefer a male or female physician. It may not matter to you or you may feel more comfortable with a physician of the same sex as your child. If you would be more comfortable with a physician of a certain age, write that in too. Older doctors have more experience but younger doctors may be more open and innovative; it depends on the personality of the physician. If you are uncomfortable asking someone's age, ask how many years he or she has been in practice.

Then begin interviewing. Call the office to set up an appointment, which should be a free-of-charge visit; tell the receptionist that you would like to schedule a "get acquainted" visit as you are choosing a physician for your child. Note the attitude of the staff on the telephone—in the future, those will be the first people you speak with. They should be friendly, helpful, and professional.

The physician, when you meet her, should be open and interested in your questions. She should feel no discomfort at being quizzed about child care and development, and how she handles situations that you ask about. You should feel a sense of humor from the prospective doctor but not a flippant attitude. Ask questions specific to your concerns about autism to determine the doctor's level of experience with and interest in ASD. The physician will likely have questions for you, too, and setting up this dialogue is important for the future of your working relationship.

The Importance of Qualified Therapists

Medical care may be only as good as the ancillary medical professionals that provide it. Different therapists will see your child more than his physician will and it is important that they are qualified, knowledgeable, and interested in their field. You should be able to tell if the therapists you are seeing care about their work; checking their qualifications is also very easy.

Speech Therapists and Audiologists

Audiologists are the head of the team that diagnoses and handles hearing disorders. They also diagnose and recommend treatment for many communication disorders. When a child has autism, an audiologist is frequently the first medical professional that sees the child, because the parents suspect deafness. Audiologists have at least a master's degree.

 **FACT**

Audiologists are trained to work with very young children and nonverbal children. They will use several techniques to determine if a child has a hearing disorder or a receptive language problem. Although they do not diagnose autism, they are important for ruling out a disorder such as deafness.

Speech therapists, or speech and language pathologists, work with people who have many varied kinds of hearing or communication problems. In an average day, a speech therapist may see a child with a lisp, an older person who has had a stroke, a nonverbal child with autism, and a person with deafness. They work with people of all ages.

Speech therapists are considered by many physicians and parents to be the primary therapist that coordinates all the therapy for the child with autism. Because they work with swallowing disorders as well as speech problems, they can coordinate therapies with physical, occupational, and sensory therapy to achieve the maximum results in the time they have with a child. An approach that combines therapies helps a child put order into his disordered world.

As your child begins therapy, regardless of what method you decide on, you will likely interact with a speech therapist. Talk to the therapist about your concerns regarding language development and what you can do at home to reinforce the therapy. Many small things that you do on a day-to-day basis can incorporate the therapy that is being used to help your child progress.

Physical Therapists

Whether or not your child sees a physical therapist (PT) will depend on her gross motor skills. Many children with autism do not have any deficits in this area and physical therapy is not necessary, but others have extensive issues, and the PT may coordinate all the therapies a child receives. The goal of physical therapy is to improve functioning. Issues such as range of motion and flexibility are primary concerns that will be addressed by the therapist. PTs work to increase a patient's independence by increasing balance, coordination, and strength.

If your physician recommends a PT, you may find your first visit with him or her to be much like a doctor visit. PTs will analyze a patient's medical history, do an evaluation of their own, and recommend a course of treatment. They will develop an appropriate therapy plan, coordinate all forms of therapy, and instruct parents on home activities to enforce the treatment plan. They may have an assistant work with the patient, but this is not always the case.

PTs are college educated, with a minimum of a master's degree being preferred by most employers. Some states require only a bachelor's degree. They will be certified and belong to a variety of organizations. Continuing education is also a requirement for licensure. As with any kind of therapist, a special interest in autism is helpful.

Occupational Therapists

One of the most important professionals your child will interact with will be the occupational therapist (OT). This person will be pivotal in helping your child build skills or compensate for skills to perform in normal everyday life. The OT may also be referred to as a sensory integration therapist. Like all other therapists your child will work with, this person is college educated, is involved with continuing education, and will belong to one or more professional organizations.

 ESSENTIAL

Many daily living skills are difficult for children with autism to perform. The lack of language, either receptive or expressive, creates difficulty for a child when she isn't sure of what she is to do or how to do it. An occupational therapist will work with a child to increase fine motor skills but also to increase reasoning and understanding.

An OT will work with a child to teach her to use various tools in her life. All of the skills taught enforce different aspects of mental function. A variety of activities will be involved over the course of a child's therapy:

- The use of a computer.
- The use of paper and pencil/crayons.

- Video games may be used to teach hand-eye coordination.
- Various exposures to sensory stimuli to decrease overstimulation problems.
- Repetitive activities may be used to teach sequencing.
- Flashcards and other language aids may be used in connection with speech therapy.

An OT will do a wide variety of things to increase your child's ability to function independently. If you need something to help your child compensate or adapt, ask the OT. If classroom equipment needs to be modified, the OT will know how to do it. Problem solving is their specialty, and they will bring many solutions to situations that puzzle you.

Licensed Clinical Social Workers

The licensed clinical social worker (LCSW) is no longer exclusively for families who have financial or social problems. The LCSW is a mental health professional that deals with a variety of emotional and societal issues that bring about conflicts in life. LCSWs are college educated with a master's degree and are required to complete continuing education annually.

If a psychologist can be viewed as treating the mental health of an individual, the LCSW can be considered as the mental health expert for society. They specialize in maintaining the social functioning of an individual in a group. Whether it be family, a group home, or society in general, the LCSW's goal is to create the best social situation possible for your child.

Social workers can be helpful when an adult child is considered for placement in a group home environment. A LCSW will also help a family determine if they are getting the financial help they are entitled to and that it is distributed properly if that is a concern. They can help a family with many issues at the school level as well. LCSW see people with autism every day and they know the community as well as their clients, and they can assist in making the best decisions for both.

Possible Treatment Programs

As you explore various options for your child's medical care, you will find many programs and treatment plans. Investigate ideas that are sound, and research all you need. But remember, there is no cure for autism. Your goal is to make your child the best person that he can be, which is a goal you will be able to reach. Following programs that promise the impossible will not cure autism and will only take your money.

There are many good treatment plans. If you are interested in any form of treatment, consult with your child's physician. It is also helpful to speak with other parents at your support group meeting. Don't try to reinvent the wheel; other people can provide you with a great deal of information. But remember that you must follow your own instincts and do what you think is best for your child and family.

 ALERT!

If something sounds too good to be true, it is. Many people will take advantage of a desperate parent's attempt to find a cure for autism. Parents spend hours searching the Internet for an effective treatment, and people willing to take their money are always available.

Neuro-Immune Dysfunction Syndrome (NIDS) Protocol

Some research has suggested a link between autoimmune disorders, autism, and ADD. NIDS treatment protocol operates to balance the immune system in an effort to reduce the symptoms of autism. The results have been very good.

The treatment protocol involves looking for various markers including allergens, and viral and bacterial titers. For the patient's family, this means that blood and urine are analyzed for things that the child may be allergic to or that may indicate levels of exposure to certain viruses and/or bacterial infections. If different disease processes appear, or allergies are determined, treatment can begin that may alleviate some of the symptoms of autism. Treatment then can begin with allergy medications, antifungals, antivirals, and SSRIs (medications used for depression, anxiety, and the control of obsessive-compulsive behaviors). People on the NIDS protocol are monitored closely with monthly or bimonthly blood work.

Applied Behavioral Analysis (ABA)

Applied behavioral analysis (ABA), also known as the Lovaas method, is one of the most popular forms of treatment of autism. This therapy does not attempt to reverse a medical condition but has been created instead to change undesirable behaviors into desirable ones. It also teaches social skills, life skills, and encourages language. It builds on small skills, creating bigger skills, and teaching motivation for learning. ABA claims to be effective in modifying the behavior of up to 50 percent of children with autism to the point that they were able to attend a normal classroom without paraprofessional assistance.

ABA is not without controversy. Some fear that children are simply responding to verbal or nonverbal cues and that the behavior mechanizes them. Proponents say that isn't the case if the child is taught properly. There is also a misconception that aversive therapy is used as punishment for undesirable behaviors, when in fact it is not. Unfortunately there is no way to determine which children will be the most responsive and successful with ABA, but younger children who spend more than thirty hours each week in ABA therapy have shown the best results. It requires a great deal of structure within the family but results begin to show quickly, and it is an ideal therapy for many children and their families.

ESSENTIAL

Don't ever begin two or more therapies simultaneously. If you have positive results, you will never be certain which treatment was the effective one. Give a new therapy at least three months before you evaluate the results and then decide if you wish to continue.

The GFCF Diet

One of the most popular treatment plans involves the use of a gluten-free, casein-free (GFCF) diet. This means exactly what it says: There are no glutens or caseins ingested by a person on this diet. It excludes all wheat, rye, barley, and oats from the diet as well as almost all milk products. Many parents maintain their children on this diet, and the results have been very positive. Although scientific studies are lacking, parental success votes in with an amazing 80 percent rate of satisfaction with the treatment plan.

The premise of eliminating gluten and casein from the diet involves a theory that autism could potentially be a metabolic disorder or an autoimmune disease. It is suspected that the body may be having a toxicological response to the molecule of gluten, and that the central nervous system (CNS) behavior is affected by the action of the molecule in a body that cannot tolerate it. Because the structure of the casein molecule is similar to that of gluten, it is also included in the elimination diet. This is very similar to celiac sprue (also called celiac disease or nontropical sprue), an autoimmune disease. Interestingly, children with celiac disease rarely have autism, but many children with autism have celiac disease.

If you decide to begin this approach to autism, do your homework first. Many products have hidden gluten in them, and even one molecule can affect the success of the diet. Learn about gluten-free eating, as it will be a dramatic change for your household.

Vitamin B$_6$

Vitamin B$_6$ is a very popular form of treatment. It is harmless if taken as directed, and the studies have shown positive results. Individuals require different levels of vitamin B$_6$, and if a person has a deficiency, the theory goes, taking large doses of the vitamin will assist them. If that is the case, autism could also be viewed as a vitamin deficiency, much like scurvy resulting from a lack of vitamin C. The key is balancing the B$_6$ intake with the other vitamins to utilize B$_6$ efficiently without causing a deficiency in another vitamin, which could cause undesirable side effects. Magnesium is used to counteract the larger B$_6$ intake and has shown to be effective as well.

 FACT

Vitamin B$_6$ therapy has shown to improve eye contact, reduce self-stimulating behaviors, reduce tantrums, improve social and environmental interactions, and improve speech. If you are interested in this therapy, contact the Autism Research Institute. Your physician may not know about this therapy; brochures from the institute have more information and will help explain the details.

B$_6$ therapy is not a cure—the founders of the treatment will be the first to admit that. But with studies showing at least half of children responding favorably to megadoses of vitamins B$_6$ and normal supplements of vitamin B complex and magnesium, it is not something parents can easily disregard.

The Experts Vs. the Parents

Something interesting happens when people enter a medical office. They quite often lose their confidence and assertiveness. Perhaps it is the environment of the clinic; a doctor is kept from the public by a vigilant staff and when they decide it is time, the doctor arrives to impart to you knowledge and wisdom. Patients have jokingly referred to their appointment as a pilgrimage, as though seeking the doctor was somewhat like seeking advice from a mysterious power.

When patients feel the doctor, or therapist, has knowledge they could not possibly understand, and they trust without question any advice, treatment, or medication given, a problem is just brewing. Many people will smile and nod their heads politely when they aren't listened to or given answers to the questions they have, but complain mightily out of earshot of the physician. It cannot be understated how important it is for the parent of a child with autism to jettison that attitude. Meeting with physicians and therapists as an equal, as a member of a team all working toward the same goal, is the approach that will help your child the most.

As a mom or dad, you are with your child twenty-four hours a day, seven days a week (with the exception of school hours and other short times away). Constantly you are monitoring and observing his behavior; you notice the smallest of changes and can sense his emotions. And you are the only one that does that.

A wise physician (and a therapist and teacher as well) wants to know exactly what the parents think and will ask them. If you feel that the experts around you aren't interested in your opinions, this needs to be addressed. If it is a school problem, call a meeting with the teachers and paraprofessionals; an IEP isn't necessary but it is important you discuss the situation. If a doctor disregards your questions or input, make an appointment and meet with the doctor in his or her private office, not in an exam room.

Trusting yourself is the most important part of any therapy or treatment. No one knows your child as you do and you can rely on your instincts. Always collect advice and listen to the experience of others, but when it comes time for the decision, you are qualified to make it.

Financial Assistance

AUTISM CAN BE an expensive condition to deal with. Having good medical coverage is important, but it isn't always easy to come by. Fortunately, there are some ways to get help. You may qualify for Social Security benefits, although the laws have changed recently, making it more difficult to get federal assistance. Your understanding of Social Security and how the system works is important in order to have your child evaluated fairly and get the benefits to which you are entitled.

Social Security Benefits

Autism is a "pervasive developmental disorder characterized by social and significant communication deficits originating prior to age 22." It seems hard for many to define autism in just a few words, but the Social Security Administration (SSA) has figured out how to sum it up neatly. They define mental retardation as a "significantly subaverage general intellectual functioning with deficits in adaptive behavior usually manifested before age 22." When a family seeks out disability benefits for their child, they will first turn to Social Security. As it is the baseline for the determination of a disability, it is important to understand how the SSA operates to determine if a child is disabled.

Educational and financial decisions are based on the results of IQ testing on children with autism. This is a very controversial area with parents, as there are concerns about the reliability of an IQ test on a child who has communication deficits.

The Wechsler Adult Intelligence Scale (WAIS) is the primary test that is used by SSA to determine if a person is mentally retarded. A psychologist or psychiatrist must give the test and interpret the results. The same person must also write an evaluation to SSA stating that the test was valid and accurately reflected the mental status of the individual who was tested. Three areas are tested: verbal, performance, and IQ. The SSA uses the lowest of the three assessments to determine a person's eligibility for benefits. But it is not only the score of the WAIS that factors into this decision; it is also how this score compares to the rest of the population.

 ESSENTIAL

Do not be alarmed if IQ testing is required for your child. The IQ score can be helpful in determining what assistance your child needs and can direct you in making medical and educational decisions; if you believe it is not truly reflective of your child's intelligence, that is fine. IQ will likely fluctuate over the years while your child hones her communication skills.

If a child is unable to be evaluated by the WAIS, other tests can be used. The Raven Progressive Matrices is for people with limited verbal ability and can be helpful for people with autism. The Minnesota Multiphasic Personality Inventory (MMPI) and the Thematic Apperception Test (TAT) are often useful if a child has other brain disorders and can help with supporting those diagnoses.

Supplemental Security Income

If you meet income and asset requirements, your child with autism may qualify for disability support through Social Security.

There was a time that a diagnosis of autism meant an automatic allowance for Supplemental Security Income (SSI), but changes at the Social Security Administration (SSA) have made it so there is no guarantee that an autistic child will receive SSI payments. A simple diagnosis is no longer enough—parents must prove that their child cannot function "normally" in society in order to be eligible.

Function, Function, Function

Social functioning is a person's ability to relate to and with others. Adults and children have different social skills, but if a person is unable to maneuver through his social environment, he will have difficulty interacting with others in an educational or vocational environment.

Function is a relative term. If you ask one person how your child functions, he or she may see an entirely different picture than you do. A physician will see function in one way, and it will be entirely different than how a teacher sees it. This can be frustrating for parents, because they see the whole picture and understand exactly what the differences are in people's perceptions of their child. The problem enters in when a disability examiner, who has never met your child and likely never will, attempts to judge and decide how much of a deficit exists in your child's functioning.

If you remember how the disability examiner is looking at the decision he or she will have to make, it is easier to understand what information will help them reach the correct conclusion. According to Social Security, a child must have a "marked and severe functional limitation," or he is not disabled. The operative word here is "and." It must be both marked *and* severe, so it is up to the people writing reports and records to show if this is the case. Another phrase that can be an issue is the requirement that a child must have "qualitative deficits in verbal and nonverbal communication *and* in imaginative activity," and again the key word is the same.

ALERT!

Do not allow phrases that are vague on reports. If someone says your child is doing well and what he or she means is that there hasn't been a meltdown in a week, it could be interpreted to mean that it is no longer a severe disability. Ask teachers, doctors, and anyone else who evaluates your child to be as specific as possible.

Try to view your child as someone would who has never seen her before. Does her autism restrict her from activities that NT children of the same age participate in? Does she have communication problems severe enough that she has difficulty expressing what she needs to anyone outside of the family? Does she lack a sense of danger? Is she unable to care for herself in a socially appropriate manner? If your answers are "yes," it is your job as your child's advocate to see that this information is conveyed to Social Security effectively and accurately.

Presenting an Accurate Picture

Knowing how the severity of your child's disability will be determined is the most important piece of information you have. Medical sources, as well as educational and social sources, can be used to support your claim that your child is disabled. This includes reports on how he lives his daily life: how he functions with others, his attention span, obsessive behaviors, tantrums, aggression, and other issues in his life that interfere with typical functioning. Reports can be submitted from any source you deem appropriate. These statements can be from immediate or extended family members, day care staff, community service workers, respite care workers, or any other person involved with your child on a regular basis.

Keep in mind that children, particularly children with autism, change from day to day and month to month. What may be true in behavior today may not be true tomorrow. In a report, you want to convey an overall impression. Do not let the temptation of making your child look good take over as you collect these reports. Save that for Sunday school. What you want now is accuracy to prove his deficits in function. If he functions in such a manner that it prohibits him from having a life that is similar to an NT child, he is eligible and you need to prove it. What must be conveyed is how he does function, not how you hope he will function eventually.

How to Apply for SSI

Applying for benefits is not difficult but it is a tedious and time-consuming process. The best way to proceed is to organize your financial records and all of the medical documentation you have so that it is at hand when you begin the application.

1. Gather all your documentation in advance: a certified copy of your child's birth certificate, tax and earnings records, name and address of medical and educational providers, and contact information for anyone who sees your child regularly.
2. Call Social Security at ☎ 1-800-772-1213, or go into a local office if there is one in your area, and request forms for the application of Childhood Disability Benefits.
3. Fill out all forms completely and accurately. It sometimes helps to photocopy the forms first so you can use one as a "practice sheet."
4. Notify all people that you have listed on the forms that they will be receiving requests for written reports, and notify physician and school offices that records will be requested. Reiterate the importance of providing accurate information.
5. About three weeks after submitting the forms to Social Security, contact them to follow up on what records and reports they have received and which ones are missing.
6. Follow up on missing reports and provide any additional information the disability examiner may need.

 **FACT**

> Any problems encountered that are not easily solved may require the expert services of a disability advocate or attorney.

Unfortunately, the SSI process can be a tedious one. Many parents feel like the disability examiners are there to disallow any application, but don't let this get in your way. The odds are high you will be rejected on the first try unless your child is profoundly autistic or has other medical conditions; this shouldn't stop you from attempting to get her disability allowed. If you are rejected, you can appeal and it is quite common for disallowed cases to be allowed in review. If you are approved on appeal, your child's benefits will be backdated to the date that the claim was disallowed, which can be a sizeable sum of money that will help offset the expenses you have incurred since then.

Medical Coverage

There are few things more important than medical coverage, particularly when a family member has a disorder such as autism. Unfortunately, most private insurances have an exclusion for autism and will not cover anything that is in any way related to the diagnosis of an autism spectrum disorder. However, there are things you can do to increase your coverage amounts:

- When you call for a doctor appointment for your child, tell the receptionist what the physician is seeing your child for. If it is a sore throat, for example, tell them that at the time of making the appointment.
- If your physician's office has a sign-in form, sign your child's name and write down the complaint that you are in for, *even if there is not a place on the form for that information.*
- When the nurse comes into the examination room and asks the reason for the visit, if it is not related to autism, there is

no reason to state that your child has autism. Unless it is a physician you have not seen before, your doctor knows your child has autism.

- When the doctor sees your child, be certain to stress at the beginning of the visit that your reason for being there is not his autism.
- Upon leaving the office, you will most likely be presented with a copy of the insurance slip. Check the section for diagnosis and be sure autism is not circled or written in—it is an irrelevant diagnosis if the problem was a sore throat or another unrelated condition.

None of this is dishonest. Most physicians and their staff include all the diagnoses a person has on an insurance form, without realizing that *only the diagnosis pertinent to the visit should be documented.* Strep throat or a checkup has nothing to do with autism, and your insurance should cover it just as it would with any other family member.

This is one of the reasons SSI is so important. With SSI comes Medicaid, which is a state-funded health insurance that does not exclude autism-related visits from its coverage. Even if your SSI drops to a level that seems hardly worth having, you will still have the Medicaid and it will ease your financial burden. If you have no other medical coverage for autism, keeping Medicaid is high on your list of priorities. You will still have to qualify for Medicaid by meeting certain income requirements, but it should be a consideration in your financial planning.

 ESSENTIAL

The disabled adult children's benefits, through Social Security, are available to adult children disabled prior to age twenty-two and whose parents are no longer able to provide for them due to retirement, disability, or death. These can help offset expenses later in life.

Creative Financial Assistance

The United States is the only "first-world" country that pays for a person's medical needs in an institution but that does not assist in keeping a family member at home. It is not sound social planning, and it certainly is poor financial planning as it costs much less to have people cared for at home. It costs 70 percent less to use respite care instead of institutional living. Parents can take a proactive approach and find many ways to secure financial assistance as they deal with the cost of autism.

Different States, Different Help

Throughout the United States, different assistance programs and benefits are available. Each of these depends on the state in which you live. Although most assistance does come from a federally funded program, it is administrated on state levels, and each of the fifty states has its own regulations.

 **FACT**

If you are on the lower end of the income scale, you still have a potential tax benefit. The Earned Income Credit (EIC) may give you a refund that is actually larger than the taxes you pay! This program was put in place to assist what the government terms the "working poor" and can help single-parent families as well as families who are struggling to get by each month.

Some states have programs known as Family Support Funds. The Developmental Disability Center (DDC) in each state manages these funds. Qualifying for these funds is easy, and parents are usually taken on their word about a child's disability. Payments can be as low as $500 a year and as high as $500 a month. The only requirement is that the funds distributed to each family must be used for the benefit of the child with the disability. Call the local DDC and ask about funds of this nature. If you are unable to find any resources, ask your support group, who will likely know what is available.

Additionally, when you file your state income tax, find out if there is another deduction for the disability that your child has. Some states will allow two deductions for a child with autism or another disability. Others do not. Check into your state's laws to be sure you are receiving every tax benefit possible.

A True Tax Incentive

Every family that pays taxes has a way to receive a lump-sum "benefit" annually. But did you know that taxes also provide a way to save money? Deductions are available to most families and although filing with listed deductions is more complex, it can make a big difference. Itemizing deductions means using the actual expenses you have incurred throughout the previous year instead of the government-estimated standard deduction. Do you know what you can deduct? You can deduct just about anything that is necessary to treat the medical condition of any member of your family!

- Health insurance costs paid by you for medical, dental, and prescription coverage.
- Physician visits that you pay for (not covered by insurance).
- Co-payments that are required for medical services.
- Medical equipment that is necessary and prescribed (and not covered by insurance) by any member of your family.
- Deductibles on your health insurance that you are financially responsible for.
- Contact lenses and glasses as well as the supplies that are needed to care for them.
- Prescribed birth control.
- Insulin.
- Transportation to medical care or therapy.

And remember, if you can reduce the amount you owe in federal taxes, you will also be reducing your state income tax. Speak with a tax expert or accountant to find the best options for your family.

FACT

It is the nature of people to not want to accept financial assistance. But you have paid into these taxes for many years, and these taxes were intended for social programs to help people in need. Do not feel guilty about accepting benefits that you are due.

Respite Care

By the time some parents hear about respite care, they are already exhausted and burned out. No one can do it all, but parents of children with autism seem compelled to attempt it, and they do quite well. The autism community has many remarkable parents who have been tested by fire and come out stronger for it. But everyone needs a break from autism—that includes you!

A Service for the Whole Family

Respite care is for both caregiver (you) and the person with a disability (your child) to have a break from the daily routine of being together. It is beneficial for the child, and it is essential for the parent. A special-needs child is not an independent element in your household. Everyone in the family is affected by his needs, and you will spend a lifetime to accomplish this adjustment. This is why respite care is a family service; it is there to assist the entire family as they care for a disabled child at home.

If your child is newly diagnosed, you may not be able to even consider leaving him with another individual. This is a normal reaction and you shouldn't do anything you are uncomfortable with. There will be a time that you will be open to the idea, but in the meantime, just keep it in the back of your mind as an option. Don't dismiss the idea completely for now, and if there is a waiting list in your area through the various agencies, get on it; you can always turn it down later if you don't feel you need it or aren't ready to try it.

ESSENTIAL

Respite care is beneficial for your child as well as for yourself. Having other people take charge at times will put some variety in your child's life and teach her that she can, and should, communicate with others. Work with the respite caregiver so he understands the communication system your child uses.

Finding a Respite Care Worker

When you discuss respite care options, have a list of questions ready. Are you interested in short-term or long-term respite? Is the care provided in your home or in another place? What kind of costs are involved and what type of assistance is available? And where do you find care? You will want to know how a service selects respite care workers and what kind of training they have and if they are experienced in first aid and CPR. Health and Human Services or the social workers you work with can guide you in finding the respite care that is appropriate for your family. Ask if you can meet the respite care worker that will be assigned to your child before your child meets him or her. It is also important, because of the routine that people with autism have, to know if the same care worker will be available each time for your child. It could be once a month or twice a month that you get to take advantage of respite care. You will be provided services based on your family's needs and the availability of respite care workers in your area.

As your child matures into adulthood, respite care can be used to assist in the building of skills. Considering that most adults with autism do live in a group home environment, the experience of respite care can help families with the transition when that time arrives. There are many services and resources available; it is just a matter of discovering them. You will likely be able to find something that you are comfortable with.

Custody Issues

It seems almost inconceivable, but in the United States, approximately 20 percent of families with disabled children are faced with a terrible decision. Because of the lack of affordable medical care and insurance, some families are forced to make a decision about parental rights. The choice? Whether to retain custody of their child or give up custody to the state in order to acquire medical care for their child. The reason? A lack of medical insurance or exclusion on a medical insurance policy for the condition the child is affected with.

In 2002, it was estimated by the General Accounting Office of the U.S. federal government that 13,000 children were given up by their families to be placed into child welfare or various other parts of the "system." Some were put into the care of juvenile justice, even though no crime had been committed. Their parents just couldn't afford their medical care or there were no services available in their community. This does not affect only families with children who are autistic, but families with any disabled children as well.

Much of the problem is a result of the medical care crisis in the United States. With health care costs as high as they are and insurances not footing the bill, parents are left to shoulder a burden they have no resources to handle. Immediate intervention is necessary in many cases and mental illness care remains the weakest link in the chain of health care. As long as autism and other spectrum disorders are listed and categorized as a mental illness, families are at a disadvantage. To add to the problem, programs for mental disorders are being cut left and right, and there is nowhere for children to receive the care and services they need.

The problem then reaches out into the school system, with special-education funds being cut; meanwhile, the numbers of children with autism continues to increase. But the true tragedy, the true fallout, happens to society. Families, who must face the grim reality that they may not be able to retain custody of their own children, are being forced to make a choice they should never have to make.

 **FACT**

Most private insurance companies have exclusions in their policies for any treatment due to autism. If you do not have medical coverage for your child, it is crucial to work with a financial consultant to create adequate resources to care for your child with the treatment and therapy you feel is best for him.

If you have a child that has been recently diagnosed with autism, begin financial planning so that a custody issue is never a problem you have to deal with. Savings, whole-life insurance policies, and equity in a home are just some of the options that can protect you financially.

CHAPTER 19

Support for Parents

I T IS NOT UNCOMMON for parents to feel a sense of isolation when they learn their child has autism. *Autism* is a word that seems very final and as one parent said, "The most devastating of disabilities." After some time passes you will feel less that way, and you will learn it is not the most devastating. Isolation is not something you have to learn to live with and, in fact, you shouldn't. There are many forms of support available to you that are worth taking advantage of.

The Importance of Support

Are you the tough go-it-alone type? Do you resist sharing openly about fears and concerns you have? Are you the kind of person that can't imagine discussing your personal life in a group setting? If so, you will likely find that the journey through autism is a bit bewildering and lonely. Looking for support does not make a person weak. Rather, it creates a foundation of stability and knowledge that imparts security and confidence.

When the Muppets were at the height of their popularity, the show featured a segment that was intended to entertain and impress people with the creativity of the puppet. It was a centipede. Not an ordinary centipede but a very special Muppet centipede with fabulous clothes and fifty pairs of oversized shoes. He had a colorful jacket, a small suitcase, a hat with a flower on it, and a very big umbrella. He sang a complete rendition of "You'll Never Walk Alone" and although the skit was humorous, there was a great deal of truth and meaning in it. How can you ever get all those feet, all 100 of them, organized and coordinated enough to walk together?

The answer is simple: You can't. And you don't have to walk this journey alone either. The centipede, looking at a higher power for authority, had the idea right. He knew he couldn't possibly coordinate all his feet, make his way through a thundering rainstorm, not lose his suitcase, and still make his destination safely if he didn't have some help. He needed support. So, he sang his song and with the support he had, he kept plugging away. And he made it in one piece; because of the support he had, he was able to travel his treacherous journey.

Autism is much like that. You may feel like the centipede at times as you try to coordinate your feet upon a path you didn't know you would have to walk. You may be drenched with the rain of everything around you falling down, and you may think your little umbrella is going to blow inside out as it tries to shelter you. But out there, beyond your immediate surroundings, there is a full orchestra playing with an entire chorus of people singing the same song. They already know the words and the way to walk to this music.

What Is Support?

Seeking support is learning how to walk and sing that same song the others are already singing and letting them teach you. It is also teaching others what you have learned yourself when you are confident in your abilities. Support is making it happen with the help of others who have "been there, done that." Support is learning to ask questions that you didn't even know existed. And support is the only way you are going to get through this.

A lot of the reason parents have problems with getting their own parents to understand what a struggle autism can be at times is simply a lack of knowledge heightened by a failure to communicate. You may approach your own mother with your frustrations, but she has no frame of reference, having not had nor raised a child with autism herself. Your frustration will be received as a question, whether you intend it that way or not, and like most moms, she will attempt to help. This just makes the situation worse, because her suggestions probably won't work; it's not her fault. She doesn't know because how could she?

Getting Support

This is the advantage of a support group. Those people know! They have been right where you are and you don't have to explain the entire autism spectrum to them in order to vent a little. Few things are more frustrating than needing to have a gripe session but before you can launch into your frustration, having to give a twenty-minute speech to explain the issues involved that have caused your frustration to begin with.

A support group for families who have children with autism won't mind if you stagger into a meeting exhausted from a lack of sleep because your child only slept for thirty minutes the night before. They may have been up all night, too. They understand you need to find a babysitter who can handle autism for two hours so you can attend one of your other children's school conferences. They probably even have a list of names and phone numbers.

 **FACT**

If you need to find a physician or dentist, ask at your support group meeting. The people there will have the information that you need and will be able to give you their opinion of the care that they received. Recommendations from people you know, especially people who may share concerns similar to yours, are a great way to find the services you need to provide for your child.

Above all, a support group, just by its presence, will remind you that you aren't alone in your daily struggles. You will learn that they, too, worry about what will happen when their child is an adult— they have the same fears and concerns that you have. They will reassure you that you did nothing to cause this to happen to your child and will rejoice with your victories and cry with your disappointments. They truly will move in the same orbit and will depend on you just as you depend on them.

Giving Support

As time goes by and autism and all its idiosyncrasies become second nature to you, you will find that you have a lot of knowledge and experience to impart to others. For some people it happens immediately and for others it takes a bit longer. You will go from being an observer to a listener in a support group, to being a parent that helps parents with newly diagnosed children. You will have ideas, solutions, and little tricks you have stumbled upon that will be of invaluable help to someone you may not even know yet.

The most important thing you can remember about giving support is to withhold judgment. It is possible that you will meet someone who has different theories than you do on the causes and the best treatments for autism. These are unknowns right now, and it is more important to work together on coping than to spend valuable time and energy debating the issues. No one is totally right and no one is totally wrong. Autism support groups are full of parents trying to get by and do the best job they possibly can, and what they need is encouragement.

 ALERT!

One rule that is absolutely followed in any support group is not to criticize other people for their decisions about treatment and therapy for autism. Keep your comments and opinions positive and helpful. Every person is entitled to his or her opinion and should be treated with respect.

Much of dealing with autism is learning by trial and error. Participating in a support group allows you to learn by the experience of others; you will save a lot of frustration and irritation if you can avoid the mistakes others have made. When you have had some experience, then you can share what you have learned and help others as they begin their journey.

Finding the Right Support Group

Just as every treatment isn't right for your child, not every support group will be right for you. Some support groups are founded on a belief in a certain treatment. If you do not feel comfortable with a particular treatment that is the foundation for a support group, it wouldn't be a good fit for you. They provide specialized support for those who follow a certain theory, and that is fine, but don't ever join a group with the idea that you can change its focus. That isn't fair to them or you.

What Are the Differences?

Different areas have different kinds of support groups. There are large ones and small ones, ones that meet weekly and ones that meet monthly, ones with and without babysitting provided, and ones that serve particular age groups. There is no one right way to have a support group. The goal is to create a community or family where the issues of raising a child with autism can be freely discussed.

If you have never been part of a support group, consider joining one that is general in its nature and approach. Their main emphasis should be on coping with autism and its behaviors. This type of group may be directed to families of children with any disorder.

General Disabilities or ASD Specific?

One of the first decisions to make in selecting the right support group for you is whether you want a group for parents of children with any disability or one that is for parents of autistic children only. There are good things about either type of group. Some of this may depend on the community in which you live—it may be hard to find very specific support groups near smaller towns.

Groups that support families who have children with various disabilities bring a great deal of variety into a discussion and the group dynamics. If you have never been to a support meeting, you may think you would have little in common with a mother holding a baby that depends on a feeding tube. You will be surprised at how much you do have in common once you begin to talk and learn about each other's daily lives. Parents of deaf children will have a lot of advice about handling simple communication issues; even though their children may have receptive speech, they know what a lack of expressive speech means to a family.

 ESSENTIAL

Walking into a support meeting for the very first time can be a little scary, but remember that everyone there is looking forward to meeting you and your family. Get there early so others walk in when you are already there and it will seem easier.

One of the most significant benefits of a group that supports various disabilities is the way it will dispel the isolation. When you see other parents dealing with issues far different from yours, yet just as (if not more so) disabling, yet surviving, you will no longer feel as alone. Meeting people who deal with children who are physically and/or mentally challenged puts life into perspective and things become more manageable.

Groups that support only parents of autistic children have some great benefits as well. Parents who deal with autism on a daily basis are not going to so much as lift an eyebrow if your child empties out your purse and lines up everything that was in it on the floor. That is "standard operating procedure" to those parents. They know what a meltdown is and won't stare at you when your child demonstrates one right in the middle of the parking lot as you are leaving. They understand elopement and how fearful it is. And they won't assume your child will talk to them; they will understand the limitations of a nonverbal child.

Specialized Groups

After some time, if you become involved in a particular treatment, you can even seek out a group that is devoted to discussion of that. They will likely touch on general coping strategies as well, but the thrust will center on a particular therapy. One advantage to a specialized support group is the information from the experiences of the members. If you, for example, want to try a particular diet to treat your child's autism, it can be helpful to be around people who are using that eating plan. There is no reason to reinvent the wheel, so be there to learn and eventually share with others.

All types of support groups have strong points that should be considered. It is likely that a group for general disabilities will have some families who have children with autism in the group. You may be limited in your choices because of location or scheduling issues, but keep looking until you find one that works for you. Making a point to join and regularly attend a support group is one step you can make that will help your life immensely.

Forming a Support Group

If you have discovered that there is not a support group in your local area, you might consider starting one of your own. You have the qualifications as the parent of a child on the autism spectrum. Beginning a support group is easy and takes a minimum of time and money.

Begin by talking with your child's physician. He or she might want to get involved on some level and at the very least will tell other patients about the group. Also, speak with the special-education department at the school your child attends or will be attending. You do not need their approval, but it would be helpful to have them involved. If you live near a community mental health center, connecting with them would be helpful, too.

Organizing

After you have some experts aware of your support group's "birth," begin to organize by setting preliminary schedules and goals. Meeting once a week is standard practice; you can also have special functions when the group is established, but for now start with weekly meetings. Compare your schedule to other schedules in your community to look for potential conflicts; if every church in town has a Wednesday night service, choose another evening.

Your next step is to find a space that would work for your meeting. Your local library may have a room they will let you use at no charge. Senior centers and community meeting halls are also possibilities. Your home is an option but it should be your last choice; you don't want the stress of making your home "just-so" when you want to create a supportive environment for families. Make fliers and posters to let people know where and when you will be meeting.

 **FACT**

Churches can be a good place for support group meetings. If you are a member of a church, ask if they would be willing to donate a room for a meeting. Have members bring cookies and muffins and you will be all ready to go.

The next step is easy. Put out cookies, coffee, and tea, and wait for people. They will show up if you have the word out. Spend time getting to know people and let your group evolve naturally. You can have guest speakers if you want and think it would be helpful. Many large support groups have started from small beginnings such as this. You may be creating a new family!

Activities for Support Groups

Many groups have planned activities. They may be educational or just for fun. They can be to raise money to help the support group in different ways or to funnel toward an autism awareness fund that the group would like to support. Whatever you plan to do, plan ahead to get as much out of the activity as possible.

Guest speakers should be scheduled about three months or more before you would like them to speak. That will allow you to organize topics of discussion that will work up to the speaker's topic and have a larger participation. When you contact someone about speaking to your group, ask about fees and what they would like to discuss. If fees are involved you may be able to cover it with a fund you have for this purpose. If there is a speaker you really want to bring in but the fee is higher than your budget, plan a fundraiser to cover the expenses.

Annual activities, such as a Christmas party or a summer picnic, are common in groups that meet regularly. Planning a yearly calendar can help with the organization of something that you know will be a regular event. Picnics often require that an area of a park be reserved and Christmas parties will need a place comfortable for adults and children of all ages. Again, you may want to establish a fund to cover such activities.

Another activity that your group might take advantage of is attending a national autism seminar. Throughout the year, many such seminars are held for two to four days. If two or three of your group could attend and bring back notes and information that they could share with the rest of the group, it could be helpful for everyone. Groups will sometimes plan for one seminar yearly and coordinate a fundraising event to cover the expenses.

 ALERT!

A great way to generate funds for your support group is to have all the families get together for a combined garage sale. If everyone donates the proceeds, your group can make a substantial amount of money quickly.

All support groups are different, so the activities of each one will vary, but one thing is true across the board. Lifetime friendships are created in these groups. The more you can contribute to your support group, the more you will receive back. Special activities serve to educate and bind people together as they work toward common goals.

Support on the Internet

The Internet may be one of the greatest inventions of the twentieth century. Never before in human history can so many people be instantly in contact with any part of the world at any time of the day or night. The cost of the equipment is reasonable in price and few areas are inaccessible. The wealth of information you can find online is staggering. If you need it, or want it, or have to understand it, you can find it online.

A Microcosm

Many people who have not yet ventured onto the Internet are hesitant and sometimes a bit fearful. They worry they won't understand it and are concerned about the dangers the media presents. Others do not think any valid information can be found on Web sites and therefore have not investigated the available resources. Others are "technophobes" and do not do well with what they perceive to be advanced technology.

Rest assured the Internet is no more than a microcosm of the "real world." It is no different than the rest of your world; it just reflects society. As in the real world, the Internet has good neighborhoods and bad neighborhoods. It has people you can trust and care for and it has people to be avoided. It has good Samaritans and it has thieves. As one child with autism proudly exclaimed as he began to grasp the concept of the computer and Internet, "There's a bunch of people in there!!"

Online Autism Communities

An autism community on the Internet is much like any other community. It has information, people, discussions, planned meetings (chats), shopping, and many personal opinions from the community population. You can find resources that can be trusted; just remember to pay attention to the source of the information.

One of the major advantages to autism communities on the Internet is the accessibility factor. They are literally open twenty-four hours a day, seven days a week. They are good for middle-of-the-night ranting and raving, and they are wonderful for people who live in isolated areas. If you have a work schedule that prohibits your attending a real-life support group, the Internet is your next best bet. And if you have a real-life support group, the knowledge you gain on the Internet can enhance your group meetings.

Appendix B in the back of this book has sources on the Internet that are valuable for anyone close to a child with autism. If you are new to the world of cyberspace, find a good book on how to get around on the Web to find the resources you are searching for. Check out various communities and discover the volume of information that can help you as you learn about autism.

Other Online Communities

There are many communities on the Internet that you could find useful. Don't limit yourself to just sites related to autism. If you take care of yourself and meet your own needs occasionally, your children will benefit from it.

Communities for spirituality can be helpful for people who feel that if that part of their life isn't functional, none of it will be. There are many sites for every faith known and they have people who believe as you do. Joining such a community will enrich your own life and, by extension, the lives of your children.

If you are a news junkie, the Internet is the place to be. All of the major news services can be found online as well as thousands of reliable news sources you have probably never heard of. Sometimes parents become so involved with a child's disability, they forget to stay in touch with the rest of the world. On the Internet, you can do that at your convenience, not on a television network's schedule.

If you have a need or are just looking for something for fun, if it is for business or entertainment, or if you are looking for something for yourself or for your children, you will be able to find a community for it online. Use search engines to find what you are looking for and just see where it might take you.

Mailing Lists and Newsletters

One primary method used online for support groups is known as a mailing list. This is like a discussion that is spread out over a period of time. People subscribe to a mailing list and e-mails are generated from one person to the entire group. Any number of people can answer a given e-mail, and their response goes out to all members of the list. It is much like standing in the middle of a party and carrying on several conversations at once. People on mailing lists tend to become friends and sometimes even expand their friendships off the list, sometimes meeting in real life.

Newsletters are another source of information for parents of children who are disabled. Web sites will often have a weekly, biweekly, or monthly newsletter that is e-mailed to a subscriber at no charge. The benefit of these newsletters is that someone else is doing the research for you. All you have to do is visit the site where they have the information posted. This can be a great service but be sure that any newsletters you receive are sent by sources you can trust.

Easier Living on the Net

The Internet can make life much easier for a family that has a child with a disability. There are features that can help you get responsibilities taken care of without having to ever leave the house. Many banks are online and allow full banking to be done on their Web site. Credit cards can be paid online, as can most utilities. There are services through many banks that will pay all the bills you request and you don't need stamps, envelopes, or a parking place.

There are also many sources for shopping. This is especially convenient if you live in a small area that doesn't have all of the retail outlets you might need. Books, music, gifts, clothes, pets, supplies for anything, and jewelry are just some of the examples of what you can find. This can be convenient for holiday shopping; taking a child with autism to a mall is difficult and stressful. Now you can bring the mall to you.

Being Cautious

Using the same common sense you use in your everyday life will prevent problems online. You wouldn't walk down a busy city street with a purse or wallet hanging open, so don't give your credit card information to a site that is not legitimate. Remember, there are people who are not reputable waiting to sell you the latest "cure" for autism, just as there are people on city streets selling things that are questionable. Just because it is legal doesn't mean it is a wise purchase. Just be practical and learn as much as you can about the environments you will visit online, and it will be a positive and helpful experience.

CHAPTER 20

The Future of Autism

THE AUTISM COMMUNITY is very diverse. There is no race, no religion, and no economic class unaffected by autism spectrum disorders. Male or female? Autism doesn't care—it is an equal opportunity disorder. This diverse community is struggling to make the best lives they can for their children affected with autism. What will this mean for the futures of those with autism?

Struggling for Unity

While parents struggle daily with autism, another problem, in some ways more insidious, enters their life. The struggle for a united front in the autism community is an issue that has yet to be conquered. The lack of unity has divided people to the point that their "strength in numbers" has substantially been diluted. And because there is no unity in approaching research, each of the major autism organizations supports research efforts in their own area of concern.

With this disjointed approach, the pharmaceutical industry views autism as a condition that does not need extensive research efforts, especially since those who have the greatest stake in finding a cure cannot agree. Federal health agencies, for example, share responsibility for dealing with autism, but each agency deals with a separate part of the picture and protects its own little piece of the research pie. This does not appear to be the case in many other childhood illnesses. There are also many illnesses that affect fewer children than autism does and yet get more attention from researchers working to develop treatments and cures.

In order to advance the quest toward finding a cure or at least a treatment for autism, the autism organizations, federal government, and medical community must put aside their own special interests and take a unified approach to the issues involved, if they are to succeed. But, before that will happen, parents need to look at themselves and their support system. The lack of unity begins at the level of the family and with dissension and conflict, moves out from there.

The Role of the Individual

People do not intend to divide the autism community; it is a situation that began many years ago and is now self-sustaining. The divisions, and all the hostile feelings around it, have infected support groups, online forums, newsletters, and almost anywhere the autism community meets for information and support. Support groups are there to help ease a burden and when people begin verbally assaulting each other, it delays just that much more progress for autism. If someone insists that they are right about their beliefs about the cause of autism, and that you are wrong, just ignore it.

ALERT!

Online verbal assaults are called flaming. If you are verbally attacked for what you think, don't acknowledge it. The Internet gives people a feeling of anonymity and things are said that might not be said in person. No one will change his or her opinion and arguing just ratchets up the stress level.

Parents do not have to agree on the cause of autism. They do not have to argue and debate endlessly on vaccinations, diet, genetics, or what star was in which quadrant that day. At the end of the day, it doesn't matter who is right. What matters is that the autism community unites so that research can be done to find the answers. It is important that we find the best treatment for each child, because very soon these children will be adults, and society will not be prepared.

If parents can unify on a grass-roots level, this will eventually influence the actions of people who can make the decisions to provide the funds for more research. Bickering will never gain one iota of information and only harms the people that are being bickered about: the children.

Looking for Answers

Of course, finding an answer necessitates finding a cause. Researchers in different parts of the world are forming theories on the cause of autism and potential treatments. Scientific studies continue with some of the world's most dedicated researchers determined to unlock the autism puzzle. Someday the cause, the prevention, and the treatment will be discovered. It could be sometime this year or it may not happen for decades; as nebulous as the questions and answers are, the question of how long this may take is even less clear.

In the meantime, coping is the best any parent or caregiver can do. No magic bullet has come along yet and life must go on. Look for answers but don't become so wrapped up in finding the answer that you forget the question. Until a 100 percent preventative treatment is found, the important question is, and always will be, "How can I best raise this child to be the best person with autism that he or she can be?"

Too Much Autism

The parents of children with autism are some of the most patient and giving people on the planet. They have had to deal with a lot; the loss they have experienced is ever-present, yet they respond with good nature, skill, and love. But there is a trap you might fall into and preventing it can be a lot easier than escaping from it. It can affect any parent of a child with any disability, but is more prevalent in parents of children with autism. And it is common for parents not to recognize that they are in the trap. The trap could be called "Too Much Autism."

When parents suffer from too much autism, they display several traits that can make their lives spin out of control

- Surfing the Internet for hours each day looking for treatments.
- Depression beginning with the diagnosis that lasts more than six months.
- Arguing with people who have differing views on cause and treatment for autism. (Debate is one thing, but public disputes that get out of hand are not helpful to anyone.)
- Unwillingness to enjoy their own activities and hobbies because it takes them away from their child.
- Having a need to discuss autism for several hours each day, which can be difficult for friends and family.

 ESSENTIAL

It is normal and natural to search for information on a diagnosis that your child receives; but after a couple of years, if searching is continuing at a high intensity, a problem exists. Anyone who continues at that rate risks encountering bad information, unscrupulous people, and promised cures with no validity whatsoever—and you may lose your sense of objectivity to evaluate all the information you're taking in constantly. The worst effect, though, will be the loss of hope. Continually exposing yourself to people who are caught in the same trap will only result in a roller coaster of rising hopes and dashed dreams.

Your Attitude Counts

If you find yourself thinking, "How do I possibly have a normal life after this? How can I do anything less?" you need to readjust your thinking. There is no such thing as a "normal" life—everyone has his or her own life with its good luck, bad luck, and just plain strange luck. Don't let autism take over your life. It is a big part of your life and, certainly, of your child's life. But you are not defined by autism and neither is your child. He or she *has* autism, but your child *isn't* autism. There is much more—he or she is a child with potential, flaws, and strengths, and above all, he or she is a little boy or little girl.

And as hard as it is, as cold as it sounds, you need to remember that you are not autistic. Your child does have this condition but you do not. Many parents, particularly mothers, subconsciously feel that by punishing themselves, a justice—or a penance, metaphorically speaking—will be done. If a mom limits her own life to only autism and her child, then she will share in the burden of autism.

If only it were that easy; if only parents could punish themselves and remove the struggle from their children. Any parent would cheerfully submit to that penalty if it worked. But not participating in things you love to do, ignoring your normal social life, and giving up your career is not going to change this. Letting your marriage slide and not tending it carefully is not going to make autism go away. Autism is like grief—you can't make it go away and you never get over it, but you can learn to live with it.

The Impact on Society

It is shocking enough to realize that autism once occurred with a frequency of 1 in 10,000, but now it shows an increase to 1 in 500 or possibly even 1 in 250. Some communities in the United States have rates as high as 1 in 100 and even 1 in 10. The sheer increase in numbers of children diagnosed with autism since 1990 is alarming.

 **FACT**

A town the size of Berkeley, California, or Green Bay, Wisconsin, will have 200 to 400 people with autism in it. A large city, such as Detroit, Michigan, or San Antonio, Texas, will have 2,000 to 4,000 people with autism in it. And instead of the numbers shrinking, they only appear to be growing. Society cannot escape the impact of this rise in numbers, which can only be considered an epidemic.

Is society ready to handle a population count of that many autistic people with the current situation and services? Can the United States handle the financial load? And with the attitude of ignoring autism because it is so poorly understood, can society take the social impact that will without a doubt occur as a result of there being so many people with communication and social deficits? Sociologists will be working hard with psychologists and physicians to determine the answers to these questions. None of this will be figured out quickly and much of it will be learned by trial and error. Unfortunately, it will be at the expense of the children with autism and their families.

Societies, and even civilizations, are measured by how they treat children, the disabled, and the elderly. If this old proverb is true, then the United States has a less than satisfactory report card. There are no easy answers. In a perfect world, we would find the cause, and then treat and prevent. But a perfect world may be a long way off. In the meantime, parents need to take the knowledge they have gained through their experiences and educate others who are not exposed to autism. The impact on our society cannot be overstated and only parents, by bringing autism to the public table, can ease the burden. You are your child's best advocate, but now you are also an ambassador for autism.

Awareness Issues

There is no national telethon for autism. People do not gather around the television with open wallets for disorders on the spectrum. Many people have never heard of it, and those who have often know only the misconceptions provided by films and television.

Funding for research is sadly limited. If any other disease or situation affected such a high number of children, it would be considered a national emergency. For some reason the attention isn't there for autism. It was not until 2003 that the Centers for Disease Control admitted that 1 in 300 children are now affected by autism. It seems inconceivable that with those numbers, people could remain unaware of the disorder.

But many in the public do not know much about autism. It is up to the parents of children with autism to bring awareness of the problem front and center. "We need an 'in your face' approach," one father said. "Don't people realize that they aren't affected by autism because they dodged the bullet? It could be any child in any family at any time." An "in your face" approach may be what it takes to increase awareness, funding, and services for these children.

 ESSENTIAL

North, south, east, or west, autism is being discussed as never before. Because of the tireless efforts of many organizations and individuals, people are becoming more aware, not only of the disorder itself, but also of the people who must live with it each and every day of their lives. But we must keep up efforts to spread the information to even more people.

Some researchers and "experts" in the field have stated that autism itself has not increased but the methods of diagnosis have improved, thus causing the rise in statistics. However, to most parents and educators, this theory makes no sense. If society simply overlooked or misdiagnosed autistic children of previous generations, there should be more adults who are now recognized as having autism, but this hasn't been the case. Parents need to start asking questions and expecting answers. Until we know what has caused this condition and how to treat it, coping and making a child with autism the "best autistic child he or she can be" is critical.

Every April is Autism Awareness Month. Every year autism societies, support groups, parents, and journalists make extraordinary efforts to draw public attention to the problem of autism. Autism ribbons are showing up and every time someone asks what the colorful puzzle ribbon is, another person learns about autism. Keep learning, and keep sharing what you know with others, and you'll do your part to increase public awareness of the urgency of this problem.

Glossary

augmentative and alternative communication (AAC): A communication aid to assist people with limited or no verbal ability. A communication board is the most commonly used tool.

applied behavioral analysis (ABA): A therapy method that uses positive reinforcement to encourage appropriate behaviors that will help an individual with autism function in society. Also called the Lovaas method, after Dr. Ivar Lovaas.

attention deficit disorder (ADD): A developmental disorder that is characterized by short attention spans and a lack of concentration on tasks.

attention deficit hyperactivity disorder (ADHD): A developmental disorder that is composed of ADD and hyperactivity within the same individual.

activities of daily living (ADL): The activities that each person engages in daily for personal care and hygiene. Dressing and bathing are examples.

Area Education Agency (AEA): Provides support services (ed consultation, psych, social work, nursing, speech and language, etc.) to local education agencies.

auditory processing disorder (APD): A disorder in which language is heard correctly but not understood or not processed correctly by the brain.

Asperger's syndrome (AS): A disorder on the autism spectrum characterized by normal speech and social difficulties. Diagnosis may not occur until the child is older.

Autism Society of America (ASA): One of the leading autism organizations in the United States.

autism spectrum disorders (ASD): A collection of disorders characterized by symptoms such as impaired verbal ability and social dysfunction.

American Sign Language (ASL): The primary sign language used in the United States. It was developed for people with deafness and is often conceptually based.

Aspie: A person with Asperger's syndrome.

autie: A person with autism.

autism: A neurological disorder characterized by communication difficulties (expressive and receptive), sensory problems, and socialization issues. Usually appears between sixteen months and two years of age.

beneficiary: The recipient of a trust fund, life insurance policy, or other assets and funds that have been designated to go to that person.

boardmaker: A device that resembles a notebook or board game created to help nonverbal people communicate.

central auditory processing disorder (CAPD): A disorder that interferes with the combination of abilities that enables a person to obtain meaning from language.

Diagnostic and Statistical Manual of Mental Disorders, 4th edition (DSM-IV): A publication used to diagnose autism spectrum disorders. The fourth edition is the most current version of this publication

echolalia: The verbal repetition of words without using those words for any communication or meaning.

elopement: The tendency of a child with autism to "escape" his or her environment and wander off, usually with no particular direction in mind.

encopresis: A bowel disorder where very hard stool forms in the rectum and liquid stool leaks out from above. Causes bowel leakage.

Exact Sign Language: A form of sign language (using much of American Sign Language) that has a sign for each word. Also known as "Exact English."

expressive speech: The ability to utilize spoken language to convey ideas, thoughts, and feelings.

facilitated communication: A controversial method of communication that uses the aid of another person for physical and emotional support.

Free Appropriate Public Education (FAPE): Programs for education that are individualized, meeting a student's needs and providing an education that progresses and is satisfactory.

flapping: The movement of the hand and forearm by a child or adult with autism that mimics a wave but occurs due to overstimulation, either physically or emotionally.

gluten-free, casein-free diet (GFCF): A diet used by many parents of children on the autism spectrum. The diet excludes all gluten and casein products.

high-functioning autism (HFA): A form of autism that is much less disabling as an individual has verbal ability and varying degrees of social understanding. IQ will be measured at seventy or above.

Individuals with Disabilities Education Act (IDEA): A United States congressional act that dictates all the rights children with disabilities have in order to receive full educational benefits from public schools.

Individual Education Plan (IEP): An official plan, written on a yearly basis, that is developed at a meeting with parents, teachers, therapists, and other experts involved in a disabled child's education.

imaginative play: The ability to play with objects using imagination. For example, toy cars, people, and houses can be a town in which an entire scenario is played out.

inclusive: A term used interchangeably with mainstreaming. Refers to a child with a disability having access to the same classroom as if he or she were not disabled.

InLv: Independent living (support group); an abbreviation used to indicate a person with autism is functioning at a high enough level to live alone with minimal supervision, such as a social worker checking in daily.

IQ (intelligence quotient): The number that is considered a standard for measuring a person's intelligence and capacity for understanding.

licensed clinical social worker (LCSW): A mental health professional licensed by each state to help individuals and families.

low-functioning autism (LFA): A more severe form of autism with IQ measuring at below seventy.

least restrictive environment (LRE): An educational term that refers to the classroom or environment a student attends daily that provides the least amount of restriction to ensure safety and the most of social and educational interaction.

multidisciplinary team (MDT): Teacher, SLP (speech/language pathologist), occupational therapist, psychologist, and parents! Used in reference to the group of individuals who are a part of development and implementation of an IEP.

meltdown: The total loss of behavioral control by a person with autism.

mental retardation (MR): Mentally retarded (IQ less than seventy).

no child left behind (NCLB): An education reform act designed to improve student achievement. All states, school districts, and schools that accept Title 1 federal grants are subject to NCLB policy.

neuro-immune dysfunction syndrome (NIDS): The likely connection between neuro-immune and/or autoimmune dysfunction and conditions such as autism, ADD, Alzheimer's, ALS, CFS/CFIDS, MS, and other immune-mediated diseases.

not otherwise defined (NOD): Often appears with a diagnosis by a psychologist. This is a term that is used when a disorder is present but it does not fall into a specific definition within the diagnostic manuals.

not otherwise specified (NOS): Used as a footnote on a diagnosis when the disorder is vague in many ways (usually seen as PDD-NOS). It is considered a "catch-all" diagnosis and is often not accepted as a valid diagnosis by insurance companies.

neuro-typical (NT): A term used for children without autism who are "normal" by definition of society.

obsessive-compulsive disorder (OCD): This is a disorder in which a person is obsessed with unwanted thoughts and feels the need to act out compulsive behaviors.

occupational therapist or occupational therapy (OT): A therapist that works with improving fine motor skills as well as developing solutions for practical day-to-day living as deficits are accommodated.

parallel play: Playing beside another child, but playing independently and not interacting with that child.

picture exchange communication system (PECS/PCS): A communication tool that uses photographs and/or drawings to replace words for language.

Prader-Willi syndrome: A disorder on the autism spectrum. PWS is a complex genetic disorder that typically causes low muscle tone, short stature, incomplete sexual development, cognitive disabilities, problem behaviors, and a chronic feeling of hunger that can lead to excessive eating and life-threatening obesity.

physical therapist or physical therapy (PT): A therapist or therapy that works to increase the functionality of gross motor skills.

receptive speech: Hearing spoken language from another person and deciphering it into a meaningful mental picture or thought pattern, which is understood and then used by the recipient.

Rett syndrome (RS): A disorder on the autism spectrum. Rett syndrome is a genetic neurological disorder seen almost exclusively in females and found in a variety of racial and ethnic groups worldwide. It is characterized by apparently normal or near normal development until six to eighteen months of life. A period of temporary stagnation or regression follows, during which the child loses communication skills and purposeful use of the hands.

savant: A person with autism who has unusual and brilliant intelligence. Appears in approximately 10 percent of people with autism.

self-contained: In reference to special education, it refers to schools or classrooms containing only a special-needs population.

sensory overload: The reaction a child with autism has when more senses are being stimulated than he or she has the ability to process.

service animal: An animal that is trained to work with and meet the needs of a disabled person.

splinter skill: This is a highly refined skill accomplished by a child or adult with autism. Other skills may be below typical age level but one or two skills, such as music or computer programming, may be far above average.

selective serotonin reuptake inhibitor (SSRI): A medication used for depression, anxiety, and the control of obsessive-compulsive behaviors, including Prozac, Zoloft, Paxil, and Luvox.

stuffing: A characteristic of autism where the child overfills his mouth with food. The biggest hazard associated with stuffing is the risk of choking.

Treatment and Education of Autistic and Related Communication Handicapped Children (TEACCH): A method of teaching children with communication deficits that encourages communication with picture boards or other assistive devices.

theory of mind: A human characteristic that acknowledges that each person has a mind and one individual may not be aware of the other person's thoughts. Communication bridges that gap.

therapy animal: An animal that is used to calm people who are either ill or disabled. The animal's job is to deliver unconditional love.

tic: A brief, repetitive, purposeless, nonrhythmic, involuntary movement or sound. Tics that produce movement are called "motor tics," while tics that produce sound are called "vocal tics" or "phonic tics." Tics tend to occur in bursts or "bouts."

Tourette's syndrome (TS): Also known as Tourette syndrome or Tourette's disorder, this is a fairly common childhood-onset condition that may be associated with features of many other conditions. This syndrome is characterized by "tics."

Williams syndrome: A disorder on the autism spectrum. Williams syndrome is typically characterized by elfin face, dental problems, characteristic stenotic cardiovascular problems (narrowing of the blood vessels) and hypercalcemia (excessive calcium in the blood.) People afflicted with Williams syndrome also have a characteristic tendency to approach strangers indiscriminately.

Additional Resources

The American Academy of Child and Adolescent Psychiatry
3615 Wisconsin Ave., N.W.
Washington, DC 20016-3007
(202) 966-7300
Fax: (202) 966-2891
www.aacap.org
The American Academy of Child and Adolescent Psychiatry provides this important information as a public service to assist parents and families in their most important roles.

Autism Options
3435 Camino Del Rio South
Suite 107
San Diego, CA 92108
(619) 280-8585
www.autism-options.com
Autism Options offers families with autistic children ways to improve attention, motivation, behavior, and motor skills using sensory techniques.

Autism/Pervasive Developmental Disorders
http://autism.about.com

The Autism/Pervasive Developmental Disorders site at About.com is one of the most comprehensive Web sites dealing with Autism and PPD. It has information, links to resources, forum communities, and chat rooms, free to all. The author maintains this Web site.

Autism Research Institute
4182 Adams Avenue
San Diego, CA 92116
Fax: (619) 563-6840
www.autism.com/ari

The Autism Research Institute (ARI), a nonprofit organization, was established in 1967. ARI is primarily devoted to conducting research, and to disseminating the results of research, on the causes of autism and on methods of preventing, diagnosing, and treating autism and other severe behavioral disorders of childhood. They provide information based on research to parents and professionals throughout the world.

Autism Society of America
7910 Woodmont Avenue, Suite 300
Bethesda, MD 20814-3067
(301) 657-0881 or 1-800-3AUTISM
www.autism-society.org

ASA has over 200 chapters in nearly every state reaching out to individuals with autism and their families with information, support, and encouragement.

The BHARE Foundation
523 Newberry
Elk Grove, IL 60007
Barefoundation@aol.com
www.bhare.org

The Brenen Hornstein Autism Research & Education (BHARE) Foundation's top priority is to fund research that will lead to a cure for autism. Good summaries for parents are available along with information regarding project funding.

Center for the Study of Autism

P.O. Box 4538
Salem, OR 97302
www.autism.org

The Center for the Study of Autism (CSA) is located in the Salem/Portland, Oregon area. The center provides information about autism to parents and professionals, and conducts research on the efficacy of various therapeutic interventions.

Children's Rights Council

6200 Editors Park Drive
Suite 103
Hyattsville, MD 20782
(301) 559-3120
Fax: (301) 559-3124
www.gocrc.com

The Children's Rights Council (CRC) is a national nonprofit organization based in Washington, DC, that works to assure children meaningful and continuing contact with both their parents and extended family regardless of the parents' marital status.

Cure Autism Now

5455 Wilshire Blvd., Suite 715
Los Angeles, CA 90036
(323) 549-0500 or 1-888-8AUTISM
Fax: (323) 549-0547
www.canfoundation.org

Cure Autism Now is an organization of parents, physicians, and researchers dedicated to promoting and funding research with direct clinical implications for treatment and a cure for autism.

Families for Early Autism Treatment, Inc. (FEAT)
www.feat.org
Families for Early Autism Treatment (FEAT) is a California-based organization with chapters in several states. Among other things, FEAT publishes one of the most comprehensive, informative, and activist newsletters in the autism community.

Federation of State Medical Boards of the United States Inc.
P.O. Box 619850
Dallas, TX 75261-9850
(817) 868-4000
Fax: (817) 868-4098
www.fsmb.org
The Federation of State Medical Boards (FSMB) Web site allows you to research if there have been any serious disciplinary actions or professional peer reviews against a physician you are considering for your child.

For Parents Only.com
www.forparentsonly.com
For Parents Only.com is a specialized search engine connecting parents and information.

Free Appropriate Public Education (FAPE)
www.fapeonline.org
The Free Appropriate Public Education (FAPE) site is intended to be a beginning point for research by parents, educators, state and federal staff members, and other interested parties into a wide range of issues involving disabilities and disability law.

From Emotions to Advocacy (FETA)
www.fetaweb.com
From Emotions to Advocacy (FETA), The Special Education Survival Guide by Pam and Pete Wright, is an excellent resource for special education information. Fetaweb.com is the companion Web site to WrightsLaw.com.

Habitat for Humanity International, Partner Service Center
121 Habitat St.
Americus, GA 31709-3498
(229) 924-6935, ext. 2551 or 2552
publicinfo@hfhi.org
www.habitat.org
Habitat for Humanity International is a nonprofit, ecumenical Christian housing organization building simple, decent, affordable housing in partnership with people in need.

International Society for Augmentative and Alternative Communication (ISAAC)
49 The Donway West, Suite 308
Toronto, ON M3C 3M9 Canada
(416) 385-0351
Fax: (416) 385-0352
www.isaac-online.org
The International Society for Augmentative and Alternative Communication (ISAAC) is an organization devoted to advancing the field of augmentative and alternative communication (AAC). The Mission of ISAAC is to promote the best possible communication for people with complex communication needs.

An Introduction to the Individualized Education Plan for Home Educators
www.altonweb.com/cs/downsyndrome.htm
This site discusses developing an individualized education plan (IEP) for your child with special learning needs for children who are taught at home. If you home school a child with autism, you need to read this Web site. Although written for children with Down syndrome, it is a very useful resource.

KeepKidsHealthy.com
www.keepkidshealthy.com
Keep Kids Healthy is an excellent pediatric medicine Web site.

Lovaas Institute for Early Intervention
11500 West Olympic Boulevard, Suite 460
Los Angeles, CA 90064
(310) 914-5433
Fax: (310) 914-5463
www.lovaas.com

The Lovaas Institute for Early Intervention is a research-based program that specializes in teaching children with autism, pervasive developmental disorders, and related developmental disabilities. The program provides services nationwide.

The Medicine Program
P.O. Box 515
Doniphan, MO 63935-0515
(573) 996-7300
www.themedicineprogram.com

The Medicine Program may be able to help you with medication expenses. This organization was established by volunteers dedicated to alleviating the plight of an ever-increasing number of patients who cannot afford their prescription medication.

MyCityMyPlace.com
Philadelphia Mental Retardation Services
1441 Sansom Street, 2nd floor
Philadelphia, PA 19102
(215) 686-0253
http://mycitymyplace.com

This Web site is a directory of resources for people with mental retardation, families, and professionals. Although this site is not specifically geared toward those with ASD, it has plenty of good information.

The National Alliance for Autism Research, National Office
99 Wall Street, Research Park
Princeton, NJ 08540
(888) 777-NAAR
Fax: (609) 430-9163
www.naar.org
The National Alliance for Autism Research is a nonprofit organization that includes family members, scientists, researchers, etc., who are involved in supporting autism research.

The National Autistic Society
393 City Road
London, EC1V 1NG, United Kingdom
44 (0)20 7833 2299
Fax: +44 (0)20 7833 9666
www.nas.org.uk
The National Autistic Society (NAS) is the UK's foremost organization for people with autism and those who care for them, spearheading national and international initiatives and providing a strong voice for autism. The NAS works in many areas to help people with autism live their lives with as much independence as possible.

National Information Center for Children and Youth with Disabilities (NICHCY)
P.O. Box 1492
Washington, DC 20013
(800) 695-0285
Fax: (202) 884-8441
www.nichcy.org
The National Information Center for Children and Youth with Disabilities (NICHCY) provides information on disabilities and disability-related issues. This organization is dedicated to providing information to parents and caregivers of children with disabilities, including autism/PDD.

National Organization of Social Security Claimants' Representatives (NOSSCR)

(800) 431-2804

www.nosscr.org

NOSSCR@wordnet.att.net

The National Organization of Social Security Claimants' Representatives (NOSSCR) has a referral service for claimants looking for a private attorney and Social Security benefit information and representation. They also have a caller hotline number for SSI children's benefits. The referral is free; the attorney will charge for the representation if the claim is successful.

National Vaccine Information Center

421-E Church Street

Vienna, VA 22180

(703) 938-DPT3

Fax: (703) 938-5768

www.909shot.com

The National Vaccine Information Center (NVIC) is a national, non-profit educational organization founded in 1982. It is the oldest and largest national organization advocating reformation of the mass vaccination system. Vaccines or immunizations are recommended for every child born in the United States. Vaccinations shouldn't hurt a child but sometimes they do. Before your child takes the risk, find out what it is.

Neuro-Immune Dysfunction Syndromes (NIDS) Research Institute

NIDS MEDICAL ADVISORY BOARD

(888) 540-4999

www.nids.net

The Neuro-Immune Dysfunction Syndromes (NIDS) Research Institute is dedicated to increasing the public's awareness of the likely connection between neuro-immune and/or autoimmune dysfunction and conditions such as autism, ADD, Alzheimer's, ALS, CFS/CFIDS, MS, and other immune-mediated diseases. If your family has an autoimmune illness situation as well as autism, you will want to check this out.

No Child Left Behind
U.S. Department of Education
400 Maryland Avenue, SW
Washington, DC 20202
(888) 814-NCLB
Fax: (202) 401-0689
www.nochildleftbehind.gov
The No Child Left Behind Web site includes a simple overview of the legislation, key dates to remember, frequently asked questions, information about what is happening in states across the country, and more importantly, where you can go to learn more and become involved. The goal of No Child Left Behind is to create the best educational opportunities for our nation's children and to ensure that they have every opportunity to succeed.

Parenting Special Needs
http://specialchildren.about.com
The Special Children site at About.com contains just about everything you need to know about raising children with special needs.

Patient Centered Guides' Autism Center
O'Reilly Customer Service
1005 Gravenstein Highway North
Sebastopol, CA 95472
(800) 998-9938 or (800) 889-8969
Fax: (707) 829-0104
www.patientcenters.com/autism
The Patient Centered Guides' Autism Center is for families of those living with a pervasive developmental disorder. Much of the material here is for those in the middle of the autistic spectrum, particularly those with a diagnosis of PDD-NOS or Atypical PDD or those still trying to find a correct diagnosis. You can find articles and resources about PDDs, diagnosis, drug treatments, therapies, supplements, education, insurance, family life, other coping topics, and resources.

Social Security Administration
www.ssa.gov
The Social Security Administration Web site.

WrightsLaw.com
www.wrightslaw.com
WrightsLaw.com is one of the most thorough Web sites regarding autism and special education. Parents, advocates, educators, and attorneys come to Wrightslaw for accurate, up-to-date information about special-education law and advocacy for children with disabilities.

Index

A

activities of daily living (ADL), 173–176, 219
adolescence, 159–171
  birth control, 168–169
  education and, 154–157
  menstruation, 165–168
  puberty, 159–161
  sexuality, 162–164, 169–171
adulthood, 173–185
  independent living, 173–176
  long-term care provisions, 179–185
  residential living, 176–179
aggression, *see* anger/aggression
American Sign Language, 62–63
anger/aggression, 5, 47, 48–51, 148. *See also* meltdowns
anxiety disorders, 30–31
applied behavioral analysis (ABA), 79–80, 156, 157, 222–223
Asperger, Dr. Hans, 6, 7
Asperger's syndrome, 6–9, 11, 40
assistive techniques/technologies, 187–198
  communication boards, 64–66, 175–176, 209–211
  computers, 187–193
  homemade devices, 196–197
  service dogs, 138, 193–195
  toys, 197–198
audiologist, 217–218
autism
  Asperger's syndrome compared, 8–9
  awareness issues, 261–262
  classical, 2–5
  impact on society, 259–260
  increase in incidence of, 21–23
  need for unity of effort, 255–257
  origin of word, 2
  possible causes, 23–27
Autism Awareness Month, 262
autism spectrum disorder (ASD), 1–12

B

behavior modification, 78–80
birth control, 168–169
bowels, *see* encopresis

C

car travel, elopement and, 53
celiac sprue, 223
children, decisions about additional, 119–122. *See also* siblings
Christmas, 131–132
communication
  in Asperger's syndrome, 8
  being positive about, 55–57
  boards for, 64–66, 175–176, 209–211
  child's difficulty with, 3–4
  echolalia, 3, 58–59
  frustration of child and, 199–201
  other methods, 66–67
  receptive and expressive speech, 59–62
  sign language, 62–64
  symptoms and diagnosis and, 16–17
  without concepts, 57–58, 61, 63–64
communication boards, 64–66
  for ADLs, 175–176
  toilet training and, 209–211
computer, as assistive device, 187–193
conceptual thinking difficulties, 4

coprolalia/copropraxia, 30–31
custody issues, finances and,
    238–239. *See also* guardianship

D

day care, 101–102, 104–105
deafness, *see* hearing
death in family, 133–134
diagnosis
    behavior/symptoms and, 3, 13–17
    increase in incidence of autism,
        21–23
    parents' reactions to, 18–21, 83–87
    physicians' reluctance to deliver,
        12
    schools and, 154
    siblings' reactions to, 112
    tests and, 228
diet, gluten-free, casein-free (GFCF),
    223
disability benefits, *see* financial
    issues; Social Security benefits
discipline, meltdowns and, 80
divorced parents, 46, 98–100. *See
    also* single parenting
doctors, *see* physicians
dogs, *see* service dogs
DSM-IV, 15

E

Earned Income Credit (EIC), 234
echolalia, 3, 58–59
eczema, 40
education, *see* schools
elopement, 51–54, 204–206
encopresis, 40, 160
environmental causes, 27
escape, *see* elopement
Exact English, 63–64
expressive and receptive speech,
    59–62
extended family, 92–93, 123–134
    grandparents, 123–126
    holidays and, 129–134
    in-laws, 98–100, 126–128

F

facilitated communication (FC),
    66–67
faith, importance to marriage, 89–92
Family Support Funds, 234–235
fathers, *see* parents
financial issues
    costs, 120–121
    custody and, 238–239
    in different states, 234–236
    long-term care provisions,
        179–185
    medical insurance coverage, 121,
        232–233
    respite care, 236–237
    see also Supplemental Security
        Income
flapping, 46–48
fluorescent lights, 137
free appropriate public education
    (FAPE), 148, 150

G

gender, ASD and, 11
genetics
    additional children and, 120
    autism's cause and, 26–27
gluten-free, casein-free diet (GFCF),
    223
grandparents, 123–126
group homes, 177–178
guardians, 181–184

H

Halloween, 130–131
hand-wringing, 11
hearing, 34–38, 217–218
high-functioning autism (HFA),
    9–10
holidays/special occasions, 129–134
housekeeping, ways to ease,
    103–104
hypersensitivity to sound, *see*
    sensory overload

I

identification bracelet, 52, 206

illness, symptoms of, 201–204

immunizations, 25–26

inclusion, *see* least restrictive environment (LRE)

independent living, 173–176

Individual Education Program (IEP), 149, 151–155, 164

Individuals with Disabilities Education Act (IDEA), 147–150

"informed consent," to sexual activity, 163–164

in-laws, 98–100, 126–128

institutionalized living, 178–179

insurance
life, 184
medical, 121, 232–233

Internet, support groups on, 250–253

interventions, 213–225
experts versus parents regarding, 224–225
physicians, 213–217
possible treatment programs, 221–224
therapists, 217–220

IQ (intelligence quotient), 9–10, 41
Social Security benefits and, 227–228

K

Kanner, Dr. Leo, 2

keyboard communication, 66

keyboards, computer, 190, 191

L

least restrictive environment (LRE), 148, 149, 150

licensed clinical social worker (LCSW), 220

lines, of objects, 33, 44–45

Lovaas, Dr. Ivar, 79

M

mainstreaming, *see* least restrictive environment (LRE)

marriage
ASD's effect on, 83–95
priorities and, 88–95
second, 106–107

masturbation, 169–170

Medicaid, 233

medication
for anger, 49
for compulsive behavior, 45
for meltdowns, 80–81
for repetitive behavior, 48

meltdowns
described, 71–72
handling techniques, 73–81
temper tantrums contrasted to, 69–71

menstruation, 165–168

mental retardation, 9–10, 41–42

migraine headaches, 72

MMR immunization, 25–26

mothers, *see* parents

mouse (computer) devices, 190–192

N

neuro-immune dysfunction syndrome (NIDS), 25, 221–222

neurologist, pediatric, 214–215

neuro-typical (NT), use of term, 160

noise, *see* sensory overload

O

obsessive-compulsive behaviors, 43–46

obsessive-compulsive disorder (OCD), 30, 31–34

occupational therapists, 219–220

P

parents
ASD's effect on, 83–95, 106–109, 257–259
fathers, daughters' puberty and, 167
in-laws and, 126–128
reactions to diagnosis, 18–21, 83–87

parents—*continued*
  single parents, 97–109
  support groups for, 241–253
  work issues of, 92, 93–94,
    100–102
PDD (pervasive developmental
  disorder), 1
PDD-NOS (pervasive development
  disorder not otherwise
  specified), 2, 5–6, 11
pediatrician, 213–214
pediatric neurologist, 214–215
physical therapist, 218–219
physicians
  kinds of, 213–216
  selecting of, 216–217
picture exchange communication
  system (PECS), 64–66
pregnancy, *see* birth control
psychiatrist/psychologist, 215–216
puberty, 159–161

R
receptive and expressive speech,
  59–62
religious services, 138–139
repetitive behaviors, 48. *See also*
  flapping; obsessive-compulsive
  behaviors
residential living, 176–179
respite care, 236–237
restaurants, 141–143
Rett syndrome, 10–12, 40
Risperdal, 48, 49
risperidone, 81
Ritalin, 48
road signs, indicating disabled
  child, 53
round objects, aversion to, 142
routine
  child's need for, 46, 101
  toilet training and, 210
  on vacation, 143–144
rudeness, handling people's, 74–75
running away, *see* elopement

S
safety issues
  elopement prevention, 51–54
  in household, 206–207
  with newborns, 116
  of single parents, 100
schools
  after childhood, 154–157
  attending functions at, 139–141
  communication systems in, 67
  IEP and, 149, 151–155
  special education law, 147–150
scrapbook, of vacation memories,
  145–146
seizures, 34, 72, 159–160
sensory overload
  in bathroom, 209
  fluorescent lights and, 137
  lines and, 44
  meltdowns and, 74
  at religious services, 138–139
  at school functions, 140
  sounds and, 37–38
separated parents, *see* divorced
  parents; single parenting
serotonin reuptake inhibitor (SSRI),
  45, 48
service dogs, 138, 193–195
sexuality, 162–164, 169–171
shopping trips, 135–137
siblings, 111–122
  older, 111–114
  reaction to diagnosis, 112
  social life and, 117–119
  younger, 114–116
sign language, 35, 62–64, 207
single parenting, 97–109
  priorities of, 100–104
  social life and, 98, 105–109
Social Security, *see* Supplemental
  Security Income
social worker, 220
society, interactions with, 135–146
  handling people's rudeness,
    74–75

religious services, 138–139
restaurants, 141–143
school functions, 139–141
shopping trips, 135–137
symptoms/diagnosis and, 15
vacations, 143–146
speech, *see* communication
speech therapist, 217–218
splinter skills, 41
state-based support programs,
234–236
stepparents, 106–109
Supplemental Security Income
(SSI), 120–121, 189, 228–232, 233
support groups, 241–253
finding right, 245–247
forming, 247–250
on Internet, 250–253
symptoms, 3, 14–17, 40–42. *See also*
diagnosis
syndromes, 2

T
tax issues, 235–236
teenagers, *see* adolescence
temper tantrums, 50, 69–71. *See
also* anger/aggression;
meltdowns
theory of mind (TOM), 4–5
therapy
occupational, 219–220
physical, 218–219
psychological, 215–216
speech, 217–218
tics, 29–31
toilet training, 207–212
touch screen monitors, 190–191

Tourette's syndrome (TS), 29–31
toys, as learning devices, 197–198
Treatment and Education of Autistic
and Related Communication
Handicapped Children
(TEACCH), 156–157
treatment programs, 221–224
applied behavioral analysis
(ABA), 79–80, 156, 157,
222–223
gluten-free, casein-free diet, 223
neuro-immune dysfunction
syndrome (NIDS), 25, 221–222
vitamin B_6, 224
trust funds, 180–181

V
vacations, 143–146
VCRs, 17
vision problems/therapy, 38–40
visual assisting sequencing, 209–211
visual thinking, 188–189
vitamin B_6, 224

W
Wechsler Adult Intelligence Scale
(WAIS), 228
wills
financial planning, 179–181,
184–185
guardianship, 181–184
work obligations, of parents, 92,
93–94, 100–102

WE HAVE EVERYTHING®

FOR PARENTING!

From addressing such serious issues as eating disorders and school violence to learning tolerance for pink and blue hair, *The Everything® Tween Book* provides sound, professional advice on coping with your child's psychological, social, and emotional needs.

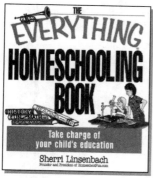

Trade paperback,
$14.95 ($22.95 CAN)
1-58062-870-2, 304 pages

Trade paperback,
$14.95 ($22.95 CAN)
1-58062-868-0, 320 pages

The Everything® Homeschooling Book is the perfect handbook to help you take control of your child's education. From researching state curriculum requirements to homeschooling multiple children, this thorough book provides up-to-date information on the best sources for curriculum guidelines by grade level, techniques for designing lesson plans, and more.

Available wherever books are sold!
To order, call 800-872-5627,
or visit us at *www.everything.com*

Everything® and everything.com® are registered
trademarks of F+W Publications, Inc.

OTHER TITLES IN THE
EVERYTHING® PARENT'S GUIDE SERIES!